Homosexuality: Power & Politics

HOMOSEXUALITY
Power & Politics

Edited by
GAY LEFT COLLECTIVE

Allison and Busby, London & New York

First published 1980 by
Allison and Busby Limited
6a Noel Street, London W1V 3RB, England
and distributed in the USA by
Schocken Books Inc,
200 Madison Avenue, New York, NY 10016

British Library Cataloguing in Publication Data:

'Gay Left' Collective.
  Homosexuality.
  1. Homosexuality
  I. Title
  301.41'57   HQ76.25   80-40640

  ISBN 0-85031-374-0
  ISBN 0-85031-375-9 Pbk

Set in 10/10 Times by Grainger Photosetters,
Unit 2, Carlton Court, Grainger Rd, Southend-on-Sea, Essex
and printed and bound in Great Britain at
The Camelot Press Ltd, Southampton

Contents

GAY LEFT is a gay socialist journal, edited by a collective of gay men, which has been published twice yearly since 1975. Copies of the journal may be obtained from all radical bookshops or direct from: 38 Chalcot Road, London NW1, England.

Introduction

The three words in out title encompass the range of concerns that have dominated the work of *Gay Left* since its foundation. We have always been concerned with the ways in which power has shaped our notions of homosexuality and resulted in a sustained sexual oppression. We have therefore sought a politics that can decisively resist and subvert that oppression.

The articles collected here do not provide an "answer" or a readily understood "programme" for some mass gay movement. They are exploratory and often tentative in form. They are designed to open up areas for intellectual and political debate rather than to foreclose discussion. They do not, moreover, represent a common political approach. Our unity comes not from holding to a set of revealed truths, but from our willingness to challenge old assumptions and investigate new responses to our situation. This open attitude has always been central to our work in *Gay Left*.

The first issue of the journal appeared in the autumn of 1975. The collective which produced it grew out of a gay male discussion/consciousness-raising group which began meeting in 1974. Some of this group had a background in the London Gay Liberation Front (GLF) and had been involved in a series of Gay Marxist discussion groups which had produced an irregular bulletin. By 1974 both the GLF and the Gay Marxist group had effectively disintegrated. Some of the latter group continued to meet, and were joined by other men who were entering the gay movement. These men constituted the beginnings of the *Gay Left* collective. By 1975 we had decided to work towards a new journal and by Easter of that year we had prepared an outline of what became our first collective policy statement.

It is difficult to recreate our sense of what was needed at the time. There was certainly a strong feeling that the gay movement lacked coherence and unity. However, we never saw ourselves as in any way attempting to make up for that lack. But what we did feel to be necessary was a serious discussion of the problems and a forum and focus to which gay socialists could relate. *Gay News* and *Sappho* provided a focus for the growing sense of a gay community, though working within obvious limits; other magazines were satisfying more specialised, even esoteric, tastes. We hoped *Gay Left* would help to create a new climate where serious and accessible political writing was not an exception but the rule. With this in mind we set out to contribute to the making of a socialist current in which sexual politics were central, but which did not ignore wider political relations.

Our first collective statement reflected that ambition. But when we re-read it now, what stands out is our desire then to integrate homosexuality into an existing socialist discourse. The result was a heavy reliance on an "economistic" form of marxism in which we tended to see homosexual oppression as a *necessary* effect of the capitalist organisation of patriarchy and the family. That analysis served a purpose in drawing our own and our readers' attention to our endeavour: to find a socialist theory of sexual oppression and to broaden the Left's awareness of sexual issues. But as a theory it was narrow and limiting, a statement of belief rather than an analytic tool. Subsequent collective statements and many articles, both by members of the collective and by other contributors, have sought to broaden our theoretical approach.

The journal has sought to cover a wide range of issues relating to sexual politics: the formation of the gay subculture and our experience of it; the tensions in the notion of "the personal is political"; and discussions of the cultural representations of homosexuality. In developing these concerns we have been prepared to examine and integrate ideas from diverse sources — the women's movement, Gramsci, Freud, and Foucault, as well as our own experiences. We have tried not to slavishly follow fashions in High Theory, but have attempted to be alive to theoretical breakthroughs and use them to enrich our work and analysis. We have increasingly moved away from our earlier simplistic and functionalist approach to one where we see the task as the understanding of the varied mechanisms by which homosexuality is constructed as a repressive category in our culture.

We have never, however, wanted to offer a global theory. Indeed, for the conventional Left, many of our concerns may have seemed microcosmic. But we have always firmly believed that the phrase "the personal is political" demands a recognition that the "personal" is fundamentally shaped by social and historical forces and is not a natural given. So an exploration of what is conventionally regarded as "private" life can often lead to wider insights into social processes. Like a torchlight in the dark, it can cast a powerful beam of light at major structural features. And in this, of course, the experiences we have started with as a collective have been those of gay men.

We have always been an all-male collective. In the early days and issues of the journal this occasioned much debate because as socialists and pro-feminist gay men we had a strong sense of our solidarity with women. However, the collective had developed as a homogeneous and closed group of gay men in response to the real division of interests and activities that existed between gay men and lesbians with the demise of GLF, with most lesbians seeing their focus of concern within the women's movement. Also, with our prehistory as an all-male consciousness-raising group it seemed appropriate to utilise the sense of common purpose and trust thus developed as the basis for personal and political explorations and to provide coherence for the journal. We have none the less sought and included articles by women in the journal and have worked with lesbians in organising conferences and other activities.

We have not sought to be the exclusive mouthpiece of "the gay left", nor to offer a comprehensive coverage for all aspects of the gay movement. We have begun with ourselves, with what we and many others felt necessary. In doing so we hope to have contributed to the creation of that socialist and radical culture which is a necessary component of wider social transformations.

Homosexuality: Power & Politics continues that range of concerns and attempts a deeper and more sustained analysis of them. Many of the topics covered by the essays in this book have been introduced in various issues of the journal: the personal experiences of lesbians and gay men; the ways of life of gay people; the historical and social sources of sexual oppression; the patterns of gay culture; the construction of arbitrary social categories ("homosexuality", "femininity" etc.); the patterns of resistance and the organisational forms of political movements.

These essays therefore act both as summations and as fresh starting-points. The vast majority are published here for the first time; the four that have been published before in *Gay Left* have been revised or supplemented for this book. The volume as a whole therefore constitutes an original contribution to the work of sexual politics. We hope it will add to the continuing debate which is essential if we are to achieve a more generous, humane, egalitarian and sexually free society.

1

Capitalism and the Organisation of Sex

JEFFREY WEEKS

In Western capitalist countries, sex is securely established on His (and it is "His") throne, Master of all He surveys. Moralists rant about its excesses, revealing in every bead of sweat their obsession with it. Liberals, rejoicing in the "ending" of ancient hypocrisies, revel in its pleasures. Sex, far from being denied by capitalism, has been exalted. Sex oils the wheels of advertising. Endless page threes sell tawdry newspapers. Sex envy is the beginning and end of personal relations. Sex has launched a thousand ships and ruined a million families. Sex has become the truth of our being, the key to our deepest secrets.

Socialists are faced with a complex problem. The sexual radical movements gained their initial impetus from the conviction that the "system" dominated by hypocrisy/puritanism denied various forms of sexual expression: female sexuality and homosexuality in particular. This in turn was theoretically related to the "need" for capitalist society to repress certain types of sexuality to secure its even functioning. The problem is to square this conviction with the active promotion of sexuality, indeed the explosive emergence of sexuality, in capitalist society over the past generation. Theories such as Marcuse's "repressive desublimation" have in fact proved totally inadequate as explanations. Instead we have to look at the forms of sexuality which have emerged as central to its capitalist organisation: the "sexually alluring", "liberated" woman who graces *Cosmopolitan*, the swinging, self-confident affluent homosexual male who lives in the pages of *The Advocate*. What we are witnessing is the creation of new sexual types which are potentially as limiting as the old stereotypes (the sexless "lady" of some nineteenth-century textbooks, the degenerate pervert of twentieth-century psychiatrists). They are models which are based on confirming sex just as the old ones denied it, but both reveal a central factor in modern cultures. What has happened is that a tendency that has always been there in bourgeois cultures has assumed a new strategic position, and we have become a sex-positive culture of sorts. But, and it is a major but, this positiveness is only being applied to certain types of behaviour, in certain ways. And in asking why this is so we might find an answer to a wider but more mysterious question: why capitalism and sexuality are so inextricably linked.

For most writers in the socialist tradition the relationship between capitalism and sexual oppression, although seen as complex, has nevertheless been treated as unproblematic. Engels wrote that true sex life had been distorted by commodity production but would flourish on a higher plane under socialism: "Monogamy, instead of collapsing, (will) at last become a reality". Contained in this (apart from an implicit heterosexual bias) are two concepts which have actually been a bar to any proper socialist evaluation of sexual oppression. The first is an assumption that sex is a natural force with direct effects on the individual and the body politic. The second is the assumption that this sexuality is channelled or directed straight forwardly and with intentionality through the nuclear family, in the interests of capitalism.

A number of assumptions have classically been made about the nature of sexuality, assumptions current both in traditionalist and left thought (and particularly evident in the writings of the Freudian left: Reich, Fromm, Marcuse). They also have the undoubted strength of appearing as commonsensical: in this view sex is conceived of as an overpowering, instinctual force, whose characteristics are built into the biology of the human animal, which shapes human institutions and whose will must find an outlet, either in the form of direct sexual expression or, if blocked, in the form of perversion or neuroses. Krafft Ebing expressed an orthodox view in the late nineteenth-century when he described sex as a "natural instinct" which "with all-conquering force and might demands fulfilment". The clear supposition here is that the sex drive is basically male in character, with the female perceived as a passive receptacle. More sophisticated versions of what William Gagnon and John Simon have termed the "drive reduction" model recur in twentieth-century thought. It is ambivalently there in part of Freud's work, though the careful distinction he draws between "instinct" and "drive" has often been lost, both by commentators and translators. It is unambiguously present in the writings of many of his self-defined followers. As G. R. Taylor wrote in his neo-Freudian interpretation of *Sex in History*:

> The history of civilisation is a history of a long warfare between the dangerous and powerful forces of the id, and the various systems of taboos and inhibitions which man has erected to control them.[1]

Here we have a clear notion of a "basic biological mandate" that presses on, and so must be firmly controlled by the cultural and social matrix. What is peculiar about this model is that it has been adopted by marxists who in other regards have firmly rejected the notion of "natural man". With regard to homosexuality, the instinctual model has either seen it as a more or less pathological deviation, a failure of socially necessary repression, or as the effect of the morally restrictive organisation of sexual morality, which is how it appears in the works of Wilhelm Reich; or more romantically, but nevertheless still ahistorically, as the "great refusal" of sexual normality, which is how Marcuse seems to present it.

Against this William Gagnon and John Simon have argued in their book *Sexual Conduct* that sexuality is subject to "socio-cultural moulding to a degree surpassed by few other forms of human behaviour", and it is in using this insight that socialists can most fruitfully explore the question of sexual oppression. A number of recent writers have taken up elements of this notion, and together they have posed formidable challenges to our received notions of sexuality.

The first consequence is a rejection of sex as an autonomous realm, sexuality as a natural force with specific effects, a rebellious energy which is controlled by the "social". In the work of Gagnon and Simon it seems to be suggested that nothing is intrinsically sexual, or rather that anything can be sexualised. In Jacques Lacan's return to Freud, desire is created as a consequence of the child's entry into patriarchal meanings at the Oedipal moment. In the recent work of Michel Foucault, *The History of Sexuality,* sexuality is seen as a historical apparatus, and "sex", far from having a life and history of its own, is a "complex idea that was formed within the deployment of sexuality".

Foucault's work is particularly relevant here because he quite clearly sees the notion of sexuality as itself an ideological construct, a product of particular historical circumstances. The notion of "sexuality" organises and unifies the various possibilities for pleasure of the body: it plays upon "bodies, organs, somatic localisations, functions, anatamo-physiological systems, sensations, and pleasures"[2] which have no intrinsic unity or "laws" of their own. In other words, our culture has developed a notion of sexuality linked to reproduction and genitality and to "deviations" from these, which have denied us (openly at least) the full enjoyment of the bodily pleasures that are potentially available to us.

The second consequence which derives from questioning the existence of a self-evident biological sexuality is that we have to question the traditional notions of "repression" of sexuality. Far from society repressing (or conversely liberating) sexuality, its main tendency lies in organising and inventing forms of sexual definition, categorisation, and hence regulation. Gagnon and Simon have written:

> To earlier societies it may not have been a need to constrain severely the powerful sexual impulse in order to maintain social stability or limit inherently anti-social force, but rather a matter of having to invent an importance for sexuality.[3]

If this is indeed the case, we must begin to think much more in terms of the various forms of social definition of sexuality and their social conditions of existence rather than try to speak in terms of "capitalism" oppressing "sexuality" as if there could be a simple relationship between the two. A major insight which both the theoretical tradition represented by Gagnon and Simon and the school of thought represented by Michel Foucault have in common is a recognition that a major way in which sexuality is regulated is through the process of categorisation and the imposition of a grid of definition upon the various possibilities of the body and the various forms of expression that "sex" can take. This in turn should direct our attention to the various institutions and social practices which perform this role of organisation, regulation, categorisation: various forms of the family, but also legal regulation, medical practices, psychiatric institutions and so on, all of which can be seen as products of the capitalist organisation of society, but all of which at the same time have a relative autonomy within the capitalist system and from the ruling class. The infinite possibilities of the human child at birth are gradually narrowed, organised and controlled as the s/he becomes subjected to the class- and gender-defined social order.

The rejection of an "essentialist" view of sexuality in turn challenges the orthodox model of the nuclear family as the sole locus of the oppression of sexuality in general and homosexuality in particular. For example, male homosexuality has been seen as a threat to the ensemble of assumptions about male sexuality, and a perceived challenge to the male heterosexual role within capitalism. As Mike Brake has put it:

> In Britain sexual intercourse has been contained within marriage which has been presented as the ultimate form of sexual maturity . . . the heterosexual nuclear family assists a system like capitalism because it produces and socialises the young in certain values . . . the maintenance of the nuclear family with its role-specific behaviour creates an apparent consensus concerning sexual normalcy.

So that,

> Any ambiguity such as transvestism, hermaphrodism, trans-sexuality, or homosexuality is moulded into "normal" appropriate gender behaviour or is relegated to the categories of sick, dangerous, or pathological. The actor is forced to slot into patterns of behaviour appropriate to heterosexual gender roles.[4]

While there is a great deal of truth in this argument, it does assume a simple functional fit between the needs of capitalism and the organisation of sexuality. In particular it makes two crucial assertions. First, it assumes some sort of intentionality on the part of the ruling class to control sexuality in this way. Secondly, it assumes a one-to-one fit between intention and actual effect. The problem is we can neither assume the first, particularly on the basis of very complex historical evidence, nor can we accept the second. The assumption generally made is that the nuclear family acts as a funnel for the control of the sexuality of the working class in the interests of the capitalist class. The problem here is that the nuclear family form was in fact essentially a product of the bourgeoisie, not of the working class. Where the working class adopted, as it has increasingly in the twentieth century, a similar family form, it is much more as an adaptation to its own particular circumstances (the organisation of work patterns, the move towards consumerism, the lowering of the birth rate) rather than as a simple acceptance of the bourgeois model. If this is so, then it is difficult to see how the nuclear family could possibly be the preordained institution for the ruling class's regulation of sexual behaviour. What this suggests is that rather than talking about a single form of sexual organisation, or indeed oppression, we must begin to think in terms of specific class organisations of sexuality and specific class forms of family and domestic organisation, each with their own specific social origins within the capitalist mode of production. Concepts of sexuality are not only culturally specific but are also class and gender specific.

Two tendencies in particular can be detected. The first, taking a clear form from the middle of the eighteenth century, is the increased stress within bourgeois ideology on the monogamous, heterosexual family as the basic unit of society. The switch is from a family model which stressed *lineage*, reproduction of the family traditions, and hence the necessary emphasis on choosing the right partner from the right family, to one which stressed individual choice, based on emotional attraction. In ideology at least the cement of the family was sex love, hedged though this was in material reality by preoccupations over property, by the inequality between men and women, and buttressed as it inevitably was by the double standard of morality. The effect of this stress which had its origins both in economics (the separation of women from social labour), in ideology (an increased emphasis on the difference between men and women and the social construction of masculinity and femininity), and politically (with the family throughout the nineteenth century being seen as an essential stabilising factor, the antidote to public tension, the private haven of peace and tranquillity) was an intensification of emotional bonding within the nuclear family. The effect of this was increased dependence of the wife economically, the changing definitions of her sexuality which was, while not denied, always seen in terms of male sexual needs, and the intensified emotional investment in children of the family. It was this family model which the leading evangelists of the bourgeoisie sought to export to the emergent working classes as a necessary element in respectability and social stability, though with limited initial success.

The second tendency associated with this was the emergence of new sexual categorisations in the course of the nineteenth century which were sustained by various social, legal, medical, religious practices: the masturbating child, the hysterical woman, the perverse adult, the congenital prostitute, the degenerate, the homosexual. At the very end of the nineteenth century there is indeed an explosion of sexual categorisations associated with sexologists like Krafft Ebing, Albert Moll, Havelock Ellis, Magnus Hirschfeld, all of whom sought to define the variations of sexual behaviour and to explore their causes. The point is that once sexuality was given priority as a necessary and central element in pair bonding, so the forms of sexual expression became more and more a matter of concern. This sexual categorisation has in turn to be associated with other social definitions which were emerging in recognisably modern forms at the same time, for example the emergence of the concept of adolescence, the redefinition of the significance of housework, the social concern with the status and redefinition of the role of motherhood at the beginning of this century, which in turn can be related to wider social needs, fear of national decline, the development of eugenics, concern with the imperial race and so on. The construction of the model of the heterosexual family and the complexly developing categorisations of behaviour and types, indeed the construction of new social beings, is one of the most characteristic but least recognised products of the way in which capitalism, complexly refracted through the whole of society, was creating new types of person to fill new social responsibilities and needs.

It is in this context that the regulation of homosexual behaviour has to be understood. Homosexuality as a complete experience has never been fully accepted in any type of society, although various forms of homosexual behaviour have been integrated into cultural norms. This has usually been organised in one of two forms: either in terms of institutionalised, and temporary, relations between older men and adolescent boys (such as in ancient Greece), or through the creation of a social role for "passive" men (and in some cased active women) who adopted all the characteristics of the opposite sex. The West perhaps has been almost alone in tabooing all forms of homosexual behaviour, though the taboos have varied throughout time and among different classes. The sodomy laws were the main source of the legal regulation of homosexual behaviour in Britain and throughout Western Europe and later North America. They were formally very severe, usually carrying the death penalty (as was the case in England until 1861), but were probably more effective in their grandeur and the terror they evoked than in their actual practical application. What is absent in Western concepts of homosexuality until the nineteenth century is any clear notion of a homosexual social role or homosexual identity. The word homosexuality itself was not invented until the 1860s and had very little general usage before the 1880s/1890s, even among specialists and small bands of self-defined homosexuals. What was controlled by the law, and indeed by public opinion much more effectively, was types of behaviour. What were punished and excoriated were *acts*, not persons. From the nineteenth century, however, what we see being defined, indeed created, in social science is a type of person; what is being condemned is not so much the activity but the state of mind. The sodomite, as Michel Foucault put it, was a temporary aberration; the homosexual belongs to a species.

From the second part of the nineteenth century, both in Britain, Germany, the USA and elsewhere, we see the emergence of new legal controls on male homosexual behaviour which had the effect of defining the narrow line between permissible and impermissible behaviour. Associated with this was the development of new ideological regulations and practices, particularly medical and psychiatric ones. These were practices and institutions that defined and in defining helped to create types of behaviour, types of persons. These definitions took changing forms from "degeneration" to "congenital madness", to unfortunate anomalies, to hereditary sicknesses, which became the regular mode of discussion for homosexuality until the 1960s.

The increasing concern and detailed manipulation and regulation of sexual behaviour has to be seen as a product of a double concern: with the life (and especially the sexual life) of the individual, a necessary concomitant of the emergence of bourgeois society; and with the life of the species, a concern with population which itself is a result of the vast demands made upon the social order by the development of industrial capitalism. The organisation of sexuality becomes an important way of organising the body politic. As Foucault puts it: "Sex becomes a means of access both to the life of the body and the life of the species." The ideologies and the social practices and institutions which began to define homosexual behaviour in a new way, as a product of a particular type of person, was part of this wider concern and regulation of sexual behaviour.

But, as against those modes of thought which speak of social control as if it were a simple imposition of ruling class ideas on a passive population, it is vitally important to recognise that the actual process of definition also creates the possibilities of a resistance and transformation, as individually and collectively we define ourselves in and against these categories. First of all there is the possibility of struggles over definition: "where there is power, there is resistance" as Foucault has put it. And this resistance can be seen in a wide range of areas, particularly in the struggles over definitions of female sexuality which went on throughout the nineteenth century among women, in opposition to husbands and doctors, and within the women's movement. There was a similarly complex but discernible resistance over the various and subtle forms of control of homosexuality. As Foucault has put it:

There is no question that the appearance in nineteenth-century psychiatry, jurisprudence, and literature of a whole series of discourses on the species and sub-species of homosexuality, inversion, pederasty,

and " psychic hermaphrodism" made possible a strong advance of
social controls into this area of "perversity"; but it also made possible
the formation of a "reverse" discourse: homosexuality began to speak
on its own behalf, to demand that its legitimacy or "naturality" be
acknowledged, often in the same vocabulary, using the same
categories by which it was radically disqualified.[5]

This reverse affirmation is in fact the history of the homosexual
rights movement from the end of the nineteenth century. It points
to the significance of the struggle over definitions, which are
actually struggles of power as to who should define. But there are
also limitations to this resistance. The resistance is all the time
going on within the terms as laid down by those who wield the
power to define, and hence the power to control and oppress.

We are accustomed when discussing homosexuality to think in
terms of a gradual relaxation of control. Thus, the Wolfenden
Report of the 1950s and its partial legal enactment in 1967 in
England and Wales is often seen as a relaxation of the legal
regulation of male homosexuality, and indeed in many ways of
course it was. But what is taking place in the deployment of the
"liberal" proposals of Wolfenden and the Homosexual Law
Reform Act (and this is characteristic of changes throughout
Western Europe and North America) is not so much an acceptance
of homosexuality as a change in its official definition: no longer as
a disease but as a condition, which has to be accepted as natural to
those to whom it occurs but which has to be quarantined as far as
possible from the majority of the population who do not
experience it. Thus the crucial factor about Wolfenden and the
1967 sexual law reform was the role of the distinction between
the public sphere and the private. Homosexuality was defined as
something which is acceptable because unavoidable, in private,
between consenting adults, but something which is not acceptable
in public: hence the tripling of the convictions of men for
homosexual behaviour in what were defined as public places after
1967. What is happening is that techniques of regulation are not
being abandoned or even in a real sense relaxed but are being
changed. Different types of sexual behaviour are becoming the
objects of regulation. There has been a switch away from the focus
on adult male homosexual behaviour, which dominated until the
1960s, towards a heightened concern with public displays of sexual
behaviour and relationships between adults and children.
Homosexuality, in other words, has not been accepted in society at
large; rather, the target for its control has switched. New
techniques of surveillance and of regulation are developing all the
time, and they are a product not simply of the needs of capitalist
mode of production nor of a simple evolution of attitudes, but of
the complex interaction of social needs, historical practices and
the self-activity of those defined.

This is the crucial significance of the gay movement since the
late 1960s because it has taken to its logical conclusion the reverse

affirmation that has always been characteristic of those homosexuals who have both accepted the definition and validated it. A homosexual identity is not given in nature, nor is it simply imposed as a social control on a deviant minority: it is the product of a long social process involving both definition and self-definition. It is a crucial stage in the rejection of stigmatisation, but at the same time it works very much within the definition presented. And all these definitions, categorisations, regulations are social impositions upon the flux of sexual possibilities there in the human animal at the time of birth. People are being defined narrowly as if they have a hidden essence, a true being which society has recognised. In taking this position, however, we are failing to challenge the restrictiveness of the definitions and beyond this the social origins of the categorisations.

What the gay movement is struggling for is not so much the freedom of an oppressed sexual minority, although the open practice of homosexuality has of course been severely restricted. We are struggling rather for the validation of a particular experience which has been rejected in sexual ideology over the last millenium. The point is that this experience is not something that belongs to a stigmatised minority alone. It is an experience which, except within limited forms of expression, has been denied within capitalist society. The tactical aim of the gay movement therefore obviously has to be in the first place to defend and assert the interests of those who define themselves as homosexual, and in the conditions of the 1980s this means the affirmation of a homosexual identity against those, especially on the far right, who would deny its validity. If there is a backlash it is here that it is located. But the strategic aim of the gay movement must be not simply the validation of the rights of a minority within a heterosexual majority, but the challenge to all the rigid categorisations of sexuality, categorisations which exist not to delineate scientifically one type of person from another but which act to control people's behaviour in very rigid ways.

But more than this, what the challenge to sexual categorisation must also involve is a challenge to the very ideology of "sexuality", that artificial socially constructed unification of the variety of pleasures of the body, not just genital, but covering the whole sensuous possibility of the human animal. We must, in other words, challenge the notion that sex, or particular types of sexual behaviour, constitutes the truth of the human individual. Foucault has captured this complex idea very well:

> I believe that the movements labelled "sexual liberation" ought to be understood as movements of affirmation starting with sexuality. Which means two things: they are movements that start with sexuality, with the apparatus of sexuality in the midst of which we are caught and which make it function to the limit; but, at the same time, they are in motion relative to it, disengaging themselves and surmounting them.[6]

The ramifications of this "surmounting" are not clear but it is apparent both that the evolution of homosexual meanings and identities is not complete or scientifically established, *and* that homosexuals are, possibly (and certainly on a large scale) for the first time, self-consciously participating in that evolution. But the logical culmination of this battle, necessary in the short, medium and perhaps even long term as it is, is the end, as Dennis Altman once put it, of the homosexual and indeed of the heterosexual, the transcendence of the narrow categories which are products of bourgeois society. And what we must affirm ultimately is not so much the rights of the homosexual, but the pleasures and joy in all their multiform ways of the whole body. It is not just the end of the homosexual or the heterosexual we must demand but the end of the ideology of sexuality. We must dethrone King Sex, and replace him with the possibilities of pleasure and sensuousness which exist in the human animal. The struggle for sexual self-definition is a struggle in the end for control over our bodies. To establish this control we must escape from those ideologies and categorisation which imprison us within the existing social order.

NOTES AND REFERENCES

1. Gordon Rattray Taylor, *Sex in History,* London, 1953.
2. Michel Foucault, *A History of Sexuality,* vol. 1, London, 1979.
3. William Gagnon and John H. Simon, *Sexual Conduct,* London, 1973.
4. Mike Brake, "I may be queer, but at least I am a man", in D. L. Barker and S. Allen (eds.), *Sexual Divisions in Society,* London, 1976.
5. Foucault, op. cit.
6. Foucault, interview in *Telos*, Summer 1977, p. 155.

2

The Struggle for Femininity

MARGARET COULSON

*"To strangle the angel in the house, that is one of the tasks
for revolutionaries, for women in politics and for militant feminists"*[1]

To examine the definition and control of women's sexuality in
capitalism is not an academic exercise. I am writing with a real
sense of political urgency which I want others to share. Since the
late sixties a new wave of feminism and sexual politics has swept
over us. It has landed some of us in places which, in terms of
politics and personal life, were almost unimaginable fifteen or
twenty years ago. It has given us new strength in our identities as
women, as lesbians, as revolutionaries. It has given us glimpses of
a "new politics"(whose history we have only now re-discovered),
of the possibility of integrating struggles in personal life and in
public politics; it has transformed the way we see politics and
ourselves and the relationship between our politics and ourselves.
We may celebrate ten years of women's liberation, ten years of gay
liberation, but we cannot take this burst of sexual politics for
granted.

Our knowledge of past struggles of women against various
dimensions of capitalist patriarchy, of past moments of sexual
politics, tells us that the waves of feminism have risen before —
and have fallen away. Dora Russell wrote of the ending of an
earlier feminist era in the late twenties: "There are periods in
human history when, without apparent reason, at first
imperceptibly, the movement in one direction, goes into
reverse.The change occurs not only in the economics and politics
of the time but even in the motivation of individual lives."[2] I think
we are again moving into such a period of human history; the
political tide is pulling back again. Perhaps an army of Queen
Canutes cannot stem the present pull of reaction (or perhaps we
can?). At least we can try to become politically conscious of the
forces which are now affecting the motivations of our individual
lives. We can look sharply and self-consciously at this period of
sexual politics, at what it has meant for ourselves, for women's
consciousness and women's struggles, for socialist politics.

The majority of women (happily for society) are not very much
troubled by sexual feelings of any kind . . . Here is one perfect example:
"She assured me that she felt no sexual passions whatsoever; that if she
was capable of them, they were dormant. Her passion for her husband

was of a platonic kind, and far from wishing to stimulate his frigid
feelings, she doubted whether it would be right or not. She loved him as
he was and would not desire him to be otherwise except for the hope of
having a family. I believe this lady is the perfect ideal of an English wife
and mother, kind, considerate, self-sacrificing and sensible, so pure-
hearted as to be utterly ignorant of and averse to any sensual
indulgence, but so unselfishly attached to the man she loves as to be
willing to give up her own wishes and feelings for his sake.[3]

There was also in the seventeenth century a repeated male complaint
about the sexual insatiability of women. "Of woman's unnatural
insatiable lust, what country, what village does not complain?"
declared Robert Burton in his *Anatomy* in 1621. . . . Apparently old
beliefs of feminine sexual evil combined with a popular view that the
active vagina and insistent clitoris were too much for any man to cope
with.[4]

Contradictory images of women and definitions of women's
sexuality have a longer history than capitalism. From her holy
pedestal the madonna was defined by her spirituality, her
suffering, her selflessness, a denial of her sexuality. By contrast
woman could be seen as temptress, representing sensuality, sexual
appetite and extravagance, the "sins of the flesh"; the witch might
be old, ugly, solitary but still mysterious, fearful, in league —
perhaps even sexually — with the devil. Woman could be sexless or
sexually dangerous; fragile, beautiful or ugly; an object of
admiration, excitement or fear; in need of careful protection or in
need of rigorous control. The ambivalence towards women
implicit in such imagery seems (superficially at least) to find
expression, in various ways, in very many patriarchal cultures.
Perhaps this is indicative of a general interconnection, within
patriarchal societies, of the subordination of women, their
subservience, with a fear of women's potential power and
potential for revolt; it suggests the interdependence of male
dominance and misogyny. These contradictory images of
femininity are framed and formulated by the oppressor, but they
both acknowledge and deny the potential of the oppressed (rather
like the nineteenth-century bourgeois fear of the unruly but
worthless mob at the base of society). They do not seem to be an
expression of women's own experiences or to reflect women's own
protests against oppression or the repression of sexuality. Such
voices seem to have been rarely heard, more rarely recorded.
    With the emergence of capitalism women began to speak more
clearly and insistently for themselves. Feminism has broken in
recurrent waves on to the political stage. Questions relating to the
position of women in society, the definition of femininity and of
women's sexuality have gradually, if uncertainly, been recognised
as areas of political struggle, at least from the perspective of the
current feminist movement. Because of this, I want to look at the

question of women's sexuality not only as an area of bourgeois patriarchal control and repression but also as an area of struggle against oppression, and to consider the broad political significance of this.

With the development of capitalism new dimensions to the contradictory definitions of women and women's sexuality began to emerge in the context of the extensive restructuring of all social relationships. The separation of labour and capital established the major classes of capitalist society; the separation of the household from social production, together with the preservation of the family and its transformation into a privatised domestic unit, created a new basis for the sexual division of labour with the woman as housewife, "domestic labourer". Among the bourgeoisie, capitalism built on an image of femininity which totally denied women's sexuality; the bourgeois lady was idle, an object to display her husband's wealth, totally dependent economically and politically, a part of his property. Yet at the same time, women (at first mainly working-class women) were also drawn out of the domestic unit and into general production. This development within capitalism seemed to suggest that the sexual division of labour could become redundant; that women might find a social position which was not determined by family status. Paid employment in social production implied the promise of economic independence, the possibility of a livelihood not dependent on the family, not involving personal dependence on men. The realisation of this possibility is blocked within capitalism; most women, most of the time, find themselves defined primarily as wives and mothers (or as failures in marriage and maternity). But while some women are required in the paid labour force, the complete and consistent operation of a division of labour allocating women to the home, to be housewives and mothers, men to work, to be breadwinners, cannot be upheld with conviction. Thus the position of women in capitalism is structured by the contradictory relationship between the private sphere of the family and the public sphere of general production.

At times the cracks around these contradictions in the fabric of capitalism widen sufficiently for a "new independent woman" to emerge into public view, and for some women to begin to claim a right to define femininity for themselves.

Alexandra Kollontai wrote about the experiences of this "new woman", struggling both for self determination in her personal and sexual relationships, and to enter fully into social and political life: "With the change of economic conditions, the evolution of production relations, the inner physiognomy of woman also changes." The single independent woman, earning her own living, develops "a new psychological sense, new needs, a new temper". She has "ceased to play this subordinate role and to be no more than the reflex of the man. She has a singular inner world, full of general human interest, she is independent inwardly and self-reliant outwardly".[5]

Kollontai was writing from the experience of her personal life and from the context of the dramatic changes brought by the development of large-scale industry in Russia early in this century, and from the perspective of her aspirations for the Russian revolution. She was both utopian and pessimistic; on the one hand all her hopes for the "new woman" were without the support of any clear concept of the structure and depth of the patriarchal relations she had to challenge; on the other hand she saw women now becoming the subjects (rather than the objects) of life's tragedies. Kollontai did not, and does not, provide many of the answers to the problems of sexual politics, but she remains important because of the significance of many of the questions which she raised. She saw sexual relations and the struggle of women for a new and more autonomous identity in the context of class struggle; she identified the ideology of sexual relationships in their relation to class relationships and to bourgeois ideology and saw the political importance of a counter-theory in the interests of the proletariat. She saw a connection between periods of social crisis and the development of crises over sexuality and in relations between the sexes which affect working-class people as well as the upper layers of society.[6] She recognised that the possibility of economic independence was crucial to smash "the dogmas that keep woman a prisoner of her own world view".[7] Besides all this, Kollontai knew the agony and the anguish which women experience in the process of struggle to redefine their identities: "The old and the new struggle in the souls of women, in permanent enmity. Contemporary heroines, therefore, must wage a struggle on two fronts: with the external world and with the inclinations of their grandmothers dwelling in the recesses of their beings."[7]

This " struggle on two fronts" must be familiar to so many contemporary feminists and women in revolutionary politics.[8] Writing more than fifty years after Kollontai, in an article which explores the relationship between fascism and sexuality, Maria-Antonietta Macciocchi identifies the struggle against "this old" femininity as the struggle against "the angel in the house, that distressing ghost which still haunts us". She quotes from Virginia Woolf's "Three Guineas":

The shadow of her wings fell on my page; I heard the rustle of her skirts in the room. Directly, that is to say, I took up my pen to review that novel by a famous man, she slipped behind me and whispered: "my dear, you are a young woman. You are writing about a book that has been written by a man. Be sympathetic; be tender; flatter; deceive; use all the arts and wiles of our sex. Never let anybody guess that you have a mind of your own. Above all, be pure. . . ." I turned upon her and caught her by the throat. . . . Killing the Angel in the House was part of the occupation of a woman writer.

Macciocchi sees "the angel in the house" as a link between patriarchy and fascist tyranny, a link which capitalism does not break. To Virginia Woolf she adds: "to strangle the angel in the house, that is one of the tasks of revolutionaries, for women in politics and for militant feminists".[9]

However, before we take on the "angel in the house" we need to understand something about how she has been constructed. In any patriarchal society the definition of women's sexuality (and men's) is embedded in the definition of femininity (and masculinity) and both develop out of and in relation to the sexual division of labour. The sexual division of labour constructs a social division between the sexes which is both an acknowledgement and a social elaboration of the biological differences between them. It establishes the social dependence of one sex on the other and seems to put a premium on heterosexuality. However, the sexual division of labour does not determine definitions of femininity, and specifically female sexuality, in a simple way. For example, in capitalism established concepts of masculinity and femininity are perpetuated not only as some sort of reflection and justification of the way relationships between men and women are structured within the privatised family unit and in relation to the capitalist economy and state. They also draw on residual pre-capitalist patriarchal concepts and assumptions which cling with a special persistence around social relations which are imposed on biological characteristics and so can appear "natural". So we have to look historically at how particular definitions of femininity and of women's sexuality have developed in the context of changes in the sexual division of labour and other social changes.

Women's sexuality is only one aspect of femininity and its relation to femininity as a whole may also be problematic. There is a tendency in capitalism for social life to be lived in separate compartments, for experience to be fragmented. Earning one's living, cleaning the house, caring for a child, making love, reading a book — each activity seems to demand a different part of one's self. It is extremely difficult to be a whole person. The compartment in which our sexuality is allowed its most direct expression seems particularly segregated from the rest of life. In the capitalist split betwen public and private life, sexual relations are hidden in the most private area of private life. Although sexuality seems to be a crucial aspect of femininity, it can also be experienced as something apart, separate from the rest of one's life and one's identity. Thus when women in the past have challenged the experience of femininity as passivity and dependence they have not always extended that challenge to the idea of women's sexual passivity and dependence. However, there is less acceptance of such a split amongst feminists today. We want economic and political independence for women; we are struggling for a redefinition of femininity which includes our sexuality, and which is seen in the context of a struggle to transform all social relationships into human relationships.

An exceedingly long patriarchal history precedes capitalism. The sexual division which develops in the context of the development of commodity production have past (specifically feudal) patriarchal traditions to draw from and wrestle with. Old definitions of femininity and masculinity, old notions about sexuality are remodelled as the new society develops. As in feudalism, the sexual division of labour has continued to be structured through the family but the family has lost the solidity it had as a unit of production in feudalism, and the sexual division of labour has lost some of the clarity *and* flexibility which were associated with that.

Internally this family unit has been structured around increasingly unequal relationships to the public world of social production, as, through the nineteenth century, women's subsidiary position in general production became more explicit, and children were excluded altogether, creating the relationships of economic dependence on a male breadwinner as a peculiarly bourgeois norm of family relationships. Sally Alexander argues that from the 1820s and 1830s, women's paid employment became defined as a problem:

> The woman as wife and mother was pivot of the family and consequently guardian of all Christian and domestic virtues. Women's waged work, therefore, was discussed in so far as it harmonised with home, family and domestic virtue.[10]

The sexual division of labour inherited from the past became more inflexible. Women lost the right to be "persons" and so were explicitly excluded from areas of the public world where — if by chance they had acquired appropriate skills or qualifications — they might previously have entered. Traditional women's skills were eroded (a process which has continued as commodity production has taken over and transformed more areas of "women's work"), while the work remaining in the home has become virtually invisible, outside the direct relations of the market where public recognition and economic rewards — however meagre — are handed out.

The woman's primary place became that of housewife, the man's that of breadwinner/worker. This polarised sexual division was at its most extreme among the upper classes where man and wife inhabited quite separate social worlds. The man's world was public affairs, rationality, discipline and action; while the wife was literally confined to the private sphere of the household, of emotionality and sickness, of idleness and reaction; one of her husband's possessions without rights over her self, her body, her children, her property, her earnings (if she had any).

Why did the bourgeoisie, in the process of establishing itself, reduce its women to this? And how did it succeed to such a great extent? Albie Sachs argues that underlying this "social brutality" was a "twofold material interest structured around gender: first that women should continue to serve men in the domestic sphere at home, and second that they should not swell the ranks of competition at work".[11] Besides, upper-class men had much to gain from the subordination of women generally (not only "their own") both in terms of direct and indirect economic advantages to be gained from a cheap pool of female labour and unpaid domestic labour, and also in terms of the complex but vast contribution which the inferiorisation of women makes to the maintenance of the political stability of capitalism. With momentary exceptions this interest does not seem to have diminished with the further development of capitalism.

In relation to the second question, it is important to recognise that besides the extraordinary effectiveness of total economic dependence, other forms of coercion contributed to the achievement of this degree of female subservience and docility. The medical profession played a significant part in this, defining femininity itself as sickness and by using (and building) its professional power and authority to intimidate many women into experiencing it as such.[12] In *The Yellow Wallpaper* Charlotte Perkins Gilman gives an account of this process from the inside. The wife of a wealthy doctor documents her captivity, watched over by her husband:

> If a physician of high standing, and one's own husband, assures friends and relatives that there is really nothing the matter with one but temporary nervous depression — a slight hysterical tendency — what is one to do? My brother is also a physician, and also of high standing, and he says the same thing. So I take phosphates or phosphites — whichever it is, and tonics, and journeys, and air, and exercise, and am absolutely forbidden to "work" until I am well again. Personally I disagree with their ideas. Personally I believe that congenial work, with excitement and change, would do me good. But what is one to do? I did write for a time in spite of them; but it *does* exhaust me a good deal — having to be so sly about it, or else meet with heavy opposition.[13]

Thus in the upper classes the bourgeois family assumed masculinity and femininity to be polarised in every way. The dual morality was one statement of this, reading back into biology to establish what appears to be a basic biological incompatibility between the sexes. Male sexual appetite was complemented not by female sexual appetite but by that longing for maternity which alone enabled women to submit to the sexual attentions of their husbands. Prostitution flourished alongside bourgeois monogamy with its insistence on premarital chastity, marital fidelity and the asexuality of bourgeois women. The other side of femininity which lurked in the subterranean areas of society also existed to supply the sexual needs of men. Behind the apparently contradictory notions of female sexuality represented by the lady and the prostitute lay a more consistent and more powerful ideology of male sexual needs, seen as active, insistent and when aroused as overpowering.[14]Thus rape could be interpreted as one expression of male sexual needs; in less extreme circumstances men demand sex and women supply it (in prostitution or in marriage), men initiate, women respond.

Lesbians have no place in this sexual ideology, except perhaps, to titillate men's sexual fantasies in pornography (it is interesting that pornographic representations of lesbians are still produced primarily for male consumption). In the later nineteenth century the definition of male homosexuality became a matter of more explicit bourgeois concern — a perversion, the property of a "queer" minority, a criminal offence — while lesbian sexuality was stifled by silence. The possibility of an active female sexuality was excluded; women without reference to men were sexless. The established model of sexual relations involved dominance and submission; one (male) to initiate, one (female) to respond — or endure. Two women together, both "utterly ignorant of and averse to any sensual indulgence", could not make any sexual connection; their passivities could lie side by side in perfect spirituality and innocence. Thus women were not mentioned in the 1885 Criminal Amendment Act, not simply because Queen Victoria would not understand such a reference to her own sex, but more fundamentally because there seemed to be no need to give such acknowledgement to women's sexuality.

The ideology of male sexual needs seems to cohere around the dominant position of the man, as breadwinner, in the sexual division of labour. As this model of the bourgeois family became more systematically upheld through the gradual but persistent intervention of the state into domestic life, the ideology of male sexual needs and female passivity permeated downwards through society. (So, my grandmother, born in the 1870s, *not* into the bourgeoisie, was guilt-ridden to her dying day because she had enjoyed sex once in over sixty years of married life. The sexual adventurousness of her son who was conceived on this occasion caused her great anguish, and she was convinced that the origins of his immorality could be traced to her one experience of any sexual pleasure.)

It is, perhaps, not surprising, that one critical response to the ideology of male sexual needs has been to argue that men should become as "spiritual" as women and that sexuality should become an insignificant feature of human society. Many feminists of the late nineteenth and early twentieth centuries held this to be the solution to the problem of sexual relations and would, perhaps, have approved the sort of sexual "puritanism" that has become a feature of some revolutionary movements in the twentieth century.

Women's commitment to motherhood has provided a convenient rationale for the sexual definition of women as an appendage to male sexual needs. Women have been mothers at all times, everywhere. During the latter part of the nineteenth century religious interpretations of this fact of nature were increasingly replaced (or complemented) by scientific theories drawing significantly from theories of evolution and from the establishment of the modern medical profession (male dominated and with a legal monopoly of knowledge and the right to practice). Women were biologically designed for maternity, and this precluded them biologically from intellectual or political endeavours or from an active sexuality. These ideas developed within a broader framework of scientific theories which have continued to dominate thinking about sexuality and human nature through the twentieth century.[15]

In the late nineteenth century women's sexuality could only be pathological, a source of venereal disease in working-class women, a source of sickness in upper-class women. Strong residues of that thinking persist now. Women who stray "too far" from sexual deference to male needs are still condemned — the nymphomaniac, the slag, the slut, the whore. Amongst juvenile delinquents girls are much more likely to be seen as sexually delinquent than boys.[16] The state has turned the definition of maternity back on to women as a means of control. "Bad" women are not fit to be mothers and their children must be "protected", i.e. taken away from them. Thus women who had committed adultery were specifically debarred from claiming custody of their children before 1873; Annie Besant lost the custody of her daughter after being charged with publishing an obscene work, a cheap edition of a pamphlet on birth control; a hundred years later lesbians are still considered unfit mothers and lose their children in custody cases.[17] Theories of children's needs have been used to tighten the knots surrounding motherhood, drawing on and intensifying women's guilt in the context of the lack of social choices available to them. John Bowlby's work purporting to show that "maternal deprivation" produces "affectionless personalities" was used, after the Second World War, to undermine mothers who went out to work, and "latch-key" children were more prone to delinquency and used to "prove" the same point.[18] The Plowden Report (a "liberal" document concerned with primary education published in 1967) recommended that "mothers who cannot satisfy the authorities that they have exceptionally good reasons for working should have low priority for full time nursery education for their children". The state, with great success, plays the needs of children (conceptualised in a totally patronising way as is shown by the symbol for the international year of the child: a child being smothered by an adult) against the rights of women as mothers. Social responsibility for children is only recognised where mothers are deemed to be "inadequate", or where there is a sudden need for large numbers of women in the paid workforce as in times of war.

Economic dependence, emotional concern about what happens to children, lack of choices, these combine to perpetuate feminine subordination, sexual passivity and submission.

Probably the most powerful theory of this femininity has been Freud's. His work provided a sharp documentation of women's oppression and specifically the repression of female sexuality; maternity was woman's compensation for lack of a penis. In an age which still upheld rationality Freud showed the significance of irrationality in human development and created the concept of the unconscious as the key to understanding it.[19] But his insights were not tempered by any sense of history. Despite his ambivalence concerning the costs and benefits of "civilisation", he offered no political answers. Freud remained a pessimist.[20]

Macciocchi has argued that the time has come (politically) to confront this pessimism; I think she is right.[21] The unconscious has become an easy dumping ground for all the things we cannot understand about human beings, about social consciousness and practice; psychoanalysis cannot cure us all of the repressions which patriarchal capitalist culture has structured into our feminine identities. We must understand that women have not always embraced the role of "angel in the house" We need now to develop a theory which recognises the contradictions structuring femininity in capitalism, and which recognises that when these contradictions have opened up there has been a basis for struggle over the definition of femininity.

Fascism has generally represented the most total denial of the possibility of such struggle. The polarisation of masculinity and femininity, the assertion of male sexual needs as against maternal longings, these have found their most grotesque expression in the theory and practice of fascism in the twentieth century. The National Front newspaper, *Spearhead,* asks:

> What conceivable point could there be in eradicating the obvious truth that women are weaker than men, that male and female have biologically based inclinations, the latter to childbirth and motherhood? What advantage is there in obscuring sexual differences and dehumanising the distinct qualities of manhood and womanhood?

John Tyndall, a Front leader, wants to "see real manhood and real womanhood once again valued".[22]

Virginia Woolf pointed to the continuity of such ideas between capitalism and fascism, comparing views expressed in the *Daily Telegraph* with those of the leaders of National Socialism in Germany. She quotes:

> Homes are the real places of the women who are now compelling men to be idle. It is time the Government insisted upon employers giving more work to men, thus enabling them to marry the women they cannot now approach.

Virginia Woolf puts this beside another quotation:

There are two worlds in the life of the nation, the world of men and the world of women. Nature has done well to entrust the man with the care of his family and the nation. The woman's world is her family, her husband, her children, her home.

She comments:

One is written in English, the other in German. But where is the difference? Are they not both the voices of dictators, whether they speak English or German, and are we not all agreed that the dictator when we meet him abroad is a very dangerous as well as a very ugly animal? And he is here among us, raising his ugly head, spitting his poison, small still, curled up like a caterpillar on a leaf, but in the heart of England.[23]

And today we can compare this to the idea, now gaining in public expression, that the new silicon chip technology which threatens so many office jobs (women's jobs) will "liberate" women from the strains of employment and enable them to rediscover the true meaning of their lives in the home.

It is because fascism has taken certain patriarchal features of capitalism to sharper extremes, and has actually mobilised support for itself on this basis that it seems important to consider the case of fascism, if only briefly, here.

In fascism woman must be above all the "angel in the house"; she has been courted by fascist leaders; eulogies about maternity have given recognition to the vital contribution which women make to the preservation of the race and to the maintenance of the state. (All this, of course, only applies to the "genetically" and "racially" pure: blacks, jews, "perverts", the physically and mentally handicapped and so on are all excluded; for them, deportation, abortion, sterilisation, suppression.) This dimension of fascism gave some basis to its appeal to many men whose jobs and status were thereby made to appear more sure. But it appealed to masses of women too, who responded to the idea that they could celebrate their enslavement as a sacred calling (for a woman, of course; Goebbels explained, "when we eliminate women from public life, it is not because we want to dispense with them, but rather that we want to give them back their essential honour"). The political problem here is "the irrationality of the consent the masses give to fascism"; this is a crucial (if less blatant) political problem in capitalism in its more everyday forms. As Reich and more recently Macciocchi have argued, it points to the significance of the part which the repression and "murder of sexuality", above all female sexuality, play in the achievement of this consent.[24]

However, even in fascism, in practice, it has not been possible to sustain the definition of femininity solely as the "angel in the house". Here is the other side of the continuity with capitalism. In nazi Germany, for example, by the 1940s the national socialist programme for women was becoming more contradictory, reflecting "the contradictory tendencies which influence the social position of women in the period of the general crisis of capitalism". One writer of that period pictures the contradictions in this way:

> One can hold out the ideal of the Sleeping Beauty, who remains in her father's castle until the beautiful prince pushes his way through the thorny hedge and wakes the dreamer with a kiss; or one can accustom the rising generation of women to work a machine gun and wear a gas mask; but one cannot think of a Sleeping Beauty with a gas mask — and that is what national socialism tries to do.[25]

Even in fascism the myths surrounding maternity have not been sufficient to contain women always in the home, and in capitalism the authority of tradition and science has recurrently been chipped away or when necessary rewritten; maternity has not always been an adequate jailer. Some women have escaped, some have even been pushed out of the "domestic prison", some have challenged what motherhood means. The ideology that femininity equals maternity equals the "angel in the house" has been disturbed by other trends working within capitalism. First, some women, especially working-class women, have always *gone out* to work; in this century world wars and the labour shortage of the 1950s and 1960s drew greater numbers of women and increasingly married women into the paid labour force (more mothers having two jobs, more women in paid employment). Secondly, the labour requirements of capital have changed; there has been an increasing concern with the quality of the labour force and of future generations (health, intelligence, education and so on); families have become smaller, state intervention in the reproduction of labour power has become larger. (Motherhood is no longer a life-long occupation; and mother does not know best.) Thirdly, there has been a dramatic increase in the range, availability and reliability of contraception, making the separation of sex and conception more of a technical possibility; so that motherhood could become a positive choice, sex could be just for pleasure. (One practical prop for a dual morality takes a knock; women don't have to risk pregnancy as an inevitable accompaniment of heterosexual sex.)

These three contradictory trends have been long-term ones, although their development has been uneven. They have become interwoven with a growing tendency for the repression and manipulation of sexuality to become a more powerful and more pervasive dimension of bourgeois political control. Gramsci, writing in the 1930s, pointed out that the new methods of rationalisation of production required a "new type of man" who "cannot be developed until the sexual instinct has been suitably regulated and until it too has been rationalised".[26] And Marcuse has provided further analysis around this theme in the context of the United States of the 1950s.[27] Reich suggested that the authoritarian basis of relationships within the family establishes particularly crucial to the control of women's sexuality; and they demonstrate many of the complexities and contradictions. They have been dominated by a number of themes concerning the "family stability" for the maintenance of law and order. Sexuality must be constrained *and* allowed some sort of expression.

The period since the Second World War has seen all of these trends intensify in the context of other changes. The marked expansion of the (literally) domestic market has focused more attention on women as consumers and on young people as consumers without responsibilities. Sex, especially as symbolised by women's bodies, has become more important as a means of selling commodities; advertising depends on the exploitation of the irrationalities of social consciousness. Commercially defined and objectified images of women now bombarded us from everywhere, telling us that women today must be sexy *and* selfless: attracting and holding their man, feeding and caring for their husbands and sons while starving themselves for the sake of the stereotype of how they should look. Women are objectified and objectify themselves. The diversity of images of femininity means women can never get it right; being a successful, selfless, smiling mum seems incompatible with being a person, with being an attractive sexual being. So we are all failures and vulnerable because of it.

Alongside the old puritanism surrounding sex, which still has a lot of institutional support, the newer permissiveness has developed. This bears the imprint of the commercial market with its compulsive emphasis on novelty and built in obsolescence, the apparent licence to search for sexual thrills, new experiences. "Open marriages", wife swapping and sexual orgies in the suburbs, and the breakdown of the ideology of premarital chastity (though still within the framework of a dual morality), these have been some of the expressions of this "permissiveness" and of its containment. The more strident sexual ideology now insists that women are sexual beings too, orgasms are not just normal but necessary; the "frigid" woman is a failure. But the idea of the primacy of male sexual needs marches determinedly onwards, over these changes, and is likely to continue to do so while women still remain largely within the constraints of general economic inequality (in work and pay) and dependence (in the family).[29]

And yet women have not been simply passive recipients of shifting — or unchanging — definitions of themselves, their sexuality. Struggles for education, for economic and political rights, for contraception and abortion, for child allowances and nurseries and so on, have simmered, been pleaded, exploded, gained concessions, been contained, assimilated, erupted again, as capitalism has developed on its contradictory path. The waves of feminism rise again and again.[30]

The relationship of such struggles to class politics has often been uneasy. Struggles around contraception and abortion have been an important pattern for the authority of the state.[28] This idea receives frequent public acknowledgement as bourgeois polititians and religious leaders pontificate about the importance of relation between sex and reproduction which have been of persisting significance across the last hundred and fifty years, despite the considerable developments in contraceptive techniques and other changes. As in other areas there has been (and still is) a prolonged battle going on, in this case about who contraception is for, what it is for, who has and should have control over it. The means of controlling fertility has been seen on one hand as an essential prerequisite of women's sexual liberation; in its absence any liberalisation of sexuality could only favour men at the expense of women. Conversely, contraception has been seen as a threat to established control of women's sexuality which has relied heavily on women's fear of conception. In the 1820s William Cobbett argued this latter case against Francis Place and Richard Carlisle. In the 1920s Stella Browne was putting a clearly feminist case: "Birth control for women is no less essential than workshop control and determination over the conditions of labour for men. . . . Birth control is woman's crucial effort at self-determination and at control of her own person and her own environment."[31]

Fifty or sixty years ago this was still rather a lonely point of view; many older feminists had seen the answer to the "sexual question" as trying to make men become as "spiritual" as women. Stella Browne's own ideas were still caught in the common assumption that a "natural" division of labour underlay relations between the sexes; she was concerned that in the present repressive sexual relations, lacking control over their fertility, more women than were "truly" lesbian would be drawn into a lesbian way of life (lesbianism might be admirable for women who really were lesbians, but they were a distinct minority). Later, the hippy movement of the 1960s brought an exuberant and disrespectful challenge to sexual repressiveness and hypocrisy. While it remained oblivious of its own heterosexist and sexist assumptions, it helped, politically, to change the framework of the discussion of sexuality and sexism which have since been taken up in the women's liberation and gay movements.

The development of contraception has also been seen as a way of breaking the "inevitable" trap of poverty and associated social problems. The long shadow of Malthus still overhangs these debates. From the latter part of the nineteenth century it has combined with theories about defective inheritance and the identification of " perversions" to raise the question: who is fit to have children? In defence of imperialism, preserving the quality of the great white British "civilisation" and British race, as the solution to poverty in the third world,[32] as a means of reducing welfare claimants in the advanced capitalist world,[33] as a central tactic of fascism, this question has had a brutal and practical significance. Socialists attacking eugenicist ideas and policies have often argued against feminists defending birth control as a woman's right, and many women proponents of birth control (like Marie Stopes), including some feminists (like Margaret Sanger), were not unsympathetic to eugenicist arguments.

Perhaps the perspectives of the latest wave of feminism and sexual politics have gone further than earlier ones to create a basis from which we can disentangle some of these political issues. It seems that we have gone further than before in raising questions about biology and the idea of a "natural" basis to relationships between the sexes, or a "natural" femininity hidden behind the layers of repression. We can recognise now that biology does not have to be destiny but that it has provided a basis on which, in its various forms, patriarchy has been built. Biological differences between the sexes are not dreamt up by the privileged, nor by men in general. Women, biologically defined, have the capacity for conception, pregnancy, childbirth, lactation and so on; men do not. The relationship between sex and reproduction differs: "While the very act of procreation insists on the male orgasm, conception can take place even without female arousal".[34] However, patriarchy is not just a conspiracy to deny us our "true natures". It is through culture, defining biology, that having babies becomes a social disadvantage, that rearing children is women's work, that sexuality is heterosexual and genitally focused, that men are the dominant sex. When we have created the conditions for controlling society and culture in the interests of humanity, rather than being controlled by them, the possibilities of liberation can really be explored and our relationship to our biology may appear quite differently from now.[35]

We have begun to analyse personal life and the domestic labour of the housewife and their relation to the public world of political and economic life. We have examined the way in which these relationships have structured the sexual division of labour in capitalism, and the ways in which the ideology of male sexual needs and the subordination of women's sexuality are organised around these. We can see, perhaps more clearly than many earlier feminists, that to redefine femininity we need to reclaim both our minds and our bodies, we need to reinterpret maternity as well as our sexuality. Strangling the "angel in the house" involves taking on all these dimensions of femininity. But we have only made a beginning on these questions; none of them is resolved, and the political situation is less and less favourable to the pursuit of them. We have to be clearer about the political significance of sexuality if we are not to be pushed into abandoning these questions, or being abandoned with them, as the pressures back to a narrower and more defensive politics gain momentum in the more reactionary context which is becoming established in the early 1980s.

NOTES AND REFERENCES

1. Maria-Antonietta Macciocchi, "Female Sexuality in Fascist Ideology", *Feminist Review,* no. 1, 1979, p. 73.
2. Dora Russell, *The Tamarisk Tree,* London, 1975, p. 216.
3. William Acton, *Functions and Disorders of the Reproductive Organs in Youth, in Adult Age and in Advanced Life considered in their physiological, social and moral relations,* 1857, quoted by Alex Comfort in *The Anxiety Makers,* London, 1968, pp. 61, 62.
4. Sheila Rowbotham, *Hidden from History,* London, 1973, pp. 6, 7.
5. Alexandra Kollontai, "The New Woman", in *The Autobiography of a Sexually Emancipated Woman,* London, 1972, p. 95.
6. Alexandra Kollontai, "Sexual Relations and Class Struggle", in *Selected Writings,* London, 1977.
7. Alexandra Kollontai, "The New Woman", op. cit., pp. 101, 102.
8. For one thoughtful discussion of this, see Jane Hawksley, Wendy Hollway, Frances Rickford, Pamela Trevithick, "How Do You Feel? Feminists, Sexuality and Social Relations", paper to Socialist Feminist Conference, Manchester 1978.
9. Maria-Antonietta Macciocchi, "Female Sexuality in Fascist Ideology", op. cit., p. 73.
10. Sally Alexander, "Women's Work in Nineteenth-Century London", in Juliet Mitchell and Ann Oakley (eds.), *The Rights and Wrongs of Women,* London, 1976, p. 61.
11. Albie Sachs, "The Myth of Male Protectiveness and the Legal Subordination of Women", in Carol Smart and Barry Smart (eds.), *Women, Sexuality and Social Control,* London, 1978, p. 39.
12. Barbara Ehrenreich and Deirdre English, *Complaints and Disorders,* New York, 1972.
13. Charlotte Perkins Gilman, *The Yellow Wallpaper,* New York, 1973, p. 10.
14. Mary McIntosh, "Who Needs Prostitutes? The ideology of male sexual needs", in Carol Smart and Barry Smart (eds.), *Women, Sexuality and Social Control.*
15. Robert M. Young, "The Human Limit of Nature", in Jonathan Benthall (ed.), *The Limits of Human Nature,* London, 1973.
16. Lesley Shacklady Smith, "Sexist Assumptions and Female Delinquency", in Carol Smart and Barry Smart (eds.), *Women, Sexuality and Social Control.*
17. Bernice Humphreys, "Lesbians and Child Custody", paper to Socialist Feminist Conference, London 1979.
18. This work is criticised by Lee Comer, *The Myth of Motherhood,* Nottingham 1972.
19. Juliet Mitchell, *Psychoanalysis and Feminism,* London 1974, for a detailed and sympathetic discussion of Freud's analysis of women.
20. See Ann Foreman, *Femininity as Alienation*, London 1977, for a short, sharp critique.
21. Maria-Antonietta Macciocchi, "Female Sexuality in Fascist Ideology", op. cit., p. 81.

22. Quoted by Veronica Ware, *Women and the National Front,* Searchlight Pamphlet, p. 8.
23. Virginia Woolf, *Three Guineas,* Harmondsworth 1977, p. 62.
24. Wilhelm Reich, *What is Class Consciousness?* and *The Mass Psychology of Fascism,* Harmondsworth, 1975.
25. Alfred Meusel, *National Socialism and the Family.*
26. Antonio Gramsci, *Prison Notebooks,* London 1971, p. 297.
27. Herbert Marcuse, *One Dimensional Man,* London 1964.
28. Wilhelm Reich, *The Mass Psychology of Fascism.*
29. Bea Campbell, "Sexuality and Submission", in *Red Rag,* no. 5.
30. Sheila Rowbotham, *Hidden from History.*
31. Sheila Rowbotham, *A New World for Women: Stella Browne – Socialist Feminist,* p. 62.
32. Bonnie Mass, *The Political Economy of Population Control in Latin America,* Editions Latin America, 1972.
33. Dwight J. Ingle, *Who Shall Have Children?,* New York 1973.
34. Roberta Hamilton, *The Liberation of Women,* London 1978, p. 85.
35. Marge Piercy explores possibilities for the future in *Woman on the Edge of Time,* Fawcett Crest, 1976.

3

Sexuality: Regulation and Contestation

FRANK MORT

A significant element in the development of struggles around sexuality has been an awareness of a sense of history. The rediscovery of earlier movements and forms of contestation — the construction of types of history that were previously unwritten — has played an important part in the formation of the political consciousness of many people in the gay movement and women's movement. Yet it seems that we are often less ready to examine the set of contemporary historical conditions which have structured our formation and emergence as gay women and men. Too often in this respect we remain unaware of many of the factors which have had a profound effect on the way we live out our lives. The process of writing a contemporary history of sexual politics which is more than a narrative of events or a "celebration" requires an examination — at once theoretical and political — of our own historical location. That is to say, it involves looking at the ways in which our sexuality as it is lived has been constructed and regulated, together with the set of specific historical conditions which have structured the emergence of particular forms of struggle and contestation.

As a result, the analysis here is not so much intended to form a history of the contemporary gay movement, but rather an attempt to understand the set of related social, cultural and political developments of the late 1950s and the 1960s which have exercised such a powerful influence on contemporary developments in sexual politics. It is therefore an argument based on the belief that people struggle to transform dominant sexual meanings and definitions under determinate historical conditions (indeed, that an understanding of those conditions is a pre-requisite for effective political intervention), and is implicitly critical of the libertarianism and spontaneism which remains as a residue in gay politics. It is a point that is particularly important in relation to the gay movement, where a failure to examine sexuality historically can lead to essentialist and universalist arguments and definitions (for example, notions of an innate sexuality) and a politics which traps us in the very structures we seek to liberate ourselves from.

A central point of reference throughout the discussion is the 1957 *Wolfenden Report. Wolfenden,* with its reformist implications and its liberalism, remains a forgotten text for the gay movement of the 1970s. Yet if it is possible to locate a particular moment which marks a radical shift in the regulation of sexuality in general, and homosexuality in particular, we should turn to the period of the late 1950s and to the debate around the subsequent Sexual Offences Act of 1967. We should be aware that politically we continue to occupy a space which is very much formed in the aftermath of *Wolfenden*. In terms both of the lived relations within the gay community, and in the formation of the identities of gay men, we are very heavily structured by the dual strategies of regulation and tolerance which govern homosexuality in the *Wolfenden Report*.

The purpose here is to understand more precisely the ways in which that moment of contemporary history is still present in its effects in the current situation. Initially, the piece focuses on the regulation of homosexuality (both through the agency of the law and through other social practices and institutions), together with the various ideological meanings which construct homosexuality as a particular sexual category, and as a specific form of sexual deviance. It goes on to examine the possible relation between the construction and regulation of homosexuality and forms of the family, the state and capitalist economic organisation. The concluding section attempts to identify the principle features of the political-moral climate of the present period; and to discuss the political strategies which have been developed in current struggles around sexuality.

Legally, the recommendations of the *Wolfenden Report* still define the current postition of gay men. The changes enacted by the 1967 Sexual Offences Act, as a result of ten years of parliamentary struggle, decriminalised sexual activity between adult male homosexuals in England and Wales. But the real significance of that legislation lies in the precise *way* in which it changed the law, and more widely, the implications this has had for the political strategies developed by the gay movement, and for the ways in which gayness is constructed as a category. The legislation introduces a new development in the regulation of sexuality and morality — it marks a shift in the exercise of the power to legally punish or not to punish, to regulate by law or to leave to the self-regulation of individuals. For *Wolfenden* the law's function in the field of sexuality is defined as essentially public: "to preserve public order and decency, to protect the citizen from what is offensive and injurious, and to provide safeguards against the exploitation and corruption of others". But the Report is also explicit that "it is not the function of the law to interfere in the private lives of citizens, or to seek to enforce any particular pattern of behaviour". And later it states categorically: "unless a deliberate attempt is to be made by society acting through the agency of the law, to equate the sphere of crime with that of sin, there must remain a realm of private morality and immorality which is not the law's business". In marking this distinction, the Report and the subsequent legislation introduce a new relation between what is legally defined as public, and what is private and to be left to individual self-regulation (though, as we shall see, still subject to non-legal forms of control). It is a relation which has had real effects on defining the space in which we are able to operate — politically, culturally and sexually.

The 1967 legislation on homosexuality can be defined as permissive inasmuch as it constructs an area of private, individual consent, while at the same time often strengthening the controls on the public appearance of "irregular" sexuality. In the introduction of this new set of legal principles *Wolfenden* should be seen in the context of the subsequent "permissive reforms" of the late 1950s and 1960s, which focus around a concern with the family, sexuality, morality and procreation. These include the Obscene Publications Act (1964), the Abortion Act (1967), legislation on divorce (1969), on theatre censorship (1968) and on the law governing Sunday entertainments (1968). Also, in the degree of attention given to a form of non-procreative sexuality, and in the intimacy of its enquiry, *Wolfenden* marks an expansion of concern on the part of the law in relation to questions of sexuality and morality. The 1885 Act which prohibited all homosexual activity between males, was a three-line amendment. In fact, homosexuality and homosexuals are isolated as the main focus for a sustained set of legal, medical, psychological and religious debates in the 1950s and 1960s, as well as being constructed as the source of repeated moral panics over sexuality. It is perhaps only now that we have become eclipsed by the increased concern over paedophilia and the "protection" of children.

Given the central place occupied by legal debates it is not surprising that the law becomes a privileged terrain on which struggles around sexuality and morality take place. The early homosexual groups were, for good reason, transfixed by the law, which was identified as the principal source of the regulation of sexuality, and the oppression of particular sexualities. The permissive legislation provides certain of the political and cultural conditions possible for the re-emergence of feminism and sexual politics in the late 1960s and early 1970s. Often the political strategies and tactics developed involved attempts to push the legal boundaries of the legislation beyond its legally defined parameters. Feminist struggles around legislation on abortion, and over legal definitions of female sexuality and dependence, together with the various and continuing campaigns for lowering the age of consent for gay people — all these political developments take as their point of departure and contestation the ground gained by these liberal reforms. And in the struggles over redefinitions, legal liberalism and tolerance come to be labelled as merely partial, and as ultimately oppressive. In fact, some of the sharpest political engagements in struggles over sexuality have involved pushing the contradictory tendencies implicit in much of the legislation to their extremes.

More generally, we should be aware that throughout the nineteenth and twentieth centuries the rule of law has occupied a central place in the construction and regulation of sexual and moral definitions — as much as it has in the sphere of capital-labour relations. Fresh legislation in the field of sexuality (such as the recent Bill on child pornography) or significant legal reversals (for example the *Gay News* Trial of 1977) act as a sensitive register of the moral climate. The law occupies a quite particular relation to debates and struggles around sexuality, in that if a specific form of sexual practice is seen to break the law it crystallises and concretises what have previously been constucted as *moral* debates. The breaking of legal barriers raises the potential threat of any action; illegal acts challenge the legal order and the social consensus on which it is based.

Yet as gay people we should also be aware that a defence of the rule of law is politically crucial to our interests. It is fundamentally misguided to dismiss campaigns over further law reforms and the legal defence of individual rights and freedoms of gay people. The legal changes of the 1960s have had pertinent personal, cultural and political effects on all our lives. And in the present political climate, with a shift to the right which is legitimated through a form of authoritarian populism and which emphasises "the rule of law", we may find ourselves hard pressed to defend the reforms we have spent so long in exposing as partial and restricted.

But if the law remains a central factor in the regulation of sexuality — with a particular history and importance for homosexuality — we should not be "transfixed" by its operation. A theory and a politics which bases its analysis too centrally on the forms of legal prohibition and censorship can easily remain unaware of the complexity of the strategies of regulation which address sexuality in its modern form. A juridically based understanding of the operation of power works with a largely negative conception of the power-sexuality couplet, which also often relies on assumptions of an innate or essential sexuality. That is to say, in such a model power relations are seen to exclude, block or refuse a basic and underlying sexuality. Moreover, the regulation of sexuality is assumed to be uniform in its operation throughout all apparatuses, institutions and social and cultural practices: from the patriarch in the family to the state apparatuses power is exercised though a coherent strategy.

In contradistinction to that model we would maintain that power, or sets of power relations addressing sexuality, operate through a multiplicity of practices and apparatuses (for example: medicine, psychology, sociology, education), each of which is distinguished by its specific structures of regulation, which are non-reducible to a uniform or single strategy. Also, we should be aware that power operates "positively" — it does not merely repress or prohibit, but is actively engaged in the construction of particular forms of sexuality which will not necessarily remain constant *across* a set of social practices (for example, the construction of homosexuality in the media may well be very different from its construction in law). It is an understanding which draws much from the work of the French theorist Michel Foucault — particularly his recent work on *The History of Sexuality* (vol. 1, 1979).

Foucault's theory of discursive practices and their power to regulate insists on the specificity of particular institutional sites and social and cultural practices in the forms of knowledge-power relations which are integral to them, the types of subjects which they construct and the strategies of resistance which are possible. Furthermore, it is a conception which differs not only from a notion of power as merely repressive, but also from current marxist understandings of ideology. In his insistence that power relations work not only ideationally (i.e. on consciousness or mental processes) but also that they are effective in shaping and regulating the physical space of the body with its attendant sensations and pleasures, Foucault draws our attention to the sophisticated and multifaceted dimensions of regulative techniques in what he terms a "disciplinary society". Within that theorisation, the law is seen to operate not necessarily as the single or central form of regulation, but rather as a "norm" — Foucault maintains that the legal apparatuses are increasingly incorporated into the general expansion of regulative structures and practices, which form a whole "microphysics of power".

How far do Foucault's general statements on the construction of sexuality help us to form a more complex picture of the regulation of homosexuality in the contemporary period? Moreover, can such an analysis provide us with a more adequate understanding of the way in which we, as gay people, have been constructed — personally, sexually and culturally — by the structures of regulation which address us? Finally, does Foucault's theory enable us to review our political strategies in a different light, and to construct new forms of political intervention in the overall struggle to transform dominant sexual meanings and definitions? It is to that set of questions that we now turn.

As we have seen, the legal changes introduced in the 1967 Act construct a new type of homosexual subject, understood as operating in the private sphere; a subject who in matters of sexuality and morality is defined as consenting, privatised and person-focused. In effect, what the reformed version of the law does is to continue to reproduce the structures through which the male gay subculture had developed over the previous hundred years, while now decriminalising it. One can speculate here that the structuring of the law across this public/private divide may have had much to do with the particular ways in which the gay subculture, and latterly the commercial gay scene, has developed from the late nineteenth century onwards. Clearly the divorce of physical sexual pleasure from marriage and procreation, together with the high degree of economic and personal freedom (though only really for middle-class men) has done much to determine the development of gay culture in the direction of leisure, pleasure and consumption. But legal structures have also been influential in that development; the legal confinement of gay people to a privatised space may have done much to structure the person-focused, pleasure-seeking and often apolitical nature of our present commercial culture.

It is that type of regulation through confinement which the gay movement, with its stress on the public process of coming out, has sought to contest. But, and I think it is here that the strategies we have developed have been caught within the historical and political structures and contradictions which define homo-sexuality, resistances are never external to the power relations they seek to challenge. They take as their necessary point of departure and contestation the specific structures and definitions of a particular historical moment. To accept that is to acknowledge the terms on which realistic political strategies can be developed. The specific problem is that political strategies which are merely based on an affirmation of gayness can serve to reproduce in a curious way the constructed definitions of homosexuality which it was *Wolfenden's* implicit aim to reinforce.

Generally, in the development of a theory and a politics of homosexuality, we should be attentive to a historical perspective. We should be aware that the homosexual subject is a socially and culturally constructed category, emerging at a particular historical moment in the late nineteenth century, and that emergence is the product of shifts and transformations in various discourses (medicine, psychology, sexology), apparatuses and institutions (the courts, the Church, social work and so on) and social and cultural practices (for example, popular culture and common sense meanings). Also, implicit in the construction of the new homosexual identity is the operation of discrete principles of regulation — as is also partly the case with the construction of the categories of "mother" and "child" in the same period. For Foucault, the processes of objectification and identification form one of the principal mechanisms for the exercise of power relations within a particular discourse or practice. In the general shift away from notions of criminality and deviance which were constructed around the *act* of transgression, the deviant subject (madman, sexual pervert and so on) comes to be awarded a particular identity, with a specific biography and set of instincts, and, in the case of the homosexual, with a differentiated anatomy and physiology.

The proposals contained in the *Wolfenden Report* operate with that type of strategy. If the Report advocates the decriminalisation of certain homosexual practices in the private sphere, it does not envisage the total abandonment of strategies of regulation. Power is no longer to be exercised through the direct operation of the law, but rather through the mobilisation of a variety of non-legal practices. Henceforward, medicine, "therapy", psychology, and forms of applied sociology are all envisaged as forming new principles of regulation. The dominant and institutionalised forms of those disciplines have indeed served to confirm the construction of homosexuality through the definitions of social deviancy, sickness or maladjustment. For example, the homosexual patient in orthodox medicine is only allowed to speak from the position of sickness or mental illness. Moreover, in the various "academic" and popular debates which proliferate after *Wolfenden* most of the arguments rest on an assumed and radical difference between heterosexuality and homosexuality. Much of the sexology, psychology and sociology of the 1960s and 1970s, with its stress on the personal history and aetiology of the sexual deviant, insists that the difference between the homosexual and the heterosexual goes much deeper than the choice of object gratification, and that it involves differences in the total personality. Almost all the discourses hierarchise and distribute the various categories of sexual deviance around the norm of marriage, the family and procreation, which provide the particular "régime of truth" for the classification of "other" sexual and moral practices. *Wolfenden* characteristically defines homosexuality as being "reprehensible from the point of view of harm to the family", and questions whether buggery should not be retained as a separate offence in that "it is particularly objectionable because it involves coitus and thus simulates more nearly than any other homosexual act the normal act of sexual intercourse". A parallel theme in the classification of deviant sexualities has been the linking of homosexuality with ideologies of nationalism and imperialism. The relation between definitions of sexual perversity and ideologies of national and imperial decline has an extensive history, dating back in Britain at least as far as the 1880s and 1890s, with the panic over national efficiency and degeneracy, class-specific underpopulation, and debates over the proposed sterilisation of the "unfit". In the 1960s those ideological truths returned with a renewed power to classify non-procreative sexualities.

That general historical awareness of the social and cultural construction of homosexuality should make us cautious of developing a politics and a culture on the basis of any celebratory notion of an essential gayness. As gay people we are placed in a privileged, though often painful, position in this respect. An awareness of the historical construction of our own identity and emergence must lead us to insist that sexual meanings are neither biologically nor socially fixed, but are involved in a continual process of construction and re-formation — both over long historical periods, and at the level of one's own individual constituted identity. Obviously it is crucially important for gay people to organise politically to defend their own sexuality and culture; and in moments of political crisis it may be as much as we can do to achieve that defence. Moreover, strategies which emphasise coming out and the general public manifestation of one's sexuality are important in the struggle to challenge and shift definitions within the dominant heterosexual culture. Also, we cannot but be aware of the fact that the social construction of our identities, as gay women and men, can make "lived relations" with heterosexuals (and particularly heterosexual men) extremely difficult and often antagonistic. We do not come together for support, or for friendship, or to organise politically through a series of accidents, but precisely because the dominant culture has constructed us in a relation of difference which is oppressive, and which has real effects on the way in which we live out our lives. (Heterosexuality *is* a continual affront to one's awareness of the world as a gay person.) For all those reasons we should continue to emphasise the specificity of our own oppression, and the necessity of a specifically gay politics. Further, within the already established groupings and tendencies involved in sexual politics we should insist that a gay perspective is present. We should enter into alliance with and offer support to feminists, and to heterosexual men who are attempting to question their own sexuality and to organise politically, but without subsuming the specificity of our own position. Theoretically too, in current analyses of sexuality, we should be ready to criticise work which marginalises or ignores non-heterosexual, non-procreative relations. *But,* and the qualification is a large one, we should also attempt to maintain a political perspective of a longer duration which involves a recognition that "freedom" for gay people cannot come solely from a greater assertion of gay rights, but must come from far wider social and cultural shifts involving the transformation of *all* sexual meanings and definitions. In the present conjuncture we can only begin to achieve this by organising politically around the historically given sexual categories and meanings. But we should be aware that our ultimate aim is the disintegration of those categories rather than their reinforcement.

The contemporary gay movement emerged out of the political and cultural climate of the late 1960s as a specific and autonomous form of struggle. In Britain, as in other metropolitan countries, its forms of appearance owed much to the general cultural and moral crisis of the period, where revolt was directed as much at the civil structures of society as at the economic point of production. A renewed emphasis on the effectiveness of ideology, and the necessity of exposing and contesting its operation through forms of cultural and ideological struggle, made it possible to develop new types of analysis and new strategies of political intervention. In the forms of its political engagement the gay movement and the women's movement have differed profoundly from existing political structures. Their origins and early strategies were often spontaneist and counter-cultural, which in retrospect we can see were developed out of the very structures of oppression which confined women and gay people.

The dialogue which has subsequently been constructed in the 1970s between sexual politics and the established forms of socialist organisation has formed one of the major political developments in the period. Theoretically, it has encouraged certain tendencies within the gay movement and the women's movement to develop a form of analysis premised on examining the relationship between the structures of sexuality and capitalist economic, political and ideological organisations. Socialist feminism attempts to provide a theory (and a politics) of the construction and regulation of sexuality, by developing marxist categories in areas which have hitherto remained undertheorised or largely ignored. As has often been indicated, this new departure has been made possible by a number of related influences: the general critique and move out of economism in the post-1968 period, together with an understanding of the "relative autonomy" of the ideological or cultural level which is seen to possess its own specificity, a revival of interest in work on and struggles around the state (with an emphasis, via Althusser and Gramsci, on the crucial ideological and cultural work performed by the state apparatuses) and more generally, an acknowledgement (often through the insistence of feminism) that certain forms of struggle are in no way reducible to the basic class contradiction at the level of the mode of production.

Yet this dialogue between marxism and feminism over sexuality has provided as many new questions as answers. Certainly, it has fruitfully challenged marxism as a coherent and defined body of knowledge. But we should be aware that these questions are not *merely* academic and theoretical; they relate crucially to the types of political intervention that we attempt to make as gay people. Questions which focus on the relation between the structures of sexuality and capitalist organisation, or on the forms and sources of power which regulate sexuality, will influence the type of political questions we formulate in developing a politics around sexuality — together with the way we envisage our own struggles relating to a more general conception of socialist politics.

Theoretically, the development of a theory of sexuality in relation to Marx's analysis of the history of capital accumulation has been made possible by the use of the concept of *reproduction*. The task of reproducing the work-force for capital, both biologically and through the forms of domestic labour historically performed by women, was seen as the point of departure for an understanding of the subordinate economic, legal and ideological position of women, and the construction of definitive forms of sexuality across a rigid male/female gender division. In certain versions of this type of analysis, capital is seen to "need" or "require" a specific form of the family and sexual organisation to secure the reproduction of labour power, the maintenance of social and political stability and the preservation of the work ethic. Those needs and requirements are met, it is argued, largely through the strategies of state intervention, whereby the state, working as "the ideal social capitalist", attempts to preserve the reproductive conditions necessary for the continuation of capital accumulation. The construction of the welfare state, with its strategies of intervention directed at the family, together with the body of legislation developed to legally regulate sexual practices are both analysed on the basis of a theory of reproduction. Moreover, given the insistence that the forms of state intervention must be seen to operate not only legally but also ideologically, the state is viewed as instrumental in the reproduction of the dominant sexual ideologies. These ideologies, it is maintained, serve to reinforce women's subordinate position in the reproductive sphere, both as mothers and domestic labourers, and help to channel sexuality into its heterosexual procreative norm, and thus to regulate other forms of sexuality as deviant or perverse. Sexual ideologies are, therefore, also understood in a basically functional or reproductive way; they are seen to act as "props" or supports for the material sexual divisions within production and reproduction. The construction of childhood, motherhood, domesticity and the structures of heterosexual morality are seen to exist in a more or less direct articulation with the needs and requirements of industrial capitalism.

More generally, such accounts of sexuality and its regulation insist that it is the relation *between* the structures of sexuality and capitalist organisation which should be examined, and which should ultimately form the basis for a politics of sexuality. From that type of analysis certain basic conclusions tend to be drawn. Namely, that the various practices and institutions which legally and/or ideologically contribute to the regulation of sexuality both "inside" and "outside" the state (the law, welfarism, medical practice, and so on) are unified in an overall strategy which exists in a definite relation to the forms of state intervention in the capital-labour contradiction. Hence *patriarchal relations,* the collective term used to describe the historically specific forms of sexual oppression, are seen to exist in articulation with the history of capitalist relations.

Two central and related problems are posed by this type of analysis. The first of these is the assumption, as a precondition for theoretical and political work, that the structures of sexuality and capitalist organisation necessarily exist in some articulation. The second concerns the identification of a unified and overall strategy which functions to regulate sexuality in an identifiably coherent way across a whole range of practices and institutions. Clearly, capitalist organisation in historically specific periods does have particular "conditions of existence" which will be influential in determining the construction and regulation of sexuality and morality — though we should be aware that there is no guarantee that those conditions will be met. Furthermore, it should be stressed that sexual oppression predates capitalist development, and exists in cultures which are not capitalist in their organisation.

But ultimately the question is a broader one, and concerns the focus of our political and theoretical attention. An analysis of sexuality which takes the history of capitalist organisation as its central point of reference will necessarily attempt to integrate the structures of sexuality into that history, whereas an analysis which begins from an attempt to understand historically the *construction of sexuality* may produce a quite different set of conclusions. Homosexuality presents very much a "test case" in this respect. It is fundamentally misguided to explain the construction and regulation of homosexuality solely in terms of the demands and requirements of capitalist organisation. More generally, we should be aware of the dangers of applying a theory, originally developed to understand the nature of *class* society, to explain the structures of sexuality.

Tentatively at this stage, we can say that the types of sexual meanings and the power relations which are produced in a particular historical moment will be dependent on the balance of relations between the various discourses, practices and apparatuses addressing sexuality, together with the forms of resistance to those structures. However, and the qualification is important, our analysis will be simplified if we impose a model derived from classical marxism, with the determination "in the last instance" being effected by the economic mode of production. In a similar way, the sets of power relations which are seen to oppress gay people should be seen as *specific* to particular practices (for example, the law, medicine and psychoanalysis). That is to say, the specific structures of oppression implicit in these practices should not be attributed to an external cause, which can be seen to inform or "shine through" each and every social and cultural institution. Too often, accounts of the regulation of sexuality are premised on an understanding that the power relations contained within a particular institution are derived from a primary or first cause. The specific structures of power are attributed to "capital", "capitalists", "men", or "heterosexuals" — individuals who are seen to have defined interests, and whose position the structures of power are thought to maintain. Politically, we should of course stress that the majority of cultural practices and institutions continue to define gay people in a subordinate relation to the structures of heterosexuality, but we should be cautious in deriving those structures from the single conspiratorial interests of capitalists or heterosexuals. Everything depends on the complex way in which particular practices and institutions are linked historically.

Politically, in what ways does the theoretical analysis have implications for the strategies we attempt to develop in the moral climate of the early 1980s and beyond? We have already focused on the law as a principal mechanism in the construction and regulation of sexuality, and stressed the importance of mobilising struggles in that area. The rule of law is central to the exercise of state power, and we should be continually alert to attempts to shift sexual and moral definitions through the use of legal strategies. Consequently the law must remain a central arena for struggle and contestation over sexuality. Furthermore, unless we hold to a simple anti-statism or libertarianism, we must be aware that the effort to shift legal definitions around sexuality involves an engagement with the law, on the terrain of the law. We need to campaign to support legislation which attempts to shift the law in a progressive direction; and to make alliances with those radical liberal and social democratic tendencies which have, in the past, helped to achieve some measure of sexual law reform.

But the potential for progressive legislation being carried through the parliamentary machinery is not merely dependent on the composition of the legal profession, or the police, nor for that matter does it depend solely on the balance of forces within the arena of parliamentary politics. It depends ultimately on the overall state of the particular historical moment, or *conjuncture* — and for us, as gay people, on the particular position occupied by morality within that conjuncture. We need to devote much more of our attention to identifying precisely and complexly the moral climate or consensus of the period of the early 1980s. The problem *is* a complex one, and again can easily invite simple or reduced theoretical-political analyses.

First, as an overall point of insistence, we should continue to stress the specificity of sexual and moral definitions and their related struggles. They possess their own history, which is not reducible to other social, cultural or economic developments, and they do not exist in any clear relation to other progressive political movements. A common response to the problem is to directly link political and economic shifts with moral and sexual transformations. An economic recession, so it is argued, is not only "expressed" by a political shift to the right, but also by a cultural regression and a moral hardening of the arteries. The appearance of fascism in the political arena is seen to confirm the analysis. The convergence of an extreme right-wing politics, together with a coherent racist and patriarchal programme in relation to women and gay people in the strategies of the National Front, lends weight to the argument that all contradictions and forms of oppression in our society are directly linked. It seems we need only sit back and wait for the appearance of a fully articulated moral and sexual conservatism in the Thatcherist repertoire.

But the problem is that moral and sexual emphases do not, as yet, occupy a central place in the policies and strategies of the new Thatcherist right. Let it be clear what is not being insisted here; it is not to deny the significance of statements made by figures such as Sir Keith Joseph on the "cycle of deprivation" in relation to single-parent families, or the repeated moral emphases in the "law and order" programmes of individual police commissioners and judges. These clearly are not accidental. But in the recent political shift to the right, with its basis in a consenting authoritarian populist support, sexual and moral debates do not occupy a central position in the complex and dense repertoire of ideological meanings that is presented. The conservative right has not actively constructed sexual and moral questions as an "issue" in quite the same way that it clearly has with the Great Debate on Education, or with immigration, or law and order (though in the last case questions of moral degeneracy are often run together with concerns over lawlessness).

Rather, what we should be aware of is the set of unsung moral and sexual assumptions which form the ground on which the more prominent political issues are articulated and debated. We are dealing here with the identification of a climate or atmosphere, rather than any clearly definable moral shift rightwards. The case is most clearly illustrated in examining the Labour Party and its programme for social democratic reform, from the 1960s onwards. Progressive statements and legislation on sexuality and morality enacted during Roy Jenkins's period as Home Secretary were often articulated to a wider set of concerns over leisure, welfare, and the general cultural climate of Britain. But they were subtly downplayed in the type of consensus that Wilson attempted to construct — a consensus which increasingly incorporated the older structures of a "moral methodism" (both in its style and mode of address) with its general stress on technological and scientific revolution. Callaghan consolidated that repertoire, with subjects always implicitly addressed through the structures of the family and family life.

Those are the terms on which sexual and moral questions are raised and debated within the political arena, and within the apparatuses of the state. Such an analysis does not rule out the possibility of a period of increasing moral and sexual reaction, but it does stress that such a movement, coming from within the sphere of "orthodox politics", would mark a radically new type of political intervention, which has only a limited set of precedents. One would suspect that an actively endorsed legal and political shift to the right on sexual and moral questions might run into conflict with certain of the unvoiced liberal moralities of the social democratic repertoire.

Where, of course, sexual and moral debates are massively carried, and where both progressive and regressive political shifts are often first noted, is in the complex web of regulatory disciplines, practices and institutions (to which Foucault among others has drawn our attention), together with the popular discourse of common-sense assumptions, meanings and definitions. The various apparatuses and practices (education, welfare, probation, social work, medicine, psychology, criminology, genetics and so on) stand in varying relations to the centrality of state power — some forming an integral part of the state apparatuses, others existing in a more mediated relation. What is clear is that it is in the day to day operation of these practices — in their practical rituals — that particular sexual and moral definitions are constructed and enforced, and local political struggles are fought out. But as we have said, we should beware of adopting any uniform or unilinear strategy of regulation in our analysis; those types of conclusions quickly become conspitatorial in their implications and vacate the terrain of a political engagement. Rather, we should assess the particular situation and operation of each specific practice, and the potential it may have for transformation through struggle.

Similarly, we should be cautious of constructing the ground of popular heterosexual culture monolithically. Clearly civil society is a fertile terrain for the growth of right-wing moral and sexual purity campaigns, of which the most famous example is Whitehouseism. But material and cultural developments since the 1950s do make any simple advocacy of a return to an older set of moral values increasingly difficult to enforce. Consumerism and its attendant values are crucial here. Despite the economic recession, we still inhabit a period in which the "erotic compulsion to spend" figures prominently. It is a development which has had partly progressive implications for the inflection of sexual definitions and meanings, particularly in its impact on women and gay people. In that area too, therefore, we should attempt to shift those definitions in a more progressive direction. Such a process involves alliances — together with continuing education and debate within our own movement.

4

What Changed in the Seventies?

DENNIS ALTMAN

One of the biggest pop music successes of 1978-9 was the American disco group, Village People. With songs like "Macho Man", "Just a Gigolo", "YMCA" and "In the Navy" they typify the new style of hedonistic male homosexual lifestyle that is becoming apparent in most large western cities. Nor is this assertion contradicted by the fact that their appeal is as great among straight as among gay audiences, nor by their protest that they are not really a gay group.[1] In many ways Village People seem a perfect symbol of a new type of male homosexual that has emerged in much of the liberal capitalist world.

The most striking change in the position of (male) homosexuals over the past decade is their visibility. There was, of course, a homosexual subculture in most large western cities as far back as the eighteenth century, and we are only now beginnning to discover its history. But it was largely hidden, and elaborate subterfuge was employed in discussing it (as in Proust's *A la Recherche du Temps Perdu* and Wilde's *Picture of Dorian Gray).* As late as the 1960s most homosexuals accepted the need to lead a double life, hiding their sexual and emotional feelings from all but a very few. *Boys in the Band* summed up much of the male gay experience just at that point in time when things began to change.

The new style of homosexual that one finds in most large western cities bears little resemblance, at least superficially, to the traditional stereotype. Homosexuality is now signified by theatrically "macho" clothing (denim, leather and the ubiquitous key rings) rather than by feminine style drag; the new "masculine" homosexual is likely to be non-apologetic about his sexuality, self-assertive, highly consumerist and not at all revolutionary, though prepared to demonstrate for gay rights. This, one might note, is far removed from the hope of the early seventies liberationists who believed in a style that was androgynous, non-consumerist and revolutionary.

Not surprisingly the new homosexual is likely to have little contact with women, either gay or straight. Among women the change in style is less easy to pinpoint, for it is clearly interwoven with changes among women in general. Gay women share the new assertiveness and self-acceptance of the men. But they have been far less attracted by the hedonism that seems the hallmark of the new male homosexual.

At the end of a decade in which the social regulation of homosexuality has changed faster than at any time in history it is worth trying to conceptualise just what this change means. Most importantly, we need ask whether this new visibility is part of a fundamental shift in the regulation of sexuality or merely a superficial change in fashion: is the new "macho" style of Christopher Street and the Castro only the latest in a long line of American fads or will Leicester and Launceston follow (as Sydney, Amsterdam and Hamburg already have)? Secondly, we need ask how far these changes are linked to other changes in social structures and attitudes. Thirdly, we need ask how far these changes are a product of the gay movement, or whether the movement is better seen as a consequence of these changes. And last we need ask whether the changes are likely to be permanent, or whether they represent only a temporary liberalisation that is likely to be reversed.

Implicit in this approach is a recognition of how far sexuality is channelled and directed by social pressures, and this requires us to talk of both the construction and regulation of sexual behaviour. To say this is not necessarily to repudiate the Freudian view, which sees some form of homo-erotic feeling as a universal, even if in most cases it is a desire that is repressed or sublimated. Indeed the evidence for this view seems to me more persuasive than those theories of inherited or purely learned homosexuality which make no allowance for the very complex pattern of repression/sublimation uncovered by psychoanalysis. The problem with Freud's theories is that they can explain everything (as in *Civilisation and its Discontents*) and hence nothing; given his premises we still need to explain how it is that particular forms of sexual behaviour and identity are created at different times and in different cultures.

It is particularly important to distinguish *homosexuality* as a form of behaviour/desire from *homosexual* (and/or lesbian) as a term of identity. The former is part of human sexual response and exists, albeit in very different forms, in all societies.[2] The latter is a specific way of channelling that behaviour/desire so as to create a particular identity based on sexual preference, and as such seems largely the product of modern urban societies. In traditional societies exclusive homosexuals, where they exist, take on particular roles, often religious (as in the case of Amerindian "berdaches") or become outcasts (literally the case for some Hindus). It is only with the breakdown of the ascriptive family and the narrowly defined role expectations of traditional cultures that it becomes possible to live as a homosexual in other than this very rigid way.

If my discussion concentrates largely on the case of male homosexuals this is less due, I hope, to male chauvinism than to the fact that there is a very different meaning to male and female homosexuality in a patriarchal society. On the one hand there seems much greater fluidity of sexual desire among many women;

in Kate Millett's *Sita* the fact that the two major characters are torn between relations with women and men seems to reflect a bisexuality that is less commonly found among men. On the other hand there is a much lesser development among gay women of the sort of commercial gay world frequented by male homosexuals, even after one allows for the lesser spending power of women in western societies. (It is clearly not merely economic factors that have prevented the emergence of backroom bars for lesbians.)

The differences between gay men and women, which have led me increasingly to question whether there is any point in using the same term to describe them, are related to two crucial points: the effect of contemporary feminism and the social and psycho-analytic factors involved in the regulation of female sexuality. The first has undoubtedly resulted in much greater intimacy between large numbers of women, leading in many cases to actual sexual involvement. The second is a more complex matter; it may well be, given the traditionally greater repression of female sexuality and its somewhat different organisation (sexual anxieties for women are of a different kind to those for men, whose sexuality is centred on an ideology of masculine supremacy and, as symbol thereof, the primacy of the phallus), that it is easier for women to escape the channelling of desire into a homo/hetero dichotomy. Ironically the writings of Freud would appear to give some support to this view.

For woman, as Simone de Beauvoir once remarked, homosexuality can be a mode of flight from her situation or a way of accepting it.[3] With the growth of feminism, lesbianism has become increasingly the latter, to the point where one can only discuss female homosexuality within the context of changing definitions of femininity and the emergence of a new feminist culture.[4] That this development is taking place at the same time as there is a "masculinisation" of male homosexuals only underlines the difficulties in discussing both together.

Furthermore, it is only in affluent liberal democracies (essentially the countries of North America, Western Europe, Australasia and perhaps Japan) that social and political factors allow for the emergence of a visible and widespread homosexual subculture. Thus even in the more traditional areas of some Southern European countries, such as Greece and Italy, where there is widespread (male) homosexuality, there are very few people who identify themselves as homosexual. In those third-world countries where homosexuality seems widespread, the absence of a concept of "the homosexual" as we know it makes many of our assumptions invalid; nor can the homophobia of many such countries be simply blamed on western influence, as recent events in Iran should make clear.

If the development of a homosexual identity requires a society that is urban, secular and affluent, so too political factors can inhibit the appearance of a homosexual subculture. This appears true in most of Eastern Europe, where state regulation of behaviour is sufficiently strong to prevent the growth of the sort of subculture found in the West,[5] while in South America and above all in the southern triangle of Argentina, Chile and Uruguay, the coming to power of repressive régimes resulted in extremely savage repression of homosexuals. The link between political liberalism and the freedom of homosexuals — most accepted in the social democracies of northern Europe — needs to be pondered by socialists.

With these caveats in mind, a number of hypotheses about changing sexual regulation can be made. In particular, there would seem to have developed over the past decade, in addition to the new visibility already mentioned, a major shift in the ideological view of homosexuality, and connected with both of these factors the development of a large-scale commercial world and of homosexuality as a political issue.

The first point is most easily established by thinking back to the end of the sixties when homosexuality, if no longer "the love that dare not speak its name", was certainly still a matter to be treated with great caution by the media. Over the past decade there has been an explosion in explicitly gay writing, films, television; a demand for a new view of homosexuality in schools and colleges; a vast increase in homosexuals themselves asserting their rights publicly. Thus Ian Young could casually begin a book column in the gay liberation journal *Gay Sunshine*: "1976 saw the public coming out of a number of writers and other public figures: culture analyst Charles Reich . . . footballer Dave Kopay, painter Paul Cadmus . . . Olympic skating champion John Curry, poets Adrienne Rich and Walter Rinder, English novelists Francis King and John Lehmann. There were also more cautious 'I've slept with men' statements by Rod McKuen, Marlon Brando and Elton John.'"[6] But homosexuality has not only become more visible; it has, at the same time, become more problematical.

With isolated exceptions the dominant view of homosexuality until the seventies was that it was inferior and to be repressed. There were differences within this overall view, depending on whether one saw it as primarily immoral, pathological or criminal, and there were a few courageous pioneers who were able to reject this view. But by and large the undesirability of homosexuality was an attitude firmly held not only by the "experts" (whether clerical, legal or medical) but by most homosexuals themselves. One has only to read the memoirs of an older generation to realise how deeply imbued they were with the sense of their own inferiority. Thus the journalist Michael Davidson, in what his publisher calls the "courageous and loveable story of a lover of boys", can extol the "insignificance" of homosexuality in Italy as proof of the Italians' "normality" and "sexual health".[7] The classic example of such self-hatred is perhaps Somerset Maugham,[8] but a whole string of reminiscences like Davidson's exist.

One of the ironies of this view of homosexuality is that a great number of the "experts" who created it were themselves homosexual, though they went to great lengths to hide it. The consequences of such an internalised sense of oppression remain to be fully explored; one needs to ask for example how far the "homosexual sensibility" (if it indeed exists) is a product of such self-hatred. It is only over the last decade that this view has seriously, and on a large scale, come under challenge, largely from homosexuals themselves. It is this that makes for the problematical status of homosexuality.

As a "deviance" is slowly being reclassified as an "alternative lifestyle", we have reached a point where neither the traditional condemnation not the insistence on its equal validity is the dominant view of homosexuality. Outside Denmark, Holland and Sweden there remain legal distinctions between homosexual and heterosexual behaviour, and while some American cities have legislated to cover homosexuals under their anti-discrimination ordinances, most American states retain the criminal sanctions against sodomy. (It is one of the many paradoxes of change that in New York, with its enormous overt homosexual population, neither state nor city governments are prepared to recognise homosexual equality.) The push in the Anglo-Saxon world for protection from discrimination is in effect an attempt to redefine homosexuals as a legitimate minority group. Such a redefinition, for all the immediate benefits that it may produce, also has the effect of reinforcing the popular prejudice that homosexuals are a distinct and recognisable group, rather than the realisation of a potential open to all. (An excellent example of this is the way in which novels with gay themes are increasingly marketed as "gay books", thus making it unlikely that readers who do not so classify themselves will see them.)

The new visibility of homosexuals is not by itself synonymous with acceptance of this new definition, as was shown in the salacious reporting that accompanied the Thorpe trial. Films and books still appear that reinforce traditional prejudices and judgements, and British television comedies in particular rely on homophobic innuendo for much of their success (think of *Are You Being Served?*, *The Benny Hill Show*, and *The Two Ronnies*). Attitudinal change both among homosexuals and the population at large occurs at a very uneven rate, which is why gay activists are forced into what seems a never-ending reiteration of the same basic arguments. The new self-accepting homosexual (and I leave aside how far any of us can totally overcome internalised guilt and oppression for the moment) co-exists with thousands of homosexual women and men who are terrified and ashamed by their desires, a new category superimposed on, but not replacing, the old.

This new problematic in the view of homosexuality is reflected in the shifting stance of many of the most influential ideological apparatuses of western society. One could cite numerous examples of debates and division among politicians, clergy, psychiatrists, psychologists, educationalists, etc. about the "proper" attitude to adopt towards homosexuality. Quite properly much of the attention of the gay movement has been directed to confronting and changing the attitudes of these apparatuses, and in some cases (e.g. the Metropolitan Community Church and various counselling and medical services) to developing alternative institutions. At the same time developments within the more liberal churches, the psychological/psychiatric/psychoanalytic professions and the social sciences have helped change the dominant attitudes.

Perhaps the most obvious form of the new visibility is the growth of the commercial gay world, again apparent, though to differing degrees, in all Western countries. Of course there have always been bars, saunas and restaurants catering to homosexuals, at least since the emergence of a recognisable urban gay identity. In the seventies these have increased enormously, and often set a pattern followed by the straight world. (New York's Continental Baths, where Bette Midler launched her career, recently reopened as a centre for swinging straights.) The whole late-seventies disco phenomenon owes much to the gay scene; *Time* has even attributed its origin to "the gay subculture".[9]

In essence the commercial gay scene represents not so much the liberation of the homosexual as his co-option into mainstream consumerist society. (I say "his" advisedly; as already noted, gay women have been much more resourceful than men in creating alternatives to a commercial gay scene.) To speak cynically, it represents the triumph of the capitalist entrepreneur over traditional morality, as in the "gay tours" promoted by some airlines. There is often de facto collusion between the police, who prevent cruising in parks, beaches, streets etc., and the businessmen who offer the same facilities at a price. (In the United States this has now reached the point that men pay to have sex with each other in what are best described as replicas of public toilets.)

At the same time there is a positive side to the growth of the commercial world; for many gays coming to terms with their sexuality, or isolated in small towns or suburbia, the ghetto is a real step towards liberation. The development of a gay press and considerable gay publishing during the seventies has had a huge impact on the self-perception of many gays, and if movement purists tend to scorn publications like *Gay News, The Advocate, Blueboy* and *Campaign,* they are for many of the men who read them the first reassurance that to be homosexual is not to be consigned to eternal misery. (The size of the gay market is shown by the success of these publications in attracting advertising; advertising executives increasingly talk of a specific "gay market".)

For most gay men, and for those gay women not touched by the

impact of the women's movement, the commercial world remains
the centre of social life. It is hardly an accident that all three acts of
As Time Goes By, Gay Sweatshop's account of gay history, take
place in commercial venues, nor that the apocryphal beginning of
the American gay liberation movement took place in a bar (the
Stonewall). The growth of a gay commercial scene and of the gay
movements have often occurred together, and are indeed closely
related; the victories of the movement help provide a climate in
which bars and suchlike can flourish, while the growth of a
commercial world can provide the beginnings of a sense of
community that the movement can in turn mobilise. This seems
truer in small towns than in large cities, and much truer in North
America than in Southern Europe, where there is a considerable
gap between the movement and the commercial bar/disco scene.[10]

The gay movement in most Western countries seems to have
experienced three phases, which are sometimes telescoped
together, and elements of all of which are present today. The
earliest, in Germany above all,[11] but also in Switzerland, the
United States, France and Holland,[12] was a period of surreptitious
groups whose main aim was to demonstrate the respectability of
homosexuality. In some cases (e.g. the Homosexual Law Reform
Society in Great Britain) the organisations stressed that their
membership was by no means necessarily homosexual.
Descendants of such groups such as Arcadie (France), COC
(Holland), CHE (Britain) and Mattachine (USA) still exist.

The second wave occurred at the end of the sixties in both the
United States and several European countries, when a much more
radical movement emerged. This involved an openness and a
willingness to use confrontation tactics that were unknown before,
and made "gay liberation" a minor press phenomenon in the
seventies. While such movements continue to exist and have come
into being recently in such countries as Spain,[13] they have tended
to be replaced by a third phase which combines their openness and
militancy with considerable interest and expertise in lobbying and
the provision of special services. This phase is most in evidence in
Northern Europe and the Anglo-Saxon world, while the second is
still dominant in Southern Europe. By far the broadest range of
homosexual groups is found in the United States, while in Italy
(where FUORI is one of the components of the Radical Party) and
Spain the links with other left-wing groups is most important.

To argue that the growth of the movement, in particular its
explosion after 1968-9, coincided with other changes in the
position of homosexuals and the regulation of sexuality in general
is merely to pose the question of "why now" in a different way.
One can hypothesise that all these changes are best understood as
part of a much broader shift in social and cultural structures that
has affected all Western countries in the past two decades. For
our purposes the most important development has been the
massive growth in mass consumption in the "advanced" capitalist

world — even if the future of such consumption seems increasingly questionable given the imperatives of ecological and resource limitations — and its effect on both values and class structure.

The transition to societies based more and more on tertiary industry and mass consumption, societies which the Americans like to refer to, probably misleadingly, as "post-industrial", has been accompanied by a very considerable erosion of the traditional values that supported early capitalist society (and that are still dominant in countries such as the Soviet Union or South Korea, where the emphasis remains on production rather than consumption.) The conservative lament that traditional values have collapsed is by and large correct, but all the rhetoric of a Carter or a Thatcher can do little to restore them, for their collapse is an integral part of the developing ideology of consumerism, hedonism and spectacle that derives from modern capitalism[14] (and of which the disco phenomenon may be the perfect symbol). In the realm of sexual morality this has meant the growth of what is often referred to as "permissiveness", which is abundantly evident in any large Western city — the increase of pornography and of sexual overtones in advertising is an essential part of the consumer capitalist ethos.

At the same time the expansion of the tertiary sector, and particularly of professional and government service, along with the growth of higher education, has created a large new middle class, less tied to traditional values than the old, and receptive to the new ideology of hedonism and "doing your own thing". It is not surprising that it is the United States, where consumerism is most advanced and the new middle class most in evidence, that has become the centre of moral and sexual experimentation.

While traditional ideological apparatuses such as the church still retain considerable influence — but more perhaps outside the affluent West (the Pope chose shrewdly in visiting Mexico and Poland) — there has been a widespread decline in the protestant emphasis on hard work, duty, respect for authority, family and nation, that went to make up the bourgeois hegemony. This ideological shift has contributed very considerably to a new tolerance for homosexuality, for to condemn it seems more and more the relic of an old-fashioned sort of moral absolutism that is no longer much in vogue.

Increasingly the dominant sexual morality is one that has shifted from an emphasis on the primacy of reproduction to one based on the primacy of enjoyment.[15] This new ideology of sexual regulation is expressed in the enormous stress on "self-awareness" so current in the United States, in literary characters such as Myra Breckinridge and Isabelle Wing,[16] in a sense the female equivalents of an already existing male genre, and in the proliferation of new magazines that extol the possibilities of "liberated sexuality" outside the framework of marriage and children. I have some sympathy with those conservatives who maintain that the mass media have completely undermined traditional moral standards.

Against this background one can point to certain political and cultural factors that triggered off a genuine shift in the social regulation of and attitudes towards homosexuality. In particular the rise of a youth-oriented rebelliousness in the late sixties in both North America and Europe allowed the emergence of a new style of homosexual, one far less willing to accept the sort of furtiveness and self-hatred traditionally associated with gay life.[17] The new wave of gay activism drew in particular on the development of the counter-culture/New Left and on the revival of feminism, which in the Anglo-Saxon world at least was the most important ideological influence on the gay movement of this period. While in many cases the influence of the United States was crucial, this does not *by itself* explain the developments in other parts of the western world; it is too easy to ascribe to "americanisation" developments that are rather part of the evolution of consumer capitalism. Gay movements reflect the particular social and cultural conditions of their respective societies, even when there are strong similarities between them.

The changes of the seventies have not occurred without reaction; the moral backlash symbolised by Anita Bryant in the United States and Mary Whitehouse in England represents a very real attempt by certain social forces to block change, and at times has succeeded in winning certain battles. It is easy to compile a long list of examples: the prosecution of *Gay News* and *Body Politic,* the defeats in referendum campaigns in Miami, St Paul, Wichita and Eugene, the seizure of gay publications by customs authorities in Canada and New Zealand, the proposed anti-homosexual laws in Greece, the strengthened campaign against "child abuse" in France.[18] Equally one could compose as striking a list of gay victories over the same period, and it is my belief that this would be the more impressive.

The very term "backlash" indicates that what is going on is a reaction to change, and in general suggests that its appearance is a sign of conservative weakness rather than strength: it is only when hegemonic values break down that demagogues arise to defend them, and as in the American south during the sixties, when white reactionaries sought to prevent desegregation, such reactions rarely succeed in causing more than temporary pauses in overall change. Indeed in the United States it could be argued that the defeat of the Briggs Amendment in California in November 1978 marked the crest of the anti-homosexual backlash.

This is admittedly a sanguine view of the phenomenon. It is certainly arguable that as economic conditions worsen there will be an increasing search for scapegoats, and homosexuals will provide an attractive target. The anti-gay backlash seems to me as much a reaction against the women's movement and general cultural changes as against homosexuals; it is just that homosexuals make a more acceptable symbol upon which to vent frustration. As Gore Vidal has said, "queer-baiting is the last socially acceptable form of minority abuse".[19] (In fact the evidence suggests that migrants and the unemployed tend to be increasingly more attractive targets.)

As homosexuals become more visible they will certainly attract the wrath of large numbers of people, motivated by a strong homophobia that in most cases seems closely linked to religiosity. Yet the overall picture drawn from experience of North America, Australia and France seems to me a hopeful one. Public opinion polls in all Western countries reveal an increasingly positive view of homosexuality, above all among the young. Hardly any politicians of consequence have been prepared to adopt the rhetoric of the backlash (Briggs was repudiated even by Ronald Reagan), although in many cases they are easily pressured by the ability of the moralists to create powerful pressure groups. No struggle for change can occur without temporary setbacks and occasional persecution, and it would be silly to ignore the real pain that the moralists are capable of inflicting. There is clearly a dialectical relationship between the gay movement and its enemies (Bryant has contributed powerfully to the new sophistication of gay politics in the United States). At the same time there is a real danger that we will allow ourselves to lose all initiative to them, rather than ourselves determining the agenda for debate.

At the end of the seventies the most striking change that is apparent in the regulation of homosexuality is the invention of the ethnic homosexual, that is, the widespread recognition of a distinct cultural category which appears to be pressing for the same sort of "equality" in Western society as do ethnic minorities. In this sense the concept of "the homosexual" seems to have triumphed over the liberationist demand to release the homosexuality that is repressed in everyone. The danger in this development is that a genuine acceptance of homosexuality will be prevented by the increasing tolerance of a commercial subculture; that is, homosexuals remain unmolested within areas carefully demarcated by capitalist entrepreneurs without any real change in broader societal attitudes towards sexuality.[20] (A good example of this danger is the strong resistance to any non-judgmental discussion of homosexuality in schools, even in societies where the ghetto is widespread and overt.)

The current emphasis on the "new homosexual" has tended to limit discussion on what may in the end be a more significant area for discussion, namely how far there is a generalised breakdown of the dichotomy homo/hetero in both discourse and practice. I have already indicated that this development seems further advanced among women than among men, but I have noted among my male students a much greater readiness to acknowledge their potential homosexuality than was true when I was an undergraduate. If this is true, then in the long run the apparent strengthening of the homosexual separatism may prove to be a step towards the disappearance of the categories altogether.

NOTES AND REFERENCES

1. See Ken Emerson, "The Village People: America's Male Ideal?", in *Rolling Stone,* 5 October 1978.
2. See Mary McIntosh, "The Homosexual Role", in *Social Problems,* no. 16, Fall 1968, pp. 182-92.
3. In *The Second Sex,* Harmondsworth, 1972.
4. See the introduction by Karla Jay in Karla Jay and Allen Young, *Lavender Culture,* New York 1979.
5. This is not to deny the existence of some form of gay world in East Germany, Poland, Hungary etc. See, e.g., Tome Reeves "Red and Gay", in *Fag Rag* no. 6, Boston, Fall-Winter 1973.
6. Ian Young, "Coming Out in Print", in *Gay Sunshine* no. 32, Spring 1977, p. 13.
7. M. Davidson, *The World, the Flesh and Myself,* London 1977, p. 191. Compare Quentin Crisp, *The Naked Civil Servant,* London 1972, where similar views are expressed.
8. See Robin Maugham, *Conversations With Willie,* New York 1978.
9. "Gaudy Reign of the Disco Queen", in *Time,* 4 December 1978, p. 68.
10. I have discussed this and other aspects of the French gay scene in two essays in *Coming Out in the Seventies,* Sydney 1979.
11. See Jim Steakley's articles in *Body Politic*, Toronto, nos. 9, 10 and 11.
12. On the early American movement, see J. D'Emilio, "Dreams Deferred", in *Body Politic* nos. 48-50, 1978-9. On Holland, see "Gayness in a Small Country", in *Body Politic* no. 53, 1979.
13. See C. and M. Valverde, "Viva Gay", in *Body Politic* no. 47, October 1978, and P. Benoit "Des Homosexuels dans l'Espagne post-Franquiste", in *Libération,* Paris, 18 June 1977.
14. This is discussed further in my *Rehearsals for Change,* Melbourne 1979.
15. Compare the critique of Christopher Lasch in *The Culture of Narcissism,* New York 1977.
16. In Gore Vidal's *Myra Breckinridge,* New York 1978, and Erica Jong's *Fear of Flying,* New York 1973, respectively. See J. Mitzel and S. Abbott, *Myra and Gore,* Dorchester, Mass., 1974, for a discussion of this thesis.
17. On the United States, see my *Homosexual: Oppression and Liberation,* New York 1971; on Britain, see J. Weeks, *Coming Out,* London 1977; on France, see D. Fernandez, *L'Etoile Rose,* Paris 1978.
18. This is argued in a symposium prepared by the review *Recherches* and entitled "Fous d'enfance: qui a peur des pédophiles?", Paris 1979.

19. Quoted by A. Kopkind, "The Gay Rights Movement: Too Many Enemies", in *Working Papers for a New Society,* July/August 1978.

20. On this, see my "Letter from Australia", in *Christopher Street,* Jan. 1977; "Within These Walls", editorial statement in *Gay Left,* Spring 1976; Tim Carrigan and John Lee, "Male Homosexuals and the Capitalist Market", in *Gay Changes,* Adelaide, Spring 1978.

5
The Ideology of GLF

SIMON WATNEY

The Gay Liberation Front (GLF) was the most important movement for homosexuals that Britain has known. The use of the word "gay" — our own word for ourselves — marked a decisive break with the institutions and discourses of heresy and disease within which all homosexuals were, by definition, previously confined. For the first time it became possible to make a positive homosexual self-identification in terms other than those of the dominant heterosexual culture. This dramatic change permitted and encouraged a significant shift away from earlier subcultural patterns which were uneasily polarised around class and sex roles, towards a less defensive and more open range of social possibilities.

In its rejection of the roles and values traditionally ascribed to gays in capitalist societies, GLF was obliged to consider the organisation of sexuality in all its forms in order to work out strategies of resistance. This led to a recognition of the fundamental political significance of sexuality as a system of social control, on the levels both of social structures and belief. The relations between these two areas have formed the axis of much subsequent analysis. In this respect it is crucial to understand how GLF theorised the position of gays in a sexual politics which at one extreme could equate the "liberation" of sexuality with the overthrow of capitalism itself.

Unfortunately many people who were involved in the early days of the movement still regard any criticism of GLF orthodoxy as an attack not only on their politics but on their most intensely held views of themselves. This is an important point. GLF gave both a sense of political identity and of personal self-identification to a generation of gay women and men. But if we are to learn from the invaluable experience of the early gay movement, it is necessary to be able to prise these two processes apart, if only temporarily, in order to grasp the emergent structure of what was taken for granted by GLF about our sexuality and its wider political implications. One of the major problems with GLF was precisely the assumption that all the most important questions had been answered. We thus inherit a critical analysis of the place of homosexuality which relies heavily on such concepts as "sexism" and "patriarchy" as if these closed all debate. If we can let go of that false sense of security which accompanies all such quests for "final" answers, then at least we might have grounds for some kind of optimism as we rethink the enormous problems concerning the relations between class, sexuality and inequality, in the face of the uncertainties of the present decade.

From its origins at the London School of Economics in 1970, GLF in Britain gathered its ideas from a wide variety of sources, many of which had been represented in London at the Congress of the Dialectics of Liberation in the summer of 1967. This was attended by such luminaries of the New Left as Stokely Carmichael, Herbert Marcuse, Paul Goodman, and Lucien Goldmann. Carmichael contrasted individual and institutional racism; R. D. Laing represented the counter-psychiatry movement; and Marcuse described a "mutilated, crippled and frustrated human existence, a human existence that is violently defending its own servitude".[1] These three themes — the analogy with racial oppression, a generalised rejection of bourgeois models of mental health, and the alienation which is inseparable from capitalist modes of production — also informed the beliefs and strategies of the American GLF movement which was the principal example for its English counterpart in 1970 and 1971.[2]

GLF, then, depended heavily upon a concept of liberation which operated across a wide range of issues. This tended to produce a special kind of elitism on the part of those who considered that they had successfully thrown off the shackles of "false consciousness". The mechanical picture of oppression versus liberation, with its attendant vision of revolutionary politics based almost religiously on the example of 1917, could never account for the diversity of gay society. If our oppression was not obvious to us, then it followed that we must be "self-oppressed", and the whole notion of self-oppression enabled the early gay movement to neatly bypass the thorny question of our complex sociology. An article in the newspaper of GLF, *Come Together,* made this point very clearly:

Self-Oppression: We become the enemy of our own liberation:
(1) When we insist that we are not oppressed:
(2) When we persist in sexual chauvinism or elitism:
(3) When we insist that gay types or a gay nature exists:
(4) When we persist in seeking a lost half (and therefore devour, expand, overlap, possess, always by bringing others to their knees by force of need and dependency):
(5) When we persist in identification with fascist war-game metaphors such as cops and robbers:
(6) When we persist in not identifying with all those held in slavery and oppression:
(7) When we persist in identifying with the master class:
(8) When we persist in accepting identification from political institutions which are neither gay nor liberated (government, church, medical, judicial, military, familial, industrial, cultural, and counter-cultural):

(9) When we insist that non-violence is an obligation and not a favour:

(10) When we insist we must wait.[3]

There was clearly a great deal to be done. It was very alarming. The litany appeared to go on forever. Was one persisting in identifying with the master class if one bought one's clothes at Take Six, or listened to Mozart rather than to the Rolling Stones? Was one persisting in seeking a "lost half" if one wanted to sleep with someone more than once? Like the parallel tendency in the women's movement of the day to collapse all issues concerning the oppression of women into an abstracted attack on The Family, so GLF tended to base much of its theory (and practice) on the rejection of an equally abstracted and monolithic notion of Heterosexuality. Hence a picture of our own gayness emerged which was simply a reversal of all the norms, values, and institutions of heterosexual society, as if these were not in themselves riddled with conflicts and contradictions. Most importantly of all, the concept of self-oppression implied that we were all equally free to "liberate" ourselves by heroic acts of will from a situation which, at the same time, was supposedly largely of our own making. This was the result of the particular historical moment of GLF. For if gays had been left out of traditional marxist class analysis — together with most aspects of sexuality, which were seen as merely superstructural and reactive in an unproblematic way to the economic "base" of society, reality — then class analysis itself was likely to be left at the back of the political cupboard in the general excitement which characterised the development of sexual politics in the late sixties, and the gradual rethinking of the base/superstructure model of society. Hence the tendency towards crude sex-versus-class theorisations of the respective positions of both women and gays, seen as homogeneous groupings, and the parallel fetishisation of the concept of patriarchy as if it explained the totality of capitalism. Hence also the women-identification of many gay male radicals, and the various agonies which resulted from their exclusion from a necessarily (at that time) separatist feminism.

The search for the roots of a specific gay oppression within capitalism was a vital precondition for the subsequent emergence of a sexual politics which would no longer be torn between the seemingly conflicting demands of political parties and autonomous movements, as if some absolute choice has always to be made between them. At the same time that search fixed a number of assumptions concerning the political status of homosexuality which need to be clarified. GLF established its own particular "commonsense" on such matters, and it is that level of taken-for-grantedness which I want to try to recover, since this may help to explain the distinctiveness of the British gay movement and our situation today.

The major division in early GLF was between the organised leninist party supporters, and the diffused forces of the alternative society. This division between what might be termed "actionists" and "life-stylers" is clearly evident in the history and theory of GLF, and in its Manifesto. This was printed in the summer of 1971 after months of discussion in the Manifesto group, one of many such groups co-ordinated by a central steering committee.[4] According to the Manifesto the oppression of gays is firmly located in the family. What is less clear is how the family relates to other social institutions. Into the figure of family life were collapsed all the frustrations and privations of a generation of young gays who had grown up watching their contemporaries from the sidelines of society, excluded from the cultural life of the supposedly "swinging" sixties. Hence the emphasis in the Manifesto and elsewhere on "role-play" in gay thought, at a time when fashionable talk of bisexuality was sanctioned in a society which was unwilling and unable to extend the notion of "unisex" beyond hairstyles. Much was made of such concepts as sexism, stereotyping, and so on, but the effect was to reinforce an inward-looking model of the nature of gay oppression as opposed to a broader consideration of the systematic connections between different modes of sexuality and differing social experience. The most urgent need at the time was to press home the fundamental validity of *all* forms of voluntary sexual behaviour. The question of the nature of that volition followed afterwards, and very much under the influence of Freud.[5]

This whole debate assumed with supreme confidence that any-one could, and should, simply throw up the family and collectivise. It was at this point that moralism set in. The Manifesto argues that gender roles are learned by indoctrination, but the process of gender socialisation was never pursued very seriously. When class was mentioned it was usually in the context of complaints that the movement was too middle-class, complaints which amounted to an attack on any and every kind of political organisation. Far more important was the accompanying concern with the language and formal structure of GLF itself. This desire to break with aggressive forms of political discussion proved to be one of GLFs most valuable and enduring legacies, even if in the early seventies this often resulted in no more than sterile linguistic fatalism concerning the possibilities of working within what was seen as a language which was innately male-defined.

The concept of "internalisation" was widely used, but was not much help when it came to trying to understand the actual mechanics of gay life. Nowhere was there any very thorough consideration of ideology, either as a general theory of implicit social beliefs and values, or as a more particular approach to the consequences for gays of recent developments in sociology concerning the social construction of the individual.[6] In this respect the remarkable speed and ease with which the later concept of homophobia was taken up as an explanation of hostility towards homosexuality shows the measure of the force of the idea that sexuality is a system of innate drives rather than a range of historically and socially constructed alternatives.[7] The tendency rather was simply to reverse all the assumptions and platitudes of mainstream bourgeois thought. Unfortunately this also tended to preserve the moralism of the original ideology, if in inverted forms. Thus one reaction to the old saw which held that homosexuals are innately promiscuous was to introduce the counter-concept of "compulsive monogamy". This certainly made sense within the fairly narrow confines of GLF, but remained incomprehensible to outsiders precisely because its meaning lay within the context of a long debate concerning the nature of relationships which was itself unstated. It was in ways like this that GLF tended to talk to itself. The dread of applying what were seen as "heterosexist" models to gay relationships had negative consequences both inside and outside GLF, in so far as it seemed to question anyone who was actually trying to sustain and develop a relationship of any kind. This was the result of regarding marriage as an exclusively exploitative property relationship rather than as a range of contradictory resolutions to the acute problems of social life under capitalism. In these terms it seemed that the wicked "one-to-one" was at least as pernicious as outright fascism; indeed, if capitalism was rooted in and stemmed from patriarchy then the latter *was* the former. . . .

This kind of logical reversal could not actually call into question the idea of promiscuity itself as a puritanical moral term. The strategy of reversing any proposition with which one disagreed, though dramatic, tended to prevent any further analysis. In this sense the tremendous and often-cited feelings of confidence and even of rebirth which GLF stimulated could, at times, prove to be its own worst enemy. The Manifesto, for example, carries on to argue that in so far as gays are "already outside the family", we are "*already* more advanced than straight people". This kind of social vanguardism was not uncommon. In a sense this is no more than a new version of the old argument that gays are somehow "innately" more sensitive/artistic than other people, but done up in a very dubious kind of radical drag.

Meanwhile, there were the problems of the so-called youth cult, role-playing and so on, but nothing that could not be solved by the sound expedients of consciousness-raising groups and communal gay life. Hence the idealism of so much GLF ideology, optimistically assuming that a kind of "Supergay" would emerge from all this guilt-free progressive living. Indeed, the belief that "homosexual liberation is not possible under capitalism" became almost axiomatic.[8] And in a bizarre way one finds a kind of radical parody of the traditional "corruption"theory of homosexuality; to live an "out" gay life is to challenge the entire structure of social relations under capitalism and, by extension, is an active revolutionary process in so far as homosexuality itself is seen as "innately" and contagiously subversive.[9]

Given the very limited results of the 1967 Wolfenden Act, this type of thinking was perhaps inevitable and even necessary. None the less, by redefining the negative clinical concept of homosexuality in aggressively positive terms, the word "gay" tended to preserve the notion of some fundamental homosexual "essence" which we all shared, over and above our actual individual social experience and sexual practice. In seeking to defend the campaign vigorously on behalf of a violently persecuted minority, GLF tended to perpetuate that same abstraction of the sexual from the social which lies so much at the heart of our situation. At the time it seemed as if a choice had to be made between a total commitment to a specifically gay politics, or else to a traditional left party framework in which issues of sexuality could not possibly be raised with the urgency they required.

Thus it was that a "radical" paper like *Ink* — "The Other Newspaper" — could report GLF responses to being banned from various London pubs in October 1971, noting that "old-style radicals would tend to classify their platform and politics as frivolous". The writer goes on to describe how gays have significantly linked their struggles to those of other minorities, concluding somewhat archly that "of course the fight continues for as long as a repressive state and government feels besieged by those who express their sexuality openly".[10] On this level of analysis gay politics has about the same revolutionary thrust as nudism. To which department of state or government the publicans of Notting Hill belonged is not made clear.

Another issue of *Ink* showed a Warhol-style Che Guevara on its cover, wearing make-up and sporting a GLF badge on his beret.[11] "Gay is Good" wrote Alison Fell, and went on to describe the history of the emergent gay movement. In an interview some GLF members explain the emphasis they place on coming out as a broad programme of "radicalisation" for both the individual and his or her society. The emphasis is on a very abstract concept of freedom: "To free the brothers and sisters . . . it is necessary to free ourselves." In this analysis "the family believes in owning things, and you have the logical extension of that, oppression of women". This marks perhaps the high-water mark of the popular assimilation of Kate Millett's *Sexual Politics,* published earlier in the year in Britain. Working-class sex roles are seen as "more rigid" because "the system has a vested interest in keeping them that way". In the absence of a socialist analysis which did not simply reduce all such questions to the notion of base and superstructure, it is hardly surprising that GLF tended increasingly towards a variety of libertarian and outright anarchist positions. This point was nowhere more apparent than in attitudes towards clothes. "By wearing drag, I feel that I am helping to

destroy the male myth."[12] The anonymous writer argues that
make-up, which objectifies women, may none the less demonstrate
or release some essential "femininity" in men. He concludes that
"those gay men who attack queens so vigorously are the ones who
are most threatened by it". This is, of course, a completely circular
argument, reminiscent of Freud's hypothetical notion of
repression. The same issue of *Come Together,* produced by the
Radical Queens' Commune in Colville Gardens, also printed
Valerie Solanas's SCUM Manifesto in full, the ultimate statement
of a certain kind of radical feminist position, representing a
surrealist vision of a "fantastic new era", in which the most
extreme version of heterosexul power relations is simply reversed,
as in the projected SCUM turd session, "at which every male
present will give a speech beginning: 'I am a turd, a lowly, abject
turd'", and so on. It was in this context that endless GLF meetings
got out of hand over the "oppression of queens", just as the
women's group became disastrously bogged down over the issue
of trans-sexuals. However important these issues were, and
remain, they came to suppress all other issues of gay sexuality in
1971, in just the same way that they themselves had hitherto been
suppressed. This was the terrible irony of GLF. As long as
capitalism was seen simply to stem (somehow) from The Family,
or else was seen to be a totally separate issue, this kind of
polarisation was inevitable. The situation was extremely
confusing. Half the leadership of GLF appeared to be maoists at
one meeting and Radical Drag Queens at the next. Drag was to call
into question the entire structure of our society. It was
simultaneously the symbol of gay liberation and an actual
revolutionary political strategy. The women in particular felt
crucified by this issue.[13] They were also angered by the ambiguous
response at the weekly All Saints Hall meeting to their report back
from the second annual Women's Liberation Conference at
Skegness that October, at which the maoist leadership had been
completely flummoxed when the GLF delegation announced
themselves as socialists, thus giving the lie to the platform's view of
lesbianism as an irrelevant and diversionary issue.

The women's situation was extremely difficult. They were
dissatisfied with the naive lifestyle politics of so many of the men
in GLF, and their sexism, yet often felt at odds at the same time
with a women's movement which seemed to be so exclusively
concerned with the problems of motherhood and childcare.
However, one of the most lasting and important influences of
GLF has been precisely the result of the gay women's insistence
that lesbianism is a fundamental issue for all feminists. Their
successful intervention into the women's movement guaranteed
the broadening of its attitude towards sexuality as a whole and its
relation to all other aspects of social relations.

The Women's Group left GLF then largely as socialists. Their
departure caused a certain amount of heart-searching. Andrew

Lumsden's response in the internal GLF Diary was to ask whether GLF had not simply created "another Boltons".[14] Sheer pressure of numbers at this time also guaranteed a fragmentation of the movement and the setting up of local groups in Camden, South London and elsewhere. Everyone agreed with the women that "we are not just fighting an economic system", but interpretations of that agreement varied dramatically.

The seminal problem for GLF was always one of political analysis. An early intoxication with some absolute ideal of freedom and liberation was understandable, particularly in a period of unexpectedly heavy-handed government. But the tactics of flower power were simply inappropriate to campaigns like that surrounding Heath's notorious Industrial Relations Act. The rejection of GLF on many demonstrations only served to reinforce the men's feelings of alienation from "straight" politics all the more, and to push them into a libertarian wilderness, in which the experience of communal living became even more cut off from the rest of society. The result was a splendid isolationism. To say this at the time, however, seemed utter heresy, the direst "reformism". And this was the way in which political identity (gay liberation) and personal identification (gay liberationist) became hopelessly confused. Demands for radical social and cultural change were interpreted solely in terms of an extremely vague theory of Total Revolution, of which GLF was to be the self-elected vanguard, piping the masses forward simultaneously from the tyranny of sex-roles and capitalism as a whole, in a gorgeous vision of sequins and personal transformation. GLF followed Marcuse's prescription for a general "revaluation" of lived experience, in the context of an individualistic philosophy which imagined that the individual was simply "free" to transform his or her life. This was the measure of the absence of any firm theory of class and ideology in relation to sexuality within the framework of GLF.

The response to the Women's Group's decision to leave GLF in February 1972 was the subject of a national Think-In at Lancaster, itself the result of an earlier decision to hold regular out-of-London meetings.[15] As Jeffrey Weeks has pointed out, "the essence of GLF was to change consciousness, but once it had begun to change it — and without a revolution! — it seemed less necessary to build the sort of radical movement that GLF claimed as essential".[16] As long as GLF could not even decide whether or not to support *Oz* magazine when it was being prosecuted under the obscenity laws, on the grounds that it was sexist, there was little hope of its own survival as a coherent movement.[17] "Repression doesn't mean that they're getting stronger — it means that we are .
. . . As our critique of the system is total so must our choice of weapons be".[18] This line was to prove a one-way ticket to any amount of pointless adventurism and unconstructive, if glamorous, martyrdom.

GLF basked in what Marcuse declared to be "the great

refusal".[19] From a crude theory of sexual repression and a generalised critique of capitalism, it advanced a set of strategies which derived from the one while they were at the same time fervently believed to be effective against the other. This was the logical consequence of that broad displacement of the social into the category of the sexual which characterises so much of the ideology of the 1960s.[20] "The oppression that gay people suffer is an integral part of the social structure of our society."[21] Such an analysis drastically oversimplified the entire set of relations between modes of production, social relations, the state, sexuality and those ideological formations which legitimate them all. The result was "an association of private and political destiny" on a particularly grand scale.[22] Anti-authoritarianism gave way all too soon into anti-rationalism and anti-intellectualism. Gays were seen as a class, a class which must be led to a state of revolutionary consciousness:

> We are fighting an entire culture. . . . If we are to gain our freedom we must focus people's attention on their frustration and their resentment on the source of it. . . . Conversion on a personal level is fundamental to our existence. . . . While the movement must have a coherent set of beliefs each individual in it must be allowed (and must be able) to give them personal expression. . . . We must be "rotten queers" to the straight world and for them we must use camp, drag etc., in the most "offensive" manner possible. And we must be "freaks" to the gay ghetto world. Our very existence must provoke a questioning of society.[23]

This kind of ultra-leftism was totally inured to its own falsity by the theory of revolutionary struggle on which it relied so heavily. It was completely unable to grasp that the politics of provocation are comprehensible only to the provocateurs.

The problem was — and remains — that sex has tended to be used as "the forum where both the future of our species and our 'truth' as human subjects are decided."[24] GLF was never able to question this use of sexuality, and, in fact, simply went along with the familiar bourgeois tendency to treat man as an *animal*, determined by "instinct" and biology, rather than objective, socio-economic factors. The emphasis on the individual's "liberation" of his or her sexuality merely continued a tendency to regard the human social being as an "abstract biological person/individual" — "the alpha and omega of modern ideology".[25] Sexuality re-emerges in this theory as some kind of *élan vital*, a life force which not only will release the individual from all the constraints of an exploitative and vicious social system, but will also transform that system itself into some form of radical libertarian Arcadia.

Gay Liberation attempted to recuperate an illusion. That illusion maintained that our sexuality is the single most significant determining aspect of our entire existence. This same act of dense moral political and social codification within the concept of sexuality stands behind all the sexual militancy of the past hundred years. We cannot "liberate" a mechanism, a way of thinking ourselves, which forces us to abstract and favour one aspect of our social make-up above all others. The real concrete oppression of homosexuals is the direct result of this total theory of "sexuality", and the tenaciously held ideologies which it has engendered. It was the tragic and heroic destiny of GLF to attempt to shift the balance of that theory in our favour as homosexuals. As the result of this we now have an altogether new and positive sense of community. We have self-help organisations, newspapers, switchboards, books like this, and so on. What we need now is a much deeper understanding of the ideology of "sex" itself, as it affects and organises all our lives, which may take us by the way to a deeper understanding of the society in which and against which we are obliged to struggle.

As gays and socialists we are involved in an ambitious task which aims to question the most basic assumptions about what it means to be a man or a woman in this society, socially, economically and sexually. That this may not appear "revolutionary" to some should not deter us. We need to realise how politically hampered GLF was by precisely this kind of romantic leninist or anarchist myth of Total Revolution, which was constantly used to attack all short-term strategies. As Sheila Rowbotham has observed, "the idea of oppression is both vague and rather static. It fixes people in their role as victim rather than pointing to the contradictory aspects of relationships which *force* the emergence of new forms of consciousness".[26] This has meant that the gay movement has tended to be treated as little more than an oyster-bed by left parties, in particular the Socialist Workers' Party (SWP). It also explains why gay politics have been so slow in making use of recent theoretical developments concerning the nature of power in capitalist societies, developments which, as in the work of Michel Foucault, offer a broader understanding of the interactions between sexuality, the state, and our sense of our own identities as individuals.

In part this problem concerns the history of popular culture in Britain. In this respect Marx tended to be kept on one side, rather like a political first-aid kit, "for use in emergency only". At the same time there is a real danger, a decade on, of painting too negative a picture of GLF and all it stood for. The significance of the denial of that fragmentation of consciousness which is perhaps the major product of the categorisation of sexuality as we know it cannot be overestimated. At the same time GLF offered in its day a relatively coherent idea of gay politics, unwilling simply to present a picture of homosexuality as a range of just and positive modes of being, and forcing the whole issue of the relations between sexuality and the social order.

This has proved to be the most significant and enduring legacy of the ideology of GLF, its original and forceful stress on the systematic and politically functional aspects of "sexuality". Out of all the hours of discussion and debate I recall one particular incident at a GLF consciousness-raising group about 1971. Someone had intervened, saying that the group was no more than a "knitting-circle". At once a keen argument followed. Wasn't this a typical male sexist remark? Didn't the metaphor suggest that women are innately different to men? Didn't it reinforce a stereo-type of women? And finally — what was so *wrong* about being members of a knitting-circle, talking quietly while being involved in useful (if unpaid?) work? This may perhaps sound trivial when written down like this. What is important I think is that such a dis-cussion could not have taken place between a group of socialist men in any other context than that of GLF. It also illustrates, I think, the practical sensitivity of the gay movement. This kind of discussion introduced a not inconsiderable number of women and men, like myself, to an altogether new and exciting idea of politics.

Nevertheless there remains a certain historically understandable reluctance to think through some of the practical consequences of such understandings. Early ideas concerning the supposedly "innately" revolutionary "nature" of homosexuality have meant that such questions as the relations between processes of sexual and political self-identification have tended to remain mystified by the convenient notion of widespread "apathy" which would seem to make the majority of gay people who are not involved in the gay movement seem guilty of some particular betrayal of their sexuality.

The whole thorny problem of the actual constituency of the gay socialist movement has thus been largely avoided. This in turn is another consequence of our reliance upon an oversimplified blanket concept of "oppression", which originally regarded all gay people as being intrinsic revolutionaries in their mode of sexuality once the veils of "false consciousness" had been revealed and cast aside. A residual version of this belief continues to sustain certain contradictory aspects of the British gay movement, in particular the French-influenced quest for some kind or recuperated psychoanalytic theory of the homosexual uncon-scious which might succeed where mechanical versions of marxism failed.[27] In America too there has been a recent tendency to attempt to isolate some kind of innate gay "human nature" on the model of sociobiology.[28] Such endeavours merely confuse the basic issue: in looking for a "natural" homosexuality rooted either in a science of the mind or an all-determining evolutionary biology, the conflicting articulations and institutions of sexuality as a whole are placed beyond analysis. This is why we need to pay much more attention to the concrete *experience* of homosexuality in all its plenitude of manifestations, not as some kind of symptomology, but rather as a direct account of our everyday being in the world, and the systematic ways in which our lives are shaped and so often distorted.

Ten years ago it seemed that we had two basic choices open to us: the glamorous anarchic possibilities of libertarianism, or the more sober rhetoric of the orthodox revolutionary left. It has not been a wasted decade if we have learned from our various struggles that neither of these positions has turned out to be quite what it seemed. We can hardly defend any all-out attack on the state when we have fought, like so many other groups, to partly reconstruct it to our own advantage. Nor can we ignore the plain fact that the organised revolutionary parties have proved signally unable to respond to that extension of the whole concept and practice of politics which is such a crucial aspect of the entire sexual politics movement. We have our own place within the political firmament of socialism, and it is up to us to affirm and defend it both outside and within such institutions as the trade unions, parties, mass movements, and so on.

If we are to learn from our own history this means, as Habermas has put it, that "we must promote reforms for clear and publicly discussed goals, even and especially if they have consequences that are incompatible with the mode of production of the established system".[29] Only in this way can we avoid the current tendency to slide back into crude economic determinism, or into a sexual politics which overdetermines the purely physical as it narrows down its grasp and concept of the political.

NOTES AND REFERENCES

1. H. Marcuse, "Liberation From the Affluent Society", in *The Dialectics of Liberation,* Harmondsworth 1968.

2. See Carl Wittman, *A Gay Manifesto,* San Francisco 1971, reprinted by Agitprop, London 1972.

3. "Self-Oppression", in *Come Together* no. 10, November 1971.

4. The original "Principles of GLF" document lists a steering committee, counter-psychiatry group, action group (actions and dances), trade-union group, schools group, media workshop, and theatre group. The list suggests the range of related concerns from the very beginning of British GLF.

5. This has been a particular feature of the French gay movement, in particular the writings of René Schérer and Guy Hocquenghem.

6. For example, Berger and Luckmann's *The Social Construction of Reality,* Harmondsworth 1967, which, despite an appallingly crude picture of homosexuality as a "wrong choice" in childhood, none the less stressed the dialectical relations between social reality and individual experience.

7. See George Weinberg, *Society and the Healthy Homosexual,* USA 1972.

8. Don Milligan, *The Politics of Homosexuality,* London 1973.

9. This position continues to be held, for example, in John Rechy's proposition in *The Sexual Outlaw,* 1977, that "public sex is revolution, courageous, righteous defiant revolution".

10. "Gays Win Out", in *Ink,* 19 October 1971.

11. *Ink,* 21 February 1972.

12. "Getting Down to the Nitty-Gritty", in *Come Together,* no. 15.

13. Conversation with Elizabeth Wilson, April 1979. See also "Socialist Women and GLF", in *Come Together* no. 15, and the two special women's issues.

14. The Boltons was, and is, a popular gay pub in West London.

15. See *The Leeds Broadsheet* no. 4, February 1972. *The Leeds Broadsheets* are the most reliable record of the various national groups through 1971-2.

16. Jeffrey Weeks, *Coming Out,* chapter 16, London 1972.

17. See "About *Oz*", in *Come Together* no. 8, August 1971.

18. "We're Getting Stronger", in *Come Together,* no. 8, August 1971.

19. H. Marcuse, *An Essay on Liberation,* London 1969.

20. See Jeffrey Weeks's "The Rise and Fall of Permissiveness", in *The Spectator,* 17 March 1979, reprinted in *Gay News* no. 165.

21. *Come Together* no. 2.

22. Jurgen Habermas, "Student Protest in the Federal Republic of Germany", in *Towards a Rational Society,* London 1971.

23. "Propaganda — Some Notes", GLF handout, c. 1971.

24. "Power and Sex: An Interview with Michel Foucault", in *Telos 32,* Summer 1977.

25. V. N. Volosinov, *Freudianism, a Marxist Critique,* Moscow 1927; London 1976.

26. Sheila Rowbotham, "The Women's Movement and Organising for Socialism", in *Beyond the Fragments,* London 1979.

27. See "Odds and Sods", a review by Philip Derbyshire of Guy Hocquenghem's *Homosexual Desire,* in *Gay Left* no. 7.

28. See Michael Ruse's review of Edmund O. Wilson's "On Human Nature" in *The Advocate,* no. 266, May 1979.

29. Jurgen Habermas, "The Movement in Germany: A Critical Analysis", in *Towards a Rational Society,* London 1971.

I should like to thank Elizabeth Wilson, Dennis Altman, and members of the Gay Left Collective for discussing aspects of this paper with me during its preparation.

6

The Politics of Tea and Sympathy

JOHN MARSHALL

The Campaign for Homosexual Equality (CHE) is a regular target for critical attack and pompous dismissal. Yet it remains the only major homosexual organisation in Britain, with over four thousand individual members and over a hundred local groups. The alternatives, whether we like to admit it or not, are small, fragmented, disorganised, and powerless. So to those who would wish to see an effectively politicised gay movement in this country, the dilemma of CHE, if we wish to view it as such, has to be taken seriously. Rather than merely dismissing the organisation as reformist and apolitical, we should attempt an analysis of CHE which roots out the underlying problems of the gay movement. We should be prepared to take the existence of CHE very seriously indeed, if only as an opportunity to develop a better understanding of our weaknesses. This article may be seen as a tentative step in that direction.

To speak of CHE as an "organisation" and to discuss the merits of its general philosophy and function is to presuppose that CHE is a thing-like body with a single identity and purpose. But of course, strictly speaking, this presupposition is unwarranted since CHE does incorporate diverse groups and varied political positions. However, even with this in mind, there is still a valid sense in which we can refer to CHE in a singular way since there are clearly identifiable characteristics which locate the organisation as being of a particular kind.

These general characteristics can be understood partly as the outcome of the organisation's history and partly as the product of the very real circumstances of homosexual oppression.

Historically, the Campaign for Homosexual Equality is the direct offspring of the campaigning efforts which had reached their conclusion with the Sexual Offences Act of 1967.[1] Such pre-1967 efforts revolved around the Homosexual Law Reform Society which had been established in 1958 to counter the reluctance of the then Tory Government to act on the Wolfenden proposals. The Wolfenden Committee itself had been formed as a response to the increasingly overt persecution of homosexuals during the late 1940s and early 1950s when there was a dramatic increase in the number of indictable offences known to the police. Such offences were willingly digested by the sensational popular press, especially those cases (and there were a number of them) which featured prominent names.

This served to create a climate in which homosexuals became ruthlessly deployed as a symbol of moral decadence. Images of the homosexual as pansy (women, as usual, were generally not considered), the homosexual as traitor, and the homosexual as corruptor of the nation's morals, were freely circulated and delightfully received by those with a hunger for an easy sense of righteousness.

The heightened hostility towards male homosexuality had a major impact on the style and content of the homosexual response. For not only did it place legal reform as the most central and pressing requirement but it also dictated the whole ideology of the battle. This was so for two reasons. First, the practical problem of securing a change in the law, given the strength of the resistance, meant that the movement was committed to a lengthy process of careful persuasion aimed at those in power. And second, there was a perceived need to avoid a too open and positive defence of homosexuality and to choose instead a more pragmatic and in some ways apologetic approach. This was thought necessary not simply because it would maximise the chances of gaining the desired legal changes. More importantly, perhaps, it reflected the uncertainty in the movement itself. Homosexuals had been much influenced by the weight of feeling against them, and lacked the self-confidence (or indeed, the ideology) to defend themselves more boldly.[2]

It was within this context that the Homosexual Law Reform Society emerged as a non-political, single-issue pressure group. Apart from "educating public opinion", its goals were dictated entirely in terms of what was thought possible by sympathetic MPs. The result, after long struggle, was the Sexual Offences Act of 1967.

Immediately after the Act, the impetus of the Society began to dwindle although of the local groups, the North Western Committee did survive. This group had tended to be more progressive and it was from within this sector that the Committee for Homosexual Equality was formed in 1969. This organisation grew rapidly in its first few years and with the impact of the more radical gay liberation movement it changed its name (in 1971) to the Campaign for Homosexual Equality.

However, despite the presence of an apparently wider perspective and despite the influence of the Gay Liberation Front (GLF), it remained the case that CHE was firmly rooted to the reformist tradition from which it sprang. Its initial response to GLF, for example, was to distance itself from an association with the new movement and to warn of the dangers of over-politicisation. And although CHE did eventually respond to the new climate, both by changing its name and by becoming a formally democratised mass membership organisation, the older style was never completely transcended. It continued with its central commitment to law reform (a new draft bill was eventually launched in 1975), the development of social facilities, and a general adherence to respectability. This is not to say, however, that it never evolved a militant style. Conferences from time to time reflected an underlying commitment to militant reformism but the organisation was never politically cohesive enough to carry through these ideals. CHE therefore remained, in practice, a rather limited force.

Having outlined, briefly, the historical tradition from which CHE emerged and the specific circumstances of homosexual oppression which largely shaped that tradition, we need now to cast our net wider and ask why CHE continues to be shaped by its historical mould and why it has failed to become a more effectively politicised movement. Why did the new confidence and militancy generated by GLF fail to flow more profoundly into the veins of CHE? And why, incidentally, was GLF such a short-lived affair with radicalism?

It is tempting in the first instance to pitch one's analysis totally at the level of ideas. That is, we could suggest that CHE has failed to become a real political force because the ideas upon which it is based reveal an inadequate understanding of the problems of gay oppression. We could say that CHE has failed to understand the nature of capitalist, family oriented, heterosexual society, and has failed to see how such values and structures, by defining the norm in a particular way, inevitably render the homosexual experience as a deviant and problematic alternative. Indeed, we could suggest that by not confronting these issues, CHE actually reinforces the very values of homosexual oppression. That is, by tacitly accepting the view of homosexuals as "a minority", it could be argued that CHE serves to reinforce the validity of the norm and the categorisation of homosexuals as deviant.

Armed with such a critique we could easily dismiss CHE as a worthy organisation. We could imagine that we have understood the failings of CHE and the failings of the homosexual movement. We might even imagine that *we* understand precisely what is required as a genuinely radical alternative.

The immediate problem, however, is that such a critique and the conclusions which apparently follow tend to assume that social change is wholly determined by choices in political philosophy. That is, it assumes (along with bourgeois political science) that there are no concrete forces which shape and constrain the political ideology of any particular group. It assumes that political difficulties can be accounted for simply in terms of the irrationality of a particular political line and that such difficulties can be overcome simply by a more rational and perceptive approach. But it should be apparent that a genuine understanding of CHE requires a movement away from the question "What is wrong with the reformist/respectable ideology of CHE?" towards the more difficult question, "What are the forces which shape the ideology of CHE and what implications do such forces have for gay socialists?"

Posing the latter question, I suggest, would redirect attention back to the precarious position of homosexuals *in this society, at this time,* and would force us to reflect on the relation between our theory and practice.

The American sociologist Laud Humphreys has observed that there are at least two major prerequisites for the politicisation of any group and the subsequent possibility of radical social change.[3] First, there must be a conscious and collective awareness of an intolerable reality in the present. And second, there must be a vision of conceivable change; a vision of a real and historically attainable alternative. Without the latter, contemporary difficulties and misgivings are likely at best to generate only a limited sense of struggle within the existing framework, or at worse, a sense of apathy or fatalism. Without the former, of course, the possibilities of struggle are even more restricted.

With this in mind, I suggest that the real dilemma of CHE (and the gay movement generally) is that conditions are such as to limit the possibility both of perceiving the present situation and of perceiving thereafter the possibility of change. It is not simply that individuals, groups, or an organisation like CHE have made mistaken political decisions. It is more the case that homosexual oppression functions to limit the possibility of political decisions being taken.

Gay activists are often keen to draw parallels between our own struggles as homosexuals and the struggles of other groups. But this is sometimes misleading since there is an important difference between "being a homosexual" and being black, being a woman or being a member of the working class. For in the latter cases there is a definite and structured lifespan through which one's being in the world is constructed in terms of the category. As such, there is a lifelong process of socialisation and identity confirmation. But in the case of the homosexual category there is no such structured lifespan. Homosexuals are not brought up to *be* homosexual. Indeed, the initial socialisation process is significantly influenced (especially for men) by the tacit requirement that one be not homosexual. As Lehne once put it: "The taunt 'What are you, a fag?' is used in many ways to encourage certain types of male behavior and to define the limits of 'acceptable' masculinity."[4]

Now in so far as homosexuals, in the first instance, have internalised a heterosexual self-conception, or at least, a sense of fear or moral aversion to the homosexual category, they immediately face a conscious *personal* struggle. "Becoming a homosexual" is a difficult process of "becoming the other" or "becoming what one has learned to despise". As such, it is an individual and privatised process, the "intolerable reality" being a confrontation with *oneself* rather than an open struggle with an easily located oppressor.

Two significant features of this process have important political implications. First, the fact that the struggle to adopt a homosexual identity is pitched on an individual and private basis means that it is extremely difficult to transcend that "personal problem" perspective. Since homosexuals do not share a common biography or sense of collective identity, they do not experience a sense of collective oppression. They are not a class or a pre-given group and to that extent they do not form a natural political community. In socio-political terms, they are simply an aggregate of persons with a common "personalised problem".

Second, the fact that homosexuals have been socialised into the orthodox social order means that they will usually retain many of the moral imperatives and value assumptions of that social order, even when these may directly contradict their experience as homosexuals. This orthodox value commitment has two aspects. In relation to homosexuality per se, the individual is likely to retain considerable anxiety about his or her homosexuality. Speaking of male homosexuals, Goffman has pointed out that "the standards he has incorporated from the wider society equip him to be intimately alive to what others see as his failing, inevitable causing him, if only for moments, to agree that he does indeed fall short of what he really ought to be".[5] A second and wider aspect of this orthodox value commitment is equally significant. It arises because homosexuals occupy diverse places within the occupational and class structure and, in the case of many homosexuals, the material and ideological forces which arise out of this location encourage a loyalty, on a deeply personal level, to a society which renders their homosexuality invalid.

These features illustrate the extent to which there are no pre-given grounds of collective conscious awareness or collective political struggle.[6] But there are also associated difficulties. The fact that homosexuals have to *adopt* their identity rather than having it bestowed upon them from birth means that the homosexual community will consist of a diverse group of people at different stages of adjustment to this personal process. And given the problems posed by the different degrees of conformity to the orthodox order, the *type* of adjustments and responses will also be diverse. Such factors serve to underline the extent to which homosexuals are an aggregate of persons rather than a pre-given social group.

A further complication is the fact that even when persons adopt a homosexual identity, this is not necessarily public. They have the capacity to pass as straight and there are some very real forces which encourage them to do so. This compartmentalisation of self finds institutional support, of course, with the existence of a separate gay subculture and it is a frustrating paradox that the increase in facilities over the last decade, while being a real and positive gain, also serves to make this double identity more comfortable to sustain.

The capacity of capitalism to incorporate and commercialise the gay world contributes to this process and it even allows sufficient free space (on its own terms) for the development of homosexual lifestyles. This again serves to neutralise much of the political potential of the homosexual movement.

Taken together, all of these considerations illustrate the difficulties in creating a social and political movement. Such difficulties are located not at the level of ideas or political disagreement but in the actual circumstances of the homosexual situation. It is only within such a framework that the weakness of CHE can be found.

The Campaign for Homosexual Equality aims to remove fear, discrimination and prejudice against homosexuals, to achieve full equality before the law, and to promote the positive acceptance of homosexuality as a valid way of life. But it also operates as a self-help group for homosexuals. It offers a befriending service for those who are struggling to define their own sexuality and it attempts to reduce isolation by developing a sense of community.

This dual function, however, immediately establishes a dilemma. First, the creation of a social community and the provision of counselling and befriending services tends to direct energy away from the business of campaigning. And second, the specific philosophy and image required for a campaigning organisation (e.g. the need to be militant, aggressive, and overtly political) tends to contradict the philosophy and image required for a befriending agency (e.g. the need to be non-threatening, approachable and, possibly, only covertly political).

For many CHE groups this dilemma is resolved in favour of the social and counselling side with the campaigning function almost entirely neglected. In other groups there is a constant struggle to maintain the correct balance although, given the tensions involved, this is never easy. But it is important to remember that this dilemma is not simply a product of poor organisation or false political priorities. It actually arises as a direct consequence of the precarious position of homosexuals in this society. It arises because there is a *need* to break down isolation, to give support, and to create a sense of community. It arises because the immediate needs of homosexuals *are* seen in personal and social rather than political terms. And it arises because there is no simple transition from a relatively private homosexual identity to a public and political identity.

In so far as CHE is a political force at all, its politics tend to be reformist and middle-of-the-road. But again, this is connected with the nature of its political constituency. Since homosexuals are not a class, with easily identifiable class interests, the organisation cannot call upon its membership *as though* it constituted a pre-given political community. For the reasons discussed above, the homosexual community is characterised by the personalisation of problems, diversity in consciousness, and different degrees of conformity to the present social order. It is therefore wholly understandable that such a diverse flock can only be drawn together under a liberal civil rights perspective.

An understanding of what one might call these "natural" limitations of CHE, however, should not lead us into the realms of political despair. Rather, we should be prepared to acknowledge the political necessity and importance of CHE. Simply by being able to affirm identities and forge the links of collectivism, CHE is performing a highly significant role.

Nor should we be too ready to minimise the importance of CHE as an explicitly campaigning force. For despite the fact that many CHE groups neglect campaigning efforts, many others do a great deal of work within their local communities and are prepared to engage in struggles of various kinds. Such efforts may not be informed by a broad sexual-political philosophy but they do constitute an important part of "the homosexual movement".

On a national level too, CHE functions as a representative voice of the gay community and is able to take initiatives on a variety of issues. Through contacts with members of parliament, the police, government departments, etc., the organisation is in a position to influence, albeit, perhaps, in minor ways, the outcome of the decision-making process. In so far as official agencies make decisions and carry out policies which affect gay people, positive engagement in these debates must be seen as a legitimate area of struggle.

The capacity of CHE to respond quickly to more immediate crises has been severely hindered, however, by problems of communication and bureaucracy. It was partly in response to this limitation that the Gay Activists' Alliance (GAA) was formed in February 1978. GAA has been a much more specifically activist organisation and as such is not restricted by the problems of a considerably more broad-based and multifunctional organisation like CHE.

It is important to stress again, however, that the differences between GAA and CHE arose not simply because one organisation was more perceptive than the other. GAA was also limited in various ways by the same forces which limit CHE. Indeed, the decision to develop GAA as a general alliance rather than a homogeneous party indicated a conscious recognition of both the problems and the diversity within the gay community.[7] The real difference between GAA and CHE lay in the fact that they emerged from different points on the map and address themselves to a rather different range of concerns. In so doing, they reflected the crosscutting and contradictory nature of the homosexual community.

It was a mistake of many involved in GLF to assume that some of these problems and contradictory forces could be conveniently bypassed in the name of radical politics. It was almost as if they assumed that history can be transformed by the purity of our acts of will. If we refuse to follow that illusion we will be better placed to understand and appreciate the real problems of gay politics, the need for a multi-dimensional movement, and the validity of CHE within it.

NOTES AND REFERENCES

1. For a more detailed account of the historical background to CHE, see J. Weeks, *Coming Out,* Quartet Books, 1977.
2. For Antony Grey's comments on the avoidance of the moral issue, see his article "Homosexual Law Reform" in Brian Frost (ed.), *The Tactics of Pressure,* London 1975. Unfortunately, contemporary critics of the HLRS tend to ignore the social and political circumstances which dictated the terms of the struggle.
3. L. Humphreys, *Out of the Closets: The Sociology of Homosexual Liberation,* Prentice Hall, 1972.
4. G. K. Lehne, "Homophobia Among Men" in D. S. David and R. Brannon (eds.), *The Forty-Nine Percent Majority,* London 1976.
5. E. Goffman, *Stigma: Notes on the Management of Spoiled Identity,* Prentice Hall, 1963.
6. It should be said that the contrast suggested between gays and other groups is not intended to imply a straightforward or *necessary* relation between pre-given collective identity and collective political consciousness.
7. For an account of GAA, see Stephen Gee, "Homosexuals Fight Back", in *Gay Left,* no. 7, and his article in this book (pp. 198-204).

7

The Politics of Autonomy

KEITH BIRCH

The modern gay movement has been in existence for a decade and has had an importance and influence much wider than the relatively small number of women and men who have been actively involved. It has been a major factor in changing the self-concepts of many gay people and on the growth and style of the gay subculture. The gay movement's influence has also been felt both in the increased public visibility of homosexuality and in the changing attitude towards sexual politics that has occurred on the left.

For some time, though, those of us who consider ourselves to be activists and socialists in the movement seem to have been at an impasse in our relations both towards the majority of the gay community and towards the socialist parties at which we have directed our energies.

At this time it is not just gay socialists who are faced with problems of how to address ourselves to a wider constituency but similarly the whole of the left in this country. The election of a Conservative government and the general ideological shift to the right confronts us with the failure to offer a wider perspective which could involve people and relate to their lived experiences.

The gay movement has been concerned with a type of politics and forms of organisation which have as their basis matters which are defined as "personal" in this society. It is this linking of the personal and political in sexual politics and the widening of the areas of struggle that have raised questions which must be central to the socialist movement in challenging the conservative hegemony.

Sexuality has become a central organising feature of our sense of being and our individuality as it is constructed in this society. The gay movement has taken this to its logical conclusion in that our sexuality has become the focus for political organisation. However, is it possible for the diverse experiences of being homosexual in this society to be an adequate basis on which a political and social movement can be founded?

The question becomes more difficult to answer when theoretically we have to oppose the notion of a discrete category of "homosexuals" as having some kind of shared history, experience and identity. In the early stages of the gay movement we took over from bourgeois ideology the view of homosexuals as a fixed minority group. The most common analogy that we made to our own position was that of black people or women. In a number of ways we had similar social and political perspectives — the demand for civil rights and equality, the assertion of a positive identity, self-activity as an autonomous movement, developing our own forms of struggle and the building of our own community.

This view, however, conceals a number of significant differences between the status of being gay and of being black or a woman in this society. It has led us into problems and a perceived "failure" when addressing ourselves to what is then conceived of as an already constituted gay community and gay identity. The path from homosexual desire and activity to one of self-identification as being gay is by no means automatic or easy. The ideological and material constraints on "choosing" a gay identity are enormous and not to recognise this can lead to a hard and unrealistic moralism over "coming out" which Gay Liberation groups have exhibited at times.

The perspective is also politically restrictive in that taking over a "national identity" limits us to the status of a fixed minority demanding our rights. This can take place largely within the present categories of sexuality, in contradiction to our earlier claim that being gay was inherently revolutionary in the sense that these changes could not be accommodated under "patriarchal" capitalism. In fact the last ten years have demonstrated yet again that the liberal capitalist societies can accommodate a growing gay subculture. In some respects if one is white, male and middle-class and living in a city or large town our "liberation" may be thought to have arrived. But even with a growing gay subculture the accommodation has been within certain well-defined boundaries regarding where, when and who.

The gay movement has got to offer a much broader challenge to the commonly held notions regarding sexuality that now prevail. Yet, in rejecting such a fixed identity, we cannot just theoretically dissolve the categories in which we now exist and the effects of which we experience in our everyday life. What the gay movement has been doing is to build and reinforce the distinct and positive identity of being a lesbian or a gay man in this society rather than breaking down the barriers between sexual categories.

Here lies an obvious contradiction between what are our theoretical and political aims and our current practice and experience. However, this will continue to be the case while homosexuality is a hidden and oppressed sexual orientation. It needs to be stressed that the process of validation of the gay experience is both constructive and necessary now, and for the foreseeable future.

Two factors that are fundamental to both the gay movement and the women's movement have been, first, the stress on self-activity, on the individual level and as an autonomous movement, and secondly, the assertion of a wider kind of politics, amounting to a redefinition of what had become understood by the term.

An important part of what has been new to our politics is summed up in the slogan "the personal is political". Entailed in this concept was a radical challenge to the politics practised by the traditional left. This ranged from our stress on the importance of subjectivity and individual experience through to the need for self-activity to fight against the specific forms of oppression faced by lesbians and gay men. The phrase also pointed to the need for us to attempt to live our politics and create the beginnings of new relationships and community now, however difficult and idealist that may be.

In their concentration on workplace organisation and what had become a narrowly economistic politics, much of the left had lost sight of whole areas of people's experiences and concerns as well as the forces which construct and limit our desires and actions. This split in much of socialist political practice mirrored an important aspect of the splits that we experience in our lives in this society. The last century of capitalist development has brought with it a great emphasis on personal life as opposed to relationships at work and in society at large. This personal sphere of the family, sexuality and subjective feelings has come to occupy an increased importance in our lives. It is, however, a site of contradiction as it is a major source for our integration into society and its values and, at the same time, a scene of frustration and conflict.

The force of sexual politics has been to make this sphere public and political, to question much of the taken-for-granted nature of our personal lives. Our sexual roles and emotional structures are largely constituted in this area of our lives and it is felt to be a sphere where we have control. However, wider social relationships of power and domination are reflected here as well as "personal" ones. The politics of the gay movement has had to confront the difficulties posed in these areas and it was in part based upon making them political issues.

The theory of autonomy asserted our right to have control of our movement and formulate our own activities, independent of existing organisations which had for so long been oppressive in their attitudes towards homosexuality and unconcerned with sexual relationships in general. The forms of organisation we developed concentrated on involvement and openness. There was a rejection of authority, hierarchy and formal structure both in small groups and large meetings. Individual groups formed to start self-help projects, produce papers and organise community centres. Alternative social events such as discos became important political actions in themselves, providing a very different and open environment compared to the major part of the commercial scene.

The process involved in consciousness-raising groups and the participation in movement activities were important steps in

building confidence and mutual support. They also enabled us to
have some sense of taking a measure of control of our lives and of
breaking down the individualisation of feelings and problems that
takes place in this society. The movement also provided the basis
of our efforts to integrate aspects of our personal and political
lives. The raising of questions about relationships and attempts to
build alternative organisations, self-help groups and discos were
the basis for a wider gay community.

Thus the gay movement was based on very different principles
to those of the left parties. Of course, the gay movement differs in
that it is a social movement rather than a political party. By its
open nature it can attract a wider section of self-defined gay people
who want to work together on various issues or on the level of
social and community involvements. This means that there is not
an allegiance to a particular political perspective as belonging to a
party implies.

This autonomy of the movement from political parties has been
central to its whole dynamic while also being a point of conflict
with some socialist groups concerning the nature of that
autonomy. The activist gay movement cannot be supplanted by a
political party even for those of us who define ourselves as
socialists. Gay socialists continue to work in the development of
the autonomous movement not just to draw links and influence it
but for our own needs and development as gay people. The left
groups themselves cannot do this for gays. It is also a fact that they
have only responded to the issues of sexuality with the emergence
of strong and autonomous women's and gay movements which
have forced them to take notice.

In defining the gay movement as being of a different character to
a party one does not mean that a movement and party have
completely separate spheres of operation. Spokespeople for some
of the socialist parties have tried to stress this separation of
concerns so that the party is given the role of bringing together the
most advanced sections of the class and of the movements,
somehow overcoming and dissolving the conflicts and contradictions that exist in the outside world. The strict dichotomy that is
constructed between the political and social spheres means that
the party remains in theory and practice largely unaffected by the
politics, ideas and criticisms of the autonomous movements.

An equivalent kind of dichotomy has also been constructed by
some revolutionary feminists and some marxists. In her book
Psychoanalysis and Feminism, Juliet Mitchell saw the class struggle
as synonymous with the economic and being carried forward by
the working class and the party. Meanwhile, the ideological and
anti-patriarchal struggle was a separate province relevant to the
women's movement. The concept of autonomous movements
does not mean agreement with there being separate realms of
struggle in this way. Rather, the self-organisation of oppressed
groups and their development would enable a more comprehen-

sive struggle for a new socialist society to take place, recognising the conflicts of interest and continuing the struggle with a broad based, dynamic socialist movement.

The accommodation or rejection of the women's and gay movements made by the main groups on the left flows from and highlights their differing political strategies. Fundamentally, the left has taken on the demands of the movements on the basis of the need for equality and civil rights, with the stress on women as workers and on gays as a distinct minority group. The wider challenge of our movements in redefining what is political and concerning methods of organising and participation has been largely ignored. "The Party" does not go in for self-inspection and the leadership remains largely unmoved from its traditional practices. The majority of the membership has little direct involvement with or discussion around such issues and therefore do not see the relevance of the criticisms and demands that are being made. It is left for women and gays to always bring up "their problem" and to confront the party and other members.

The particular responses of the main parties have differed. The Communist Party has in recent years been supportive of women's and gay struggles, giving publicity in their daily paper the *Morning Star*. After what seemed an initial attempt to ignore the women's movement the CP has come to strongly support the autonomous social movements. This has been part of their general reassessment of their political role in Britain and the nature of the process towards socialism. Within their concept of a "broad democratic alliance of progressive forces" the space exists for broad-based autonomous movements which extend the scope of struggle and advance political consciousness. Problems remain, though, in regard to how much issues of sexual politics have touched the majority of the membership and affected the nature of the organisation and its internal democracy.

The line of the International Marxist Group has in practice been similar to the CP, though based on a different political perspective. It has supported the growth and role of the autonomous movements and has taken up some of the issues of sexual politics strongly. However, it adheres to the dichotomy between the roles of party and movement. Its political perspectives on the party and the attainment of socialism have not been seriously revised from their traditions based on trotskyism (see Philip Derbyshire's article in this volume, "Sects and Sexuality").

The other most important left group, the Socialist Workers' Party, has always had a more difficult relationship with the autonomous movements, some aspects of which have been detailed in issues of *Gay Left*. Their stress on building the vanguard party containing the most advanced elements of the class and of oppressed groups leads to a dismissal of the autonomous groups. It has tended to classify work in the women's and gay movements as reformist and middle-class and therefore not worthwhile political activity. The way forward for socialist women and gays is to join the party and the "class struggle", thus totally denying the relevance of autonomous movements.

It is a measure of the continuing hegemony of the conservative traditions of much of the trade-union movement and of the Labour Party that we find ourselves having to address and challenge the practices of these parties as the focus of relevant socialist activity in this country. However, the traditions, theories and organisation which flow from trotskyism still dominate the groups to the left of the Communist Party and they often seem to stand in the way of changes that an open and developing socialist politics demands.

Sheila Rowbotham in *Beyond the Fragments* has described the experiences of feminists in relation to the leninist parties. She describes how the notions of the vanguard party and democratic centralism in the leninist tradition crush and exclude the experiences, theories and developments of the women's and gay movements among others. The development of a relevant and dynamic politics in the socialist movement is weakened by that refusal of the left groups to be open to ideas and criticisms that emerge from others involved in socialist activity.

At the basis of the attitudes of many of the socialist groups are a number of simplistic assumptions concerning the political organisation and notions of consciousness and ideology. Both of these areas are problematic for the gay movement as well as the socialist movement as a whole.

What constitutes class consciousness or a gay consciousness? Why does the working class not organise in its own objective interests for the transition to socialism or gays flock to the gay movement? Theoretically, the left resorts to a number of different explanations — it is a false consciousness, the betrayals of reformist leaders or that the vanguard party with the correct analysis has not yet been built.

The women's movement and gay movements played an important part in the impetus of recent years in the discussions relating to consciousness and the role of ideology. Within the socialist movement important openings have been made in these areas since the 1960s. The political and social upheavals of that time saw the left largely unprepared and unable to take up any vanguard, unifying role as they proclaimed for themselves. Despite major conflicts there were few signs of imminent revolution by the working class who remained wedded to social democracy, as in Britain to the Labour Party. Thus a greater concern became apparent in the socialist movement about the role of ideology and culture in reproducing and maintaining social relations and "common sense" ideas of this society. There was a renewed interest in the work of Gramsci, the intervention of Althusser and his followers, and a reassessment of Freud and psychoanalysis. These concerns intermeshed with the problems being confronted in the women's movement — the social construction of sexuality, the basis of women's oppression and its ideological and cultural forms, and the practices and institutions which define and regulate aspects of our lives and feelings.

What is a common theme in all of these concerns is to understand the complexity of relationships at all levels rather than simplistic theories of immediate determination such as the base/superstructure dichotomy, of consciousness as a mere reflection of social situations or of social conditioning which could be simply transformed with "the revolution".

The gay movement has had to confront the issues regarding consciousness, culture and ideology in a very direct way. Those of us who are marxists initially felt a need to validate ourselves within the traditional theoretical frameworks of the left. This resulted in rather narrow and limited analyses of gay oppression under capitalism. In the editorial of *Gay Left* no. 1 we stated that part of our project was to come to a materialist analysis of the position of gays under capitalism, the role of the family and women's position in it, and sexual oppression. However, in the intervening time the attempt to fit an understanding of ideology and gay oppression in particular into a narrow, economic marxism has been shown to be inadequate. Theoretically such an attempt does not stand up to close historical or contemporary scrutiny.

The moves that have occurred in our theories in the past few years have been to try to understand the much more complex links between institutions, ideology and out sexuality. The concept of "reproduction", economic and ideological, was central in broadening our political analysis and in trying to understand the strength and complexity of the economic and social system. It also provided a framework in which work progressed on theories concerning the social construction of sexuality, masculinity and femininity. We have come to understand that sexuality is not a drive that is simply oppressed and confined by society and which can therefore be liberated to achieve some natural form. It is a socially constructed category whose definition, regulation and meanings change historically. The work of Foucault has led us to investigate more rigorously those practices, especially medicine, psychiatry and the law, which have been central in defining present notions of sexuality. This effort may help us to identify the forces at work and those areas of contestation in which we might more successfully intervene.

It is perhaps true to say that what much of this recent theorising has done is to acknowledge and justify the political practices that the autonomous movements have evolved and to make more coherent our criticisms of traditional left politics. If our understanding of the complexities of relationships has increased we have not yet developed our politics to take us further forward.

What then do our politics and theories mean for us in the present conjuncture of political and social forces? One of the problems we have is the desire to see the gay movement as being equivalent to a political party, wanting to initiate national campaigns and organisations and then feeling we have failed when this does not succeed. We should recognise that the gay movement as it has evolved until now takes a multitude of forms rather than being a coherent organisation with agreed goals. The involvement of lesbians and gay men in projects like switchboards, journals, centres and theatre groups as well as organisations such as CHE, GAA and many women's groups is likely to remain the dominant kind of focus for some time. The unifying element in this diversity is the validation of the gay experience and identity and the development of the gay community in which we as gay socialists can participate. It will only be through activities at all levels such as these that a stronger and more widely based community can be built and from this have the power to challenge the oppression we face as gays.

8

Bringing It All Back Home: Lesbian Feminist Morality

SUE CARTLEDGE

Morals — like "thrift" and "backbone" — have not been very popular for some years. Along with the rest of the permissive society in the swinging sixties, many of us rejected the bourgeois and religious morality we had been brought up with. Externally imposed moral codes were decried as uptight and square, and replaced by Doing Your Own Thing, Letting It All Hang Out, and exploring a wide variety of experience in the name of peace, love and flower power. The women's liberation movement grew up at the tail end of the hippy era, and shared its rejection of traditional morality. Our specific contribution, however, was to scrutinise far more carefully both the old morality and that which had replaced it.

Feminists began to develop a critique of bourgeois morality, not just because it stopped us having fun, but for deeper reasons. We explored the ways in which the moral codes constructed around the family, the work ethic, and law and order, served to keep workers, and particulary women, in their place. Of special interest to us was the role of religion, with its associated burdens of sin and guilt. Another target was the sexual double standard, which elevated us as virgins or mothers, or wrote us off as whores (men, meanwhile, remaining just men, with overriding "natural" sexual instincts). We began to analyse the task assigned to women and the family, of transmitting bourgeois ideology to the next generation.

At the same time, we became increasingly uneasy with the place of women in the counter-culture. Who wanted to be a swinging chick, sexually available to any dope-smoking groper? Nor did we relish the role of earth mother, attached to some particular self-appointed guru, for the purpose of bearing his babies and baking his bread. The growing gay movement did not escape the woolly liberalism of this era. But at least it served to point out an additional dimension: the counter-culture was not only sexist, but extremely heterosexist. And it became increasingly clear to feminists and socialists that it could rapidly be absorbed into a modernised capitalist mainstream. A range of highly profitable enterprises sprang up to cater for the new consumers — from musicals like "Hair" to boutiques called "Che Guevara".

Our ten-year-old battle against the twin faces of bourgeois capitalist morality is still, of course, in its infancy. The trendier women's glossies continue to hector us to be liberated, orgasmic, and prop up male egos. Meanwhile Rhodes Boyson, Margaret Thatcher and Callaghan gird up their loins for a renewed elevation of "family life" and moral codes.

In our search for alternatives, feminists could draw little inspiration from the mainstream of left-wing movements (let alone what was known of practice in socialist countries). As Jeffrey Weeks pointed out in *Coming Out*, "Marx and Engels inherited from the utopian socialists a classically romantic belief in the all-embracing nature of true love between men and women", and envisaged that under socialism "monogamy, instead of collapsing, [will] at last become a reality". In the hundred years since Marx, left-wing visions of socialist morality and personal relationships have hardly shifted. Of course, some socialists and feminists in other generations (Kollontai, Carpenter, Reich, Simone de Beauvoir) have recognised the political importance of personal life. And many women and men who are not famous as writers or political activists lived through the same problems of personal politics that we face now. But on the whole their insights and their struggles have not been absorbed into the political mainstream. More old-fashioned socialists — if they ever consider the subject — seem to share Marx's idea of a better form of monogamy (once women get their equal pay and nurseries sorted out and become less irritating and nagging). The revolutionary left, though no doubt more inclined to sleep around, has given serious consideration to sexual politics only under heavy pressure from the women's movement and the gay movement.

And so, once feminists began to examine the role of sexuality, the family and morality in the oppression of women, we were pushing to the centre of the stage those aspects of life hitherto dismissed by the left as "personal", "private", "marginal", or even "trivial". Pursuing the causes and effects of sexism, we swam at first in largely uncharted waters. We could only start from our own experience and move outwards. In so doing, we developed a new theory and practice. "The personal is political": this phrase expresses, in a condensed form, our determination that the things we felt were important — love, friendship, sexuality, our children, our parents, pornography, housework, and many, many more — should no longer be dismissed as "not political questions". We began to develop an analysis of how these "marginal" areas are in fact crucial to the processes, not only of oppression, but also of revolt. We began to destroy the division between public and private life.

The practice of consciousness-raising was crucial. To break down the walls of our isolation and discover a common oppression linking our "personal problems": to do this we need to know and trust one another. In the context of small women-only groups, meeting regularly, we began to be able to admit that we sometimes feared or hated our children; that our marriages were empty; that we had never had an orgasm; that we loved other women. From these admissions we developed an understanding and an analysis. We also began to change our personal lives. To begin on this project (seldom deliberately, but propelled by our inability to live any longer with the contradictions we were bringing to the light of consciousness), we needed a support far more basic than that of rallies or meetings dominated by chairmen, agenda, and platform speakers. The small-group, polycentric formations of the women's movement provided this support.

In constructing a politics of personal life, we have to work with a crucial paradox at the heart of the struggle. Our only material for building a new world is the ruins of the old. In our trek towards the future, we are loaded with the emotional baggage of the past. This inevitable contradiction lies behind many of the heartbreaks and heartaches of personal politics. Rejecting the old and new bourgeois morality, we are still imbued with a mass of hidden moralities — our own family upbringing, religious ideas, libertarianism, individualism. As we try to develop our understanding of the way in which relationships are not a private enterprise but are structured by patriarchy and capitalism, we still, only too often, blame ourselves and each other for our personal failures. It is extremely unlikely that in one generation we could change the material basis of these structures, and their effect on our own feelings and needs. Yet personal politics too often slips from understanding to judgement. The burden of private guilt, instead of being lifted, can simply become public guilt. We have redefined "moral" questions as "political", but the undertones of praise, blame and failure remain.

The women's movement is an intensely moral project, in which everything we think, say or do is up for questioning. Unless we are clear about the political basis for this process, we could end up with a new moralism as oppressive as the old. As a recent revolutionary feminist paper put it, "Do we want a feminist analysis aimed at changing the world, or a code of right-on and right-off behaviours aimed at policing women?" Equally dangerous is the possibility of a retreat. As the first euphoric explosion of possibilities founders on the inevitable difficulties of changing our lives, we could draw the wrong conclusions. Instead of developing a more solid, if more gradual approach, based on the actual practical conditions of women's lives, we could retire wounded to the apparent safety of couples, homes, babies and individual solutions.

For those of us who have forgotten, re-reading some of the papers produced in the late sixties and early seventies provides a fascinating reminder of innocence and enthusiasm. An article called "Fuck the Family", in a 1972 edition of *Lesbians Come Together*, begins:

> Our collective is made up of six people, Jenny, Lorna, Richard, Julia, Barbara and myself, Carolyn. When we first moved into the house I

don't think any of us imagined what would develop. We intended to live closely of course, but as we all soon realised this was not enough. After about a week we decided to share all our clothes; these were moved into one big cupboard. We pooled our money for food, Tampax, toilet rolls and catfood. Around about the same time a women's awareness group was started. It met at the house. Although the group was important itself, what was much more significant was that after each session, which usually lasted all night, women would stay for days talking and talking, in a way they hadn't been able to before. . . . Because it was not always possible (for us in the collective) to be in one room all the time, we decided that if two or more of us got together and talked then anything said should be repeated to whoever was missing. This helped to fight couples and factions.

In practical terms some beautiful things started to happen. It was fabulous to see Richard walking around in Lorna's cardigan, Jenny in Richard's underpants, and Julia in my shoes. Soon it was possible not to feel that a particular article belonged to anyone. . . . Our attitudes towards the opposite sex have changed radically. Even Jenny, an ex SCUMite now enjoys cuddling Richard in bed, and loves without hangups many of the brothers who come to the house.

By 1974, when a London Women and Socialism workshop was held on sexuality, it was already becoming apparent that full frontal attacks on old patterns of relationships could be more destructive than constructive. One of the papers from the workshop describes the rules of the writer's commune:

RULES

My husband said, "All scenes out front. Our relationship will improve if we sleep with more people." (Up to then we had both slept with other people secretly. I had done it more than he had.)

Smash monogamy and couple relationships was a huge rule — get in touch with your jealousy, your deepest, most possessive emotions. (I had no trouble doing that and when my husband started another serious relationship I fought him and her. I pulled her hair and pinched her, I bit and hit and kicked and threw chairs. One day I threw all our plates of scrambled eggs into the garden . . .). We attacked the problem too brutally. We did everything that was hurtful right in front of the person it would hurt.

Romantic love was out. The theory was that naked we could respond to each other freely. Clothes served to mystify. Romance came through inhibition and repression. I find this quite brutal now. We expected to be able to jump into bed and make love to anyone on the basis that we lived together and were therefore not strangers. . . . We kissed everyone hello and goodbye. It had to be everyone so no one would feel paranoid but they still did.

The paper ends with the heartfelt cry: "I don't want to share everything. I don't want to analyse everything."

With the hindsight of ten years on, we can smile at the naïveté of some of our experiments. Yet, as Sheila Rowbotham pointed out in a recent interview, it was easy enough, in the afterglow of May 1968, to believe that we could change the world overnight: "It seemed such an amazing thing to have this different consciousness, and have that consciousness confirmed in lots of groups, it seemed as though the world must just fall open. What's evident now is that it takes longer."

It would take ten volumes to discuss all the moral questions that have been thrown up by the women's movement, and the attempts that we have made to resolve them. Not only love, friendship, sex, jealousy; but work, money, power, relationships with parents and children, even class and race, have all been discussed as moral issues. The lines between what is practicable or possible, and what is desirable, have often been fuzzy. Often our attempts to change the ways we act have been based on liberal notions of individual freedom and spontaneity. Or else we have veered towards the imposition of a feminist straight-and-narrow. But the wealth of questions that have been raised, and of the lived attempts to resolve them, is astonishing.

Feminists have questioned whether our "feelings" — of love, romance, dependence, attraction, jealousy — are "natural". Many of us would agree that they are, to some extent at least, a product of the structures that we live in. But to what extent, and how much can we alter the feelings? The roots of our need for a Great Love, in the exclusivity and one-to-one dependence of a nuclear family, have been examined. But breaking down this exclusivity has proved more complex than the slogan "Fuck the Family". The feminist moral code prescribes that our sexual relationships should not be private and "coupley". There are sound reasons for this prescription, in the damage that exclusiveness does to the sexual relationship itself, as well as in the barriers it puts up against other people. Indeed, the fragility of the bourgeois myth of the happy couple is demonstrated daily outside the feminist ghetto as well as within it. Most of us have first-hand evidence of the danger of monogamy, in the bitter and barren lives of our own parents.

But the attempt to fulfil our needs for emotional security other than in monogamous relationships has thrown up enormous problems. Lifelong monogamy is of course, not only often destructive, but for most of us, quite unrealistic. For now that we have destroyed the external bonds, do we really want to forge new ones? But with what, exactly, is monogamy to be replaced? Often lifelong monogamy has simply been replaced by serial monogamy: a succession of exclusive relationships ending more or less painfully as a new lover comes on the scene. Our lives are broken up into discontinuing chunks of time: the three years I spent married to X, then the two years with Y. . . . Our loves still erect barriers against the rest of our lives; and what we gain in variety of sexual and emotional experience we perhaps lose in the continuity and depth of shared lifetimes. Conducting more than one sexual relationship at the same time does not always solve the problem. It can simply be what has been labelled "parallel monogamy", where overlapping relationships raise a host of problems of their own. What is the morality of triangular relationships when one partner would prefer monogamy? Are they alone responsible for their pain, suffering because they haven't tried hard enough to destroy their possessiveness?

Structuring into "primary" and "secondary" relationships, while it may be a convenient solution for the two halves of the primary, can be agony for the unfortunate secondary lover, condemned to second place by the historical accident of arriving on the scene second. Sexual and emotional jealousy cannot simply be wished away. If we have been brought up to feel that our security depends on owning another person, body and soul, then their involvement with somebody else is really a threat. And jealousy has proved one of the most recalcitrant of our "feelings". The cost, in time and anguish, of trying to resolve these contradictions, is immense. Is it, indeed, worth it? A woman at a recent Socialist Feminist workshop on sexuality confessed, "I struggled for two years to suppress my pain and anger at my lover's other relationship — and then I heard a woman say that if her bloke ever slept with anyone else she'd walk out straightaway — and I thought, 'Isn't she wonderful!'" Sometimes it can only be the knowledge that, however hard it is to go forward, it would be infinitely worse to go back — to the world of disenchanted lifetime bondage and secretive extra-marital affairs — that consoled us.

We have tried to steer a difficult path between widening our sexual relationships and sexual consumerism. Should all sexual acts be based on a Meaningful Relationship? Should you always know somebody well before you sleep with them? Is casual sex objectifying? Feminists have tended to answer these questions in the affirmative — even if our practice does not always live up to our theory. Casual sexual relationships, based more on physical attraction than on spiritual, intellectual or political communion, have been frowned on —and often identified as "male" behaviour. On the other hand, does the avoidance of sex except in the context of a more complex relationship, elevate it to an undue importance? Does it then become something sacred, only to be embarked on after due ritual? Attempts to demystify sex by sleeping with our friends instead of falling in love with strangers, have helped some of us to dent Romance. But the mystification clings. . . . We may foul up our friendships in the attempt to liberate our loves. Some feminists have advocated celibacy as a way out of these contradictions: a brave stand in the face of the general opinion that there must be something wrong with you if you don't have a lover.

Notions of sexual attractiveness have come under heavy fire. Is it sexist to be attracted to someone on the basis of their personal appearance? On the other hand, is it realistic *not* to respond to appearance? Obviously feminists would criticise stereotypes of beauty and ugliness. The pressures that consumer capitalism puts on women to worry about their appearance and clothes have rightly been criticised. But the women's movement has its own unwritten codes of looks and dress. After almost every Women's Liberation conference a women who is older than most of us, or who has made the mistake of wearing a dress, will write to a women's movement journal to say how out of place she felt.

One of the most powerful themes of feminist personal politics has been its stress on the importance of friendship. This emphasis grew from the early days of the movement, as we discovered, for the first time, it seemed, our solidarity and identity with other women. The excitement of this discovery was tremendous. We were no longer the traditional rivals for the affections of men. We were sisters. Our first realisation of the beauty of friendship has developed into a recognition that giving importance to our friendships is crucial if we want to shift the pivotal importance of sexual relationships. Of course, as friendships have become more important, they have attracted some of the emotional loading and subsequent rivalries, rows and betrayals hitherto reserved for love affairs. On the whole, however, the development of friendships, often based on shared political activity, has been one of the greatest gains of the women's movement. But friendship networks can be elitist. If they coincide, as they often do, with political groups, they can exclude other women. Can we be friends with everybody? Obviously not. But what happens to women who are lonely and who do not know many other people? In a world constructed on friendship, what is the fate of women whom nobody likes very much?

The question of where and how you should live (begging the question of how many women have a choice) has often been seen as a moral, rather than a practical, issue. Is it wrong to live with your lover — and thereby reinforce the extent to which your identities are bound up? But if you do not, can you stand always being stranded at their place with the wrong book and no clean socks? If you live with other people, what should be the limits of collectivity? Should incomes be shared? How do people who are earning feel about sharing their hard-earned cash with the others who only have to get up at nine if it is their signing-on day? Should you mind if people borrow your clothes or bike without asking? What happens if someone will not do their share of housework? How should you deal with the tensions and frictions of shared domestic life? With a lover, domestic tensions are usually resolved — or not — along with other problems in the relationship. With co-dwellers, the alternatives often seem to be heavy-handed house meetings or a crescendo of irritation about putting out the milk bottles or boiling drip-dry shirts. Is it wrong or peculiar to want to live by yourself? Some of us have felt a conflict between the desire for independence (crucial to the liberation of women from dependence on men or the family circle) and the desire to be close to other people.

The questions of life and love have a whole different perspective for women with children. The practical and emotional needs of children both limit our areas of choice and raise a whole set of moral issues of their own. A contributor to the 1974 socialist feminist sexuality workshop wrote: "As far as personal relationships with adults are concerned, I do not relate as an individual. I relate as a set of relationships. Anyone who has any kind of close relationship with me has to have a relationship with the kids — women as well as men. I do not move as an individual entity; I am committed and tied to my relationship with my children. I am a walking relationship in myself. . . . It seems that discussing the question of monogamy where there are children becomes a discussion of sexuality in a practical context, and one in which monogamy (or relative monogamy) need not be oppressive, repressive, but part of an ongoing commitment to a practice of emotional and practical politics with children, where the complexities of dealing with a lot of new/ different people in brief sexual encounters can be destructive and quite reactionary". (This comment, on the destructive effect on children of a succession of brief encounters, might well be extended. Do not our adult friends, as well, suffer from the side effects of our changing partners? And certainly the time and emotional energy needed to orchestrate the changing of the guards can leave us too shattered for work or organised political activity.)

As our children grow older, go to school, and come into contact with other lifestyles, they are faced with the gap between what they learn and see at home, and what school and society teaches them. Feminists have to decide whether to take up instances of sexist teaching materials or practices with their child's school, and face the possible conflict and labelling for the child. We have to decide how far to give in to the pressure to be more like other mothers (Mum, please wear a dress to parents' assembly). For lesbian mothers, of course, these pressures are particularly painful. Assuming that we do not want to conceal our sexuality from our children, how explicitly should we discuss it with them? Should we introduce them at an early age to a distressing discussion about the fact that many people they meet will regard their mothers as sick or wicked? Or should we leave them to discover this fact gradually, possibly from remarks by their friends?

In some ways the problems of our relationship with our parents are similar to those with our children. As time transmutes our parents from repressive authorities to our emotional dependants, how much do we want to risk wounding them by our beliefs and way of life? If we are, or want to be, emotionally close to our parents, we have to take this risk, for otherwise no real closeness is possible. Sometimes honesty with parents pays off handsomely, as they respect our freedom or even share our beliefs. For others of us this does not happen, and our relationship with one or both parents feels like a long stretch of guilt punctuated by interludes of recrimination or non-communication. Again, this problem is especially painful for lesbians. Few parents, however progressive, are actually pleased to have a homosexual child. Most people are aware of being in some sense a disappointment to their parents — for few lives can bear the burden of expectation that parents are encouraged to place on their children's shoulders. But gays can be charged with having deliberately, wickedly blighted their parents' lives. The question of sexuality is always dangerous ground between parents and children. When the sexuality in question is homosexual, it becomes a minefield. It is no accident that the subject of "coming out to your parents" has had reams of paper and hours of agonised discussion devoted to it. We can all understand the importance for ourselves and others of eroding the assumption that homosexuals are those funny people in the theatre or in criminal cases, but never your nearest and dearest. But if parents show every sign of not wanting to know the truth, how far should we make them a testing-ground for our beliefs?

Many women, when they first became involved in the women's movement, were students, or on the dole, or working in "alternative" situations. We had plenty of time for political activity and for experimenting with relationships. We were surrounded by like-minded people. Many of us now, however, have full-time jobs and/or children. We work with people who do not share our ideas or politics. This creates both practical and emotional problems. Our spare time is drastically reduced. Work can exhaust us, at the same time as it offers a world of involvement (and for some women, of success and status) separate from the rest of our lives. Sandy Kondos and Lucy Draper described some of their feelings about work in a recent paper:

> Genuinely, honestly, truly being interested in your work and worrying about it, and your friends not believing it because it doesn't fit in with the way they see you, and it takes you apart from them. And worrying about it, and feeling that this is really you, it's not only alienated 9-5, it involves a lot of your real deep feelings. But not being able to talk about it.
>
> Also being alienated 9-5. Being tired, and having to get up in the mornings, and not wanting to get pissed out of your head on Sunday nights, and not feeling able to stay up all night talking about life, because you know that next day you will not be able to cope with feeling shitty. So losing your old spontaneity and feeling like you are old and boring.

In this whistle-stop tour of problems of feminist morality, the question of lesbianism has been raised separately only in discussing relationships with parents and children. This is because it seems to me that lesbian and heterosexual feminists face broadly the same dilemmas, and have followed the same paths in attempting to resolve them. Certainly they have more in common than have most lesbians with most gay men. The sexual politics of the film *Nighthawks* is positively Neanderthal compared with even the most fumbling feminist attempts at changing our personal lives. But there are, of course, specific problems facing lesbians (some of which they share with gay men). Morality, or rather immorality, is the context in which all homosexuals are seen by heterosexist society. We are defined by our sexual orientation; and we are usually defined as immoral, unnatural, sick or wicked. We can just about escape damnation if we refrain from acting on our desires. Anita Bryant and Mary Whitehouse, while hating the sin, will then deign to love the sinner. This would all be a bit of a joke if these judgements were not also deeply engraved in our views of ourselves — let alone in the views of our friends, relatives and colleagues. Even if via the gay movement and the women's movement we struggle to respect ourselves, it is still not easy to come out at work or to one's family. What risks can we take, and how far should we push ourselves? How many of us are strong enough to walk about *everywhere, always,* with a Lesbian Liberation badge glowing from our lapels?

Our conflicts are not always with heterosexuality. Feminist and non-feminist lesbians have clashed on a number of issues. Is role-playing acceptable or not? Are inclinations to be butch or femme harmful echoes of the power inequalities between men and women? Or are they harmless games? Is it okay as long as you switch roles from time to time? Overt sexism among lesbians has shocked some feminists. I visited a lesbian nightclub recently with two friends and we sat feeling, as one of us put it, like the unsmiling Russian delegation at a decadent Western cabaret, as we watched a tinselled belly dancer perform a near-strip.

Perhaps one consolation for lesbians is that, while from time to time we may no doubt oppress our lovers, this is not built directly on a bedrock of structural inequalities. We at least escape the heartsearchings of our heterosexual sisters about whether it is right for feminists to sleep with men at all.

Caught between the nightmare we have fled, and the vision of a new world whose material foundations have not yet been laid, we can only go forwards. The path winds on through a forest of contradictions. But which of us really wants to go back? We cannot relinquish the responsibility we have taken for our own lives. We must continue to chip away at the patriarchal and capitalist mould. But we must do so with an understanding of the limits. We cannot change our ways of living and working overnight, when the material basis of our lives, the ideological basis of our feelings, retain their real and recalcitrant power. We have to attack the causes as well as the effects. We have to find practical ways in which the freedom of all women can be extended (not just that of white middle-class childless women with a little room for manoeuvre). Otherwise history — herstory — will judge us as a quirk of late twentieth-century decadence, swapping partners and experimenting with communes while the fires of destruction raged outside. We must construct relationships and ways of behaving which are both practical, and moral in a feminist and socialist sense — truly liberating and not based on exploitation. And we must detach from this project the faded penumbra of guilt and obligation. We must keep the ideals that give us our force, without relapsing into cynicism or despair when — as is inevitable — we encounter failure. The task is enormous — but then whoever said changing the world would be a picnic?

9

Sects and Sexuality: Trotskyism and the Politics of Homosexuality

PHILIP DERBYSHIRE

The left in Britain is in crisis, a crisis that manifests itself in the appalling electoral defeat of the Labour Party, the fragmentation of the Communist Party and the disarray of the far left. Within that crisis, and the more general decomposition of social and political culture, the gay movement, for all the proliferation of lesbian and gay groups, commercial facilities and magazines, shows an apparently similar crisis of coherence and direction. The time of the Gay Liberation Front is well and truly dead, and attempts at successor organisations such as Gay Activists' Alliance seem otiose and moribund. That political vacuum has allowed the trotskyist left to claim for itself an importance that other conjunctures would not have warranted, and indeed other national situations have not produced (for example Germany, France, Italy). The revolutionary left now represents itself as one of the few cohesive strands of theory and practice within the broad milieu of the gay movement, that has broken with liberal conceptions of sexuality and reformist notions of action, and claims to integrate the struggle for sexual liberation with the struggle for socialism. To that extent it becomes even more crucial to analyse and criticise the trotskyist conception of sexual politics, and more specifically the understanding of the politics of homosexuality that underpins the programme which is offered as *the* way forward for the gay movement, and by implication all those involved in "the politics of everyday life".

The encounter between trotskyism and Gay Liberation has been long and fraught. Despite the Bolshevik liberalisation of the Russsian laws against homosexual activity, as well as the legalisation of abortion and the granting of formal equality to women, sexual politics played almost no part in the programmatic positions of the Fourth International (FI). This was perhaps unsurprising in the light of the violent marginalisation of the FI by stalinism: it was enough to keep alive a tradition of critical marxism in the face of the degeneration of the Bolshevik revolution and the atrophy of the Communist International, never mind extend and deepen marxist theory in areas where Marx and Engels themselves had demonstrated a remarkable purblindness. However, that historical marginalisation and determination by the struggle against stalinism proved a serious obstacle to trotskyism in coming to terms with the growth of the autonomous movements of women and gay people in the late sixties and early seventies. Trotskyism had become, in its political isolation, dogmatic and fetishistic. The failure of the proletariats in the West to choose revolution, their acquiescence in a position of co-opted support for imperialism in the post-war boom, had deprived trotskyist groupings of the practice that might have shifted their political conceptions away from a reverential regard for the "moment" of October 1917.

Used to an unchallenged because untested model of radical social change, trotskyism was bewildered by the rise and success of movements that articulated different forms of oppression to that of class and used different conceptual tools to understand that oppression. And, significantly, those movements first arose in the USA, where the local section of the Fourth International, the Socialist Workers' Party (USA), was engaged in a tortuous struggle against the ideas that flowed in the late sixties from the student rebellions, the anti-war movement and the practice of urban terror by the Weathermen. Battling against "ultra-leftism" in mass movements that had little time for the Old Left, the SWP (USA) saw nothing but libertarianism and diversions in the demands of the women's and gay movements.

Trotskyism was only pushed to a realisation of the nature and importance of sexual politics by the rise of the self-organised movements that articulated different forms of oppression to that of consequence of previously held positions, and that pragmatic inclusion of the women's and gay struggles in trotskyist politics is apparent in contemporary positions.

In the early seventies, the FI refused to take positions on the question of homosexuality: "the principle underlying the slogan 'Gay is Good' is a scientific question, and the revolutionary party does not take positions on scientific questions" was the line, and at the same time, 1971, homosexuals were discouraged from joining the organisation on grounds of security. The British section, the International Marxist Group, followed this line, and in consequence there were walk-outs and resignations by gay comrades who felt betrayed by the way in which the revolutionary organisation was merely refracting bourgeois, anti-gay attitudes. Similarly the International Socialists in Britain, who had broken from the FI in the fifties, and who later became the Socialist Workers' Party — SWP (UK) — despite praiseworthy openness in other areas of politics, for example community struggles, and despite a self-conscious break with the sectarian self-righteousness of orthodox trotskyist groupings like the Socialist Labour League, saw fit to issue statements to the effect that homosexuality would vanish under socialism, denied gay members the right to form groups inside the organisation, and refused to endorse statements of support for homosexuals and validation of homosexuality.[2]

Trotskyism had no theory of sexual oppression beyond a reiteration of Engels's *Origin of the Family* and Trotsky's own writings on the problems of everyday life, and reacted to the suggestion that here was an area that might need thinking through and might have serious implications for the rest of marxist thought with a mixture of contempt, arrogance, hysterical hostility and self-satisfied indifference. The shift in ground came only as a result of the pressure of women and gay comrades inside the revolutionary organisations themselves, who took support from the auto-nomous movements outside.

The SWP (UK) includes a statement in its "Where We Stand" to the effect that it is opposed to all forms of discrimination against homosexuals, and the IMG states, rather more sententiously, that it seeks to "unite the fight of the workers against the bosses with that of other oppressed layers of society — women, blacks, gays — struggling for their own liberation". The SWP has produced a pamphlet on the "gay question", "The Word is Gay", includes articles in its journal *Socialist Review,* and holds regular meetings on "Gay Liberation and Socialism". The IMG has produced internal documents and a submission to the FI world congress, and plays a leading role in the GAA. The Chartist grouping, a trotskyist tendency inside the Labour Party, has produced a summary document on gay liberation and has attempted a much broader theorisation of sexual politics.[3]

Thus there has been a shift in the overt political and programmatic positions of the trotskyist groupings, and trotskyist cadres are very much in evidence in the gay movement in a way impossible to imagine ten years ago. But it is questionable whether this shift indicates a real integration of the politics of sexuality, rather than a serial inclusion of homosexuals as another category of the oppressed. The essential structure of trotskyism remains unchanged, and the political practice is analogised from struggles in the labour movement that bear little relation to the complex specificities of sexual oppression.

Trotskyism regards itself as the historical legatee of the Bolshevik revolution, and it is *de rigueur* for each trotskyist group to claim its place in the apostolic succession . . . Marx, Engels, Lenin, Trotsky, *et al.* The lunacy of fourteen trotskyist organisations in Britain each claiming to represent *the* pure current of revolutionary thought needs little underscoring, and is yet a further consequence of the political economy of sects divorced from political practice.[4] However, for our purposes, most of the trotskyist groupings can be ignored, in that they have ossified to such an extent that sexual politics is not even on their agenda. Only the IMG and SWP in Britain have done so to any serious extent, and arguably only the IMG has made a contribution that merits serious discussion.

While both the IMG and SWP have similar positions on the need for the revolutionary party and the seizure of state power as a prerequisite for the establishment of socialism, and both would adhere to a notion of the dictatorship of the proletariat, they can be distinguished by their respective stances toward the autonomous movements. The SWP sees the function of the party as absolutely primary: the party is not merely a necessary tool for the overthrow of capitalism, it is a sufficient one. All struggles are to be co-ordinated through the party, and the party is seen as the vanguard *tout court.* From this flows a negation of the importance of struggles carried on outside the aegis of the party, and particularly a dismissal of the gay movement and the theory and practice that it has engendered. The IMG, on the other hand, makes great play of its support for autonomous movements, and even its most hardline leninist spokespeople[5] recognise that in a post-revolutionary society, it will still be necessary for autonomous movements to exist and to stuggle against the remnants of bourgeois power and ideology, and such movements would include that of gay people.

The SWP, in its particular interpretation of leninism, already excludes the possibility that homosexuality presents any notable problems for orthodox marxism. If the very autonomy of the gay movement is rejected *a priori*, then it can be hardly expected that the SWP would conceive of the oppression of sexuality as carrying any further difficulties in understanding, nor in the political practice which attempts to resist and end that oppression.

The clearest instance of this is an article in *Socialist Review* by Lionel Starling,[6] which expresses the SWP's present position on the "gay question". As befits a tightly knit, self-designated "democratic-centralist" organisation, the SWP's attitude to homosexuality is exactly the same as on any other question, that is, all political tactics have become conflated to the single imperative of "Build the Party". The routes to this end have included the Right to Work Campaign, the Anti-Nazi League, Women's Voice etc. For the SWP the political problem of homosexuality becomes the organisational question of the recruitment of homosexuals.

> Our conclusions for the immediate struggle around gay politics are totally different to the libertarians . . . the gay struggle should be directed towards involving the best organised and most exploited sections of the working class.
>
> We have to . . . intergrate the gay struggle into class struggle as a whole, to concentrate on drawing in militants, rather than looking specifically to "homosexuals" . . . going into an ANL rather than fighting nazis as "homosexuals" in gay anti-fascist groups . . . having homosexuals on the Right to Work marches arguing for gay liberation, setting up a very broad base for campaigning against police harassment in all its forms.

The gist of Starling's article is that homosexuality is a specific orientation of a delimited population: there are homosexuals, and there are bourgeois ones and working-class ones, and the point is to recruit working-class homosexuals to the SWP, after which homosexuality is annulled as an issue. Despite his making noises about gay oppression stemming from class oppression, Starling offers no analysis of that oppression: why should it be that homosexuality is subject to repression under class society, and why is it that it is only in the last ten years that a movement which has shown success in combating that oppression has managed to emerge? Similarly, he offers no explanation for the somewhat chequered history of the IS/SWP's response to homosexuality, thereby reinforcing the fetishised vanguard conception of the infallible party.

"The gay liberation tendency is not based on the ranks of the manual working class." Starling's observation is correct, but hardly illuminating. The Bolshevik tendency in the early days of the Russian Social Democratic Labour Party was scarcely the most "proletarian" tendency, in the almost biologistic sense that Starling uses class membership. The reduction of political position to class origin was one of the worst defects of stalinism, and it bodes ill to see it used by Starling as weapon against criticism, a stick to beat those who reject the SWP's line. The parallel to earlier vulgar versions of marxism recurs in the stagist rendition of how gay liberation is to be achieved: "Gay Liberation is pie in the sky unless the foundations are built for the working class to overthrow the state", i.e. first one has to build the party, then overthrow the state, and then one can think about Gay Liberation.

But the most insidious feature of the whole article, and the SWP's positions on sexuality generally, is the liberal understanding of homosexuality that pervades it. Homosexuality is not seen as a social construction but rather belongs almost as a natural gift to a small minority. Sexuality is not seen as a complex formation within an imbricate structure that connects mode of production, consciousness, family, culture and ideology, but rather as a label that marks off one oppressed group who are to be accommodated within the leninist party. Sexism, heterosexism and the dominant models of what it is to be a woman or a man, all, by implication, cease to be problematic inside the party, which floats serenely and without contradiction above the messiness of subjectivity, leading the masses to a clearly descried victory.

The SWP's line marks a dead-end in the attempt of trotskyism to appropriate sexual politics. Within this vision of infallible, contradiction-free party, a biological theory of class and innate sexuality, the questions which the gay movement has asked and which remain problematic are ruled illegitimate. The problem of how capitalism maintains itself at all, as if what were needed were merely some vast recruiting drive by a well-oiled machine, is obscured in a clamour of zealotry and self-publicity.

Turning to the IMG's positions on homosexuality, we find an approach very different from the SWP's vulgar reductionism. There *has* been an attempt to theorise gay liberation, albeit within the traditional conceptual apparatus of trotskyism. Similarly, although the end goal of the IMG's strategy is the seizure of state power by the proletariat under a vanguard leadership, and the reconstruction of society in the direction of socialism, there is an attempt to articulate a strategy and tactics that come to terms with the specificities of gay oppression, within a broad counter-strategy to that of the bourgeoisie. To make a critique of this more complex response, it will be necessary to give a fuller exposition of the IMG's theoretical bases. In turn, some of these theoretical considerations lead outward into areas problematical for the whole of marxism, and not just sexual politics. In consequence this section will be schematic, and perhaps over-sketchy: the debates that began after May 1968 have not yet finished, but it is precisely those debates that the politics of homosexuality finds signally important.

The most recent theoretical contribution by the IMG has been a document submitted to the most recent world congress of the Fourth International by the gay commission of the IMG.[7] This attempts to give an account of the historical appearance of homosexuality and the nature of its repression, and the consequent oppression of homosexuals. I intend to give a resumé of that account, offer three major objections to it and then move on to discuss the practice of the IMG within the gay movement, offering a critique of the notions of politics that underlie that practice. In this latter section, again, the debates are not merely localised within gay politics but ramify outwards into the core problems of the contemporary left.[8]

Trotskyism is founded on a conception of marxism as a positive science, from which flows logically its understanding of revolutionary politics as a technology of social transformation. There is an intimate link between its model of science, nineteenth-century in origin, and its practice, which owes much to contemporaneous models of social engineering. Fundamental to both these conceptions is a model of history as objectively knowable, society as manipulable in its totality and reason as abstracted from history, the latter viewed from a distance. That site of historical observation is the party, which provides the epistemological justification for the claim of the party to be the vanguard of the proletariat. (This position differs very little from Lukács's defence of leninism, where the party is the consciousness of the class-for-itself.) Furthermore, it makes possible claims that there are certain and true propositions — scientific laws of society — which provide the bedrock on which all other phenomena find their explanation.

This becomes clear in the IMG account of gay oppression, the starting-point for which discussion is the economic role and function of women's oppression. An orthodox periodisation of history is assumed, and it is the extension of commodity production which gives rise to the dominance of the bourgeoisie and the subjection of all social relations to the accumulation of capital and the maximisation of profit. The economic is determinant and not merely in the last instance. (This adherence to orthodox base-superstructure models finds its classic expression within the trotskykist corpus in Mandel's economic works, such as *Late Capitalism*). The problem of women's oppression is to find a functional fit between the capitalist mode of production and the subordinate position of women, which is duly given by the analysis of domestic labour (i.e. the servicing of male workers by unpaid women, whose work, lacking exchange value, lacks value altogether), and an analysis of the family as the primary agent of socialisation. Importantly, the family is seen as an institution foisted on the working class during the mid-nineteenth century, after the ravages of industrialisation had all but broken up the extended family of the predominantly rural labour pulled into the factories. Thus women occupy their subordinate position solely by virtue of their relation to the means of production, and their privatisation in the domestic sphere of reproduction. Ideology reflects this relation.

Homosexual oppression is seen as a consequence of this. Given the "naturalness" of both homosexual and heterosexual behaviour, the construction of a specific grouping of homosexual individuals is seen as a result of the strengthening of the family in the mid-nineteenth century. While homosexuality occurs throughout history, the times of its efflorescence are the times of decline of the dominant classes (e.g. imperial Rome, late feudalism, and now "late" capitalist societies), where the extant social relations, primarily the family, cease to be effective in organising sexuality. In this situation of crisis, as norms lose their hold, a last-ditch effort is made to reinforce those norms by the legal, moral and social proscription of deviant sexuality, its production as a specific category and its marginalisation. This is exacerbated by a reflection within social relations of the dominant commodity form of production. In much the same way that commodities are fetishised, i.e. made into things rather than products of social labour, so human beings are conceptualised in terms of character, individuality, having fixed properties — in a word reified, no longer subjects of a self-transforming praxis. The gay male identity is explained as a modelling on the decadent values of the aristocracy, where the evasion, irony and dissimulation of a class in decline are appropriated by gay men (who first take up such an identity within the ruling class) to sidestep their oppression: camp as identity and tactics of survival.

Thus gay oppression is founded in class society, and homosexuality, as a discrete category, is socially constructed, produced within the contradiction between an outdated family form and the new social possibilities constantly produced by capitalism. It follows from this that gay oppression can only be overcome by the replacement and transformation of those social relations which in turn can only be achieved by the move to socialism. Emphatically, then, gay liberation is hooked to the struggle for revolution.

There could be a number of factual objections to this account. Was the bourgeois family really an imposition on a working class which was agitating for protective legislation? How does the notion of modelling account for the development of a "macho" gay male identity? And what is it to make a vast historical generalisation like "homosexuality occurs in times of decadence"? What notion of homosexuality is being operated with here?

But beyond these objections, it is possible to criticise the account on a more abstract level, and such a critique illustrates the systematic failure of trotskyism both to account for sexual oppression and to offer an adequate understanding of social change.

(1) The account of history and the production of particular forms of oppression is both teleological and determinist. The broad historical sweep both excludes specific analysis, and demonstrates a necessity in history, that is at least questionable, and in the light of recent analyses fallacious.[9] The economic is seen as the primary motor of history, producing in an unmediated way causal effects on every section of society. This relationship of efficient causality is presumed rather than demonstrated, and immediately constructs the question as one of finding a functional relation between class oppression and any other mode. As the analysis unfolds, the theory of epochs, the inevitable transition between modes of production and the historically imminent telos of socialism, is a metaphysic already organising the question under consideration, and as such preselects the evidence and anticipates the links that are to be discovered. Despite fears of bureaucracy, well-developed and articulated in other areas of trotskyist thought, a shift in the economy is assumed to have an immediate effect on all social relations. There is a model of society as a whole which moves from one articulated, functionally coherent moment to another, even if much play is made of the notions of contradiction and dialectic. Those contradictions are known, the course of the dialectic predictable. Yet at the same moment, the IMG's vision of society is one of utter permeability by the intentions of the ruling class. There is a major paradox at the heart of the theory, an antinomy that goes unacknowledged yet provides the apparent explanatory flexibility of the theory.

(2) This paradox results from the twofold explanation in terms of an economic determinism and, simultaneously, an ascription of intentionality to classes that act as historical subjects. Thus, on the one hand, there is a functional relation between the family and the capitalist mode of production, yet on the other, the ruling class acts out a strategy, effective (though without any analysis of the mechanisms and mediations that permit that effectivity) and successful, which strengthens the family, imposes it on the working class, and in process constructs the marginal sexualities. The ruling class is seen as competent and knowledgeable, a mirror image of the party, competent and in possession of truth and certain knowledge.

(3) That contradiction finds its site in the lack of a developed theory of consciousness, and an understanding of subjectivity and ideology, which finds its most notorious expression in the consistent fetishising of leadership and the constant discourse of "betrayal" in trotskyist thought. More needs to be said about this in the section on practice: here I will just draw out the strands of implicit theory and criticise them.

Subjectivity appears only on a class level, is mass and homogeneous within a given class, save only for the contradiction of false/real consciousness. As remarked above, in this account, the ruling class perceives its interest transparently, and with it the means to further that interest. The proletariat on the other hand, does not have such a pellucid relation to its class interest, rather it is enmeshed in the toils of false consciousness, which is defined as a holding to be true of propositions about the world which are in fact false. The proletariat is systematically misled and mystified with respect to its true interests and possibilities either by the deceits of the ruling class, or by the deceptions practised by its own reformist leadership. Subjectivity is thus explained by a rationalist model of clear/opaque vision of an objective world. The world is there, albeit transformed by human practice, but in a crucial sense separate from human beings, disguised by a mist of false and prejudicial ideas. Human beings are such and such *in reality,* but are persuaded to think of themselves otherwise. Thus, by an understanding transposed from the economy, people are persuaded to have beliefs about themselves — that they are individuals, that there is an ontological separation between the individual and society, that human beings have fixed, natural properties, character and so on. Sexual identity is one among a set of such false understandings.

This rationalist mode, however, seriously simplifies the nature of ideology and the complex articulation of a world constantly shifting in response to human practice. Most importantly, it gives only a superficial account of sexuality, which has less to do with the holding true of sets of false propositions (though one cannot underestimate the importance of discursive orderings of beliefs as justification and motives for action), and much more to do with the organisation of desire and the living out of gender roles which are never coincident with conceptions thereof.

We live our lives as men and women, homosexual and heterosexual, with deeply rooted and *involuntary* needs and desires. Sexuality, though constructed, not a natural essence, is the form through which we live our bodies, the way our pleasures are organised. The signal importance of gay politics is that it has to take up these questions, not seeing the problem as one of a mischievous misrepresentation of a well-ordered reality, and then go on to explain how the apparatus of sexuality has come into being, by what techniques and methods it is maintained, and crucially, how it is that the "ideology of sex" is so tenacious and pervasive. The rationalism of the IMG's position leaves off just where the complexity begins. Ideology is not a set of ideas propagated by the media which can be combated by a counter-theory, a matter of choosing in some free space between alternative descriptions of the world. Ideology is not merely a way of looking at the world, rather it is a mode of production of that world. A rooted faith in rationalism gives the reason for the IMG's refusal to look seriously at psychoanalysis, discourse theory, and the complex understandings that are emerging as a consequence of the interrogation of language. If that rationalism is abandoned, then it becomes necessary to find a much more wide-ranging account of gender, sexuality and the construction of sexed subjects with which to underpin a theory of gay oppression and liberation.

The present organisation of sexuality rather than beginning in the mid-nineteenth century finds its roots in the development of a whole set of apparatuses, techniques and discourses on the individual which antedate that time. It was not the consequence of a strategic intent by a near omniscient ruling class, but rather the confluence of technologies of intervention on the body and in populations. That configuration was not a univocal production, rather it was a product of competing powers, strategies and resistances. Economic and class interests were not negligible, but the psychiatrisation of the homosexual owes as much to the development of notions of criminality, the extension of avowal and confession as the means of production of truth about the individual, the shift in the site of application of power and so on, as to a grand strategy to quell proletarian restiveness.

I have remarked that there is a logical connection between trotskyist theory and its organisational form and the political practice it follows. In the preceding section I have tried to uncover the models of self, society and knowledge that underpin the theory, but I have left untouched the question of power which lies at the heart of the matter.

Power, for the IMG, is state power, and the power of the capitalist class. It is univocal and stems from a single source, the ownership of the means of production. The point of the IMG's strategy is the seizure, the appropration of that power: politics is defined as those questions pertaining to the confrontation with the state. Strategy is the means of centralising and making effective those struggles, and the prime tool is the party. To that extent, the criticisms I levelled at the SWP are appropriate here too (that is, considerations of sexism, heterosexism, gender and so on are underplayed as political problems inside the party); the difference is that the IMG does not claim to be the "party", rather only the embryo of a future revolutionary organisation. However, in the light of the previous discussion, further criticisms can be raised.

(1) The party is constituted as the site of knowledge, historically and epistemologically privileged. In the light of the IMG's self-understanding as "scientific marxists", the claim is made both to a

more veridical understanding of society as a totality, and to an ability accurately to assess the direction of movement of that society. Equally, the party is in a position to offer the rational alternative that will disperse the mists of false consciousness that hide the proletariat and the oppressed from their true interests. From this position, and armed with the tool of the programme, the party makes interventions in resistances organised outside the party's aegis. The aim is to provide correct leadership, and to effectively articulate the demands of those resistances so that they challenge the state and permit the consummation of the revolution. (One might note here the insistence on national structures in the IMG's interventions in the gay movement, which follows from this idea of centralised leadership and effectiveness.) While the autonomous movements (feminists, gays, blacks) are granted an importance, they cannot of themselves effect real shifts in power. This is a restatement, in a different key, of the principle that only trotskyists can lead a real revolution. Once, however, the contradictions of economism, voluntarism, the weakness of the theory of consciousness and the inappropriateness of rationalism are demonstrated, the coherent cluster of justifications for the party, the tactic of interventionist politics and rational, global, alternative programmes falls apart. The party is now no more epistemologically privileged than any other section of society, indeed cannot be, in that society is not that kind of knowable object.Rationalism neither explains nor provides any direction for change in a domain characterised by the persistence of and permeation by the involuntary. And the programme which takes its pragmatic value from a notion of functional coherence dissolves into a set of slogans, moralistic and seemingly of little appeal to "the masses".

(2) As the explanation of desire, gender and sexuality fail, the tactics of building mass campaigns which assume that the "methods of class struggle" are appropriate to all forms of resistance, cease to have more impact than exhortations, ungrounded imperatives and empty words. The discursive space that would permit the theorisation of specific struggles and allow the development of singular, relevant tactics is absent: the sense of the body as a site of struggle is completely missing. The conceptual framework of the IMG sees only the "masses" as political agents, and this refuses to acknowledge the problem raised by the social production of individuals and the operation of a felt, "internal" oppression. Even questions of "coming out" and the assumption of identity are glossed over, with the consequence that the scattered, sporadic yet persistent resistance by homosexuals, and the spectacular growth of a gay subculture, remain untouched by the slogans and organisation of the IMG.

I have tried to tease out the assumptions, lacunae and inadequacies of the SWP's and IMG's political understanding of homosexuality in order to counter the claim that they offer a better theorisation of homosexuality and a viable way forward for the gay movement. I have tried to show that sexuality has not been "integrated" into their marxism but remains outside: their politics is responsive, a reaction to the growth of the autonomous movements but not with its own dynamic. This becomes clear in the downgrading of sexual politics at the end of the seventies.

I have not tried to construct an alternative theory, since I would maintain that such a new politics is only beginning to form, with the real important contribution being made within feminism and with the work of people like Deleuze, Foucault and others, some of whose notions I have used.[10] That politics would make sensible the present organisation of sexuality of which homosexuality is but one facet, and would enable us to construct effective resistances and strategies of oppostition. The question of the organisation of desire, the regulation of bodies and populations, and the construction of individuals both as objects of knowledge and as "subjected" subjects, leads to a retheorisation of the domain of politics itself, and of power as productive and not merely constraining. The state becomes de-reified under such a theory, and the notion of its seizure becomes problematical.

Trotskyism fails to address itself to these new tasks, becoming itself an object of scrutiny. It is not a question of revamping it, abandoning worthless sections and holding on to its truth, but rather asking why it has been influential, what its appeal is: why it was capable of organising resistance. A task, for anyone who thinks it important, of writing its genealogy.

NOTES AND REFERENCES

1. Sheila Rowbotham et al., *Beyond the Fragments,* London 1979.
2. Bob Cant, "I.S.: A Grim Tale", in *Gay Left* no. 3.
3. *Intervention,* no. 2.
4. Jim Masters, "Revolutionary Politics as a Hobby", in *Intervention*, no. 2.
5. J. Ross, "The Personal and the Political", in *Socialist Woman,* Summer 1977.
6. Lionel Starling, "Glad to be Gay", in *Socialist Review,* no. 12, May 1979.
7. IMG Gay Commission document to the Ninth World Congress of the Fourth International.
8. Rowbotham et al., op. cit.
9. M. Foucault, *The History of Sexuality*, vol. 1, *An Introduction,* London 1979; and M. Foucault, *Discipline and Punish,* London 1978.
10. See N. Poulantzas, *State, Power, Socialism,* for a critique of Foucault's ideas, especially the functionalism (plural as opposed to unitary) of Foucault's account of the development of "disciplinary" society and the role of the state.

10

New Politics – Old Struggles

BOB CANT and NIGEL YOUNG

In this article we want to try to explore how the development of our sexual politics as gay socialists led to a new type of politics which tried to connect with the straight left: through the unions, parties, the workplace and the development of a gay workers' movement (GWM). What does seem vital to us is that any new strategies for gay socialist activity build on the developments of autonomous movements and continue to stress new ways of organising and the importance of relating our politics to our personal lives. In consequence the concerns of gay socialists must become integral to left politics and not something which can be hived off to gay caucuses, gay groups or gay commissions.

We feel our own political experiences are not universal in the gay movement because of our involvement in the politics of the sixties and the fact we are both London-based teachers. It therefore seems necessary to give a brief account of our past political activities. These political practices obviously helped to shape our experience as gay socialists and our perception of gay socialist activity. We hope they have not obscured our vision.

Nigel Young
I was born in and have lived most of my life in London. My earliest planned political experience was as a marcher on the Ban the Bomb demonstrations in the sixties. From there I moved into the Labour Party as a Young Socialist and within it I worked for what I mistakenly thought would be a socialist government in 1964. By 1966 it already began to dawn on me that this was a mere dream. By the late sixties I was out of the Labour Party and had become a not very active student radical supporting student rights, going on pro-Hanoi and anti-Rhodesia demonstrations and occupying the London School of Economics. Eventually I became a teacher and joined the National Union of Teachers. This period, the early seventies, heralded new political activity for me: working in the union and trying to sort out what the differences were between the Communist Party, the International Socialists (now the Socialist Workers' Party), the International Marxist Group and the left of the Labour Party. It was all very confusing, and as I became more involved in the gay movement and therefore more aware of sexual politics, I felt none of the parties dealt adequately with the new politics of the early seventies. The left was beginning to take some

notice of the oppression of women and gays, but the prevailing attitude still seemed to be that the core of oppression was felt by the working classes at the point of production, so if you were not an industrial worker struggling on the shop floor it was hard to relate to the left. Consequently I have not joined a party, but I work with the revolutionary left in my union activities because they fight for the rights of classroom teachers, raise wider political issues than any other groups in the union and stand up against a reformist trade-union leadership. I have been involved with the Gay Teachers' Group since 1975.

Bob Cant
I was born in Dundee in 1945. I was an inactive member of CND at university and I campaigned for Labour in the elections of 1964 and 1966. Two years' teaching in Tanzania made me aware of poverty on a scale which I had never seen in Northern Europe. On my return to England I was inevitably drawn towards activity in the solidarity campaigns for the struggle against imperialism in South Africa and the Portuguese colonies.

My gayness I regarded as something private and incidental. But when I began a permanent teaching job in 1971 and also, therefore, became involved in serious union work, I was simultaneously becoming involved in London GLF. It was possibly because of the fact that I felt torn so many ways — between union work, anti-imperialist work and sexual politics — that I was eager to join an organisation with a world view. When I joined the International Socialists (IS) in 1973, I was aware that they had no position on the gay question and was prepared to struggle for its integration into the wider programme of IS. IS was, however, in its most economistic period, and the Gay Group was totally routed. After three years I left, as most other members of the Gay Group had already done.

I remained committed, however, to the principle of rank-and-file involvement in union politics and I struggle in my union, NATFHE (National Association of Teachers in Further and Higher Education), towards that end. I have been branch secretary and am also active at regional and national levels. The leadership of the union is left-looking but remains bureaucratic in its approach to activity. Some of us set up a Gay Group in NATFHE, and with the support of the rank-and-file caucus we succeeded in having the union adopt a policy of opposition to discrimination against gay teachers. There is a strong reluctance on the part of the union leadership to publicise this policy and so it remains (like many gay members of NATFHE) in the closet.

The importance of the early seventies for gay socialists was that the gay movement gave us both an awareness and a confidence in ourselves. In the early seventies that confidence was being formed within the movements, but by May 1975, the eve of the first Gay

Workers' Conference, people across the country had begun to take their new-found confidences out of the gay movement and into the wider community.

It was a very exciting time: gay groups and caucuses were being formed in the probation service, the social services, the medical profession, amongst teachers, the unemployed; lesbians were making demands in relation to their specific needs and in one or two places, gay centres were being set up in working-class areas. At the same time there were also developments in left parties concerning sexual politics in general and gayness in particular. Within the IS, later the SWP, gay members had struggled for some time to get the party to take sexual politics seriously and to take a positive stand on the question of the oppression of homosexuals. Because of the difficulties of that struggle, some gay members within IS felt unable to continue as members (see Bob Cant, "A Grim Tale", in *Gay Left* no. 3), but what they achieved as a starting position enabled newer gay members to start up an SWP gay group, and eventually the SWP paper, *Socialist Worker*, listed "an end to all forms of discrimination against homosexuals" in its column on what it stood for. The International Marxist Group (IMG) also has gay members, and debates were conducted and leaflets produced on the question of homosexuality, while the Communist Party made a statement against the oppression of homosexuals at their annual conference in 1976.

Of course, not all of these developments arose from gay activity; much of the new awareness of sexual politics arose out of the demands and work of the women's movement. But the important point concerning gays and the left was that for gay socialists the debate was begun. Those in parties and outside them had a base from which to organise. No longer were we placed in the position of arguing for socialist and sexual politics in some kind of vacuum. The left groups now had policy statements, and as Sarah Benton wrote in "Communists' Comment" (*Gay Left* no. 5):

> The gay movement will finally discover a political party (parties) making a statement about homosexuality which is more radical than a lot of gays are prepared to state. I think that brings into focus the question what is a movement and what is a party. I think this means certain gays will ask themselves questions about political parties which would have been completely irrelevant before. If all the political parties you knew were all anti-homosexual, then the possibility of your involvement with a political party would have been absolutely nil unless you were going to be secretive. Whereas I think now, that question has been brought up as a valid one for discussion in a way that it wasn't a valid one before.

With all this variety of activity occurring, there was a need for gay socialists to share their experiences and give each other strength and support to continue the struggles. At the same time there was a growing feeling that we needed to organise around specific sets of demands which in themselves could give groups a cohesion and a sense of continuity. However, there were certain intrinsic problems which surfaced at the first gay workers' conference and which were never really to be resolved. A major difficulty was the nature of campaigns for gay socialists. Somehow these programmes had to attempt to unite our commitment to gay liberation with our commitment to socialism. Many of us had already been involved in a wide variety of gay groups, but their activities and many of the people in the groups could not be described as "socialist". This is not a criticism of these groups, more a statement of reality. People needed the groups for social and support reasons. Many people went to gay workers' groups because of the isolation they felt at work, some went along as a first step in coming out. In other words the groups functioned as part of an autonomous movement.

The question of broader political activities required a different set of premises. Our experience of the gay movement, with its emphasis on sharing experiences, its commitment to involving everyone in the process of making decisions, and its determination to evolve ways of acting which did not rely on committees or executives or diluted forms of democratic centralism, was its strength. But on the other hand when we decided to mount a campaign around a gay workers' charter, we needed to think about and at least discuss concepts which arise out of traditional left politics; programme, organisation, commitment and discipline — concepts which were often in total contradiction to the aims of an autonomous movement. Thus our past experience did not prepare us for this discussion — a discussion which we would still consider necessary today in order to work out ways of taking the alternative politics and ideas of an autonomous movement to outsiders.

As far as the gay workers' movement was concerned, levels of consciousness, needs and degrees of militancy varied enormously. The Gay Workers' Newsletter, produced by a collective in Nottingham, highlighted these difficulties. In Newsletter no. 1 there were articles on the need to fight conspiracy laws, a gay workers' charter, a huge list of workshops for a future conference ranging from "gay chauvinism" to "gay workers' International", plus a statement exhorting us to "seek a base for action within the organised labour movement". In Newsletter no. 2 there was criticism of the politics of the previous issue (too jargonistic and not enough campaigns specifically relating to gayness), a demand to replace the charter with a slogan and a rather tokenistic commitment to give as much space as possible to lesbian activities, although the presence of lesbians in the GWM was as usual very small compared with the number of men. Most politically active lesbians were working in the women's movement, while the proliferation of the gay subculture had been centred on male needs. In addition to this, lesbians at work tended to be more isolated and more exploited with less union involvement. For lesbians working in the GWM, therefore, it meant a move from one male-dominated area to another equally dominated by men.

Coming out was a topic which always dominated workshop discussions at GWM conferences. People were interested in programmes and plans of action, but we always returned to the problem of coming out in the workplace. We recounted our own experiences and the responses of our workmates and we argued for hours over the most effective way of doing it. Some argued that we should wear a badge right from the start so that there could never be any doubt about it; others argued that we should only come out when we knew the workplace and had built up some support from two or three people to whom we had come out individually.

These discussions also revealed the way in which class was a major feature in determining the nature of the coming out experience. In the middle-class "professions" people are expected to have career aspirations, and the pursuit of these involves professional workers in a constant process of selling themselves and presenting an acceptable identity and private life at their places of work. This is far more marked in the private sector than it is in the public sector, but even in the professions there are strong constraints on one's lifestyle. One need not be particularly ambitious, but most people adhere to these constraints for the sake of survival and job satisfaction. For those of us in the caring professions, coming out could mark the beginning of a long period of discussion resulting in a redefinition of the constraints in that particular workplace. Silence from such articulate and well-educated colleagues would be a statement of some significance. It is highly unlikely that anyone in these circumstances could be sent to Coventry, but one would be allowed to feel a misfit.

For those of us in jobs where verbal communication was neither part of the job nor very easy — such as in a typing pool, a factory, a ticket collector's booth, a mine, etc. — coming out would be clearly rather different. The competitiveness between workmates is less common and the social constraints of the workplace are controlled not so much by ideas about careers as the need to survive in unpleasant surroundings. This is not to romanticise the collective consciousness of the manual working class; but such work conditions do result in cultural patterns based on the shared knowledge that everyone concerned needs some form of escape from the grimness of work. Lunchtime window shopping and visits to the pub are important ways of asserting identities other than those imposed on us by work. To come out as gay, therefore, amidst the discussion of engagement rings or page 3 of *The Sun* is making a threat to something apparently created by the workers themselves. People who have come out in these circumstances have often been greeted with verbal abuse and periods of total rejection when no one will speak to them.

Despite these class differences, the fact remains that a heterosexual lifestyle is an important part of workplace culture. The pinups on the walls and the pre-wedding parties both in their different ways celebrate the heterosexuality of the workforce. They make some workers feel that work is not totally alienating. Radio One and Capital blare away in countless workplaces — the repetitive and conformist heterosexism of the lyrics interrupted by the DJ's banal witticisms and a string of dedications ("Tony of Wapping sends his love to Linda of Romford"). Teachers and social workers may not be subject to quite the same barrage of heterosexist pulp, and for them the workplace may appear less heavily heterosexist and sometimes even sympathetic to alternative expressions of sexuality. It is noticeable, though, that the new openness permitted to such workers remains very much within the framework of heterosexual monogamy. They no longer have to pretend to be happily married if they are not and they no longer have to claim to be in a stable relationship if they are not, but people who cannot sustain such situations are seen as unfortunate, and those who choose not to are seen as immature.

We have a situation, therefore, where heterosexual assumptions are central to the workplace culture. These assumptions will vary from the male chauvinist to the liberal, but there can be few workplaces in Britain where they are absent. Some of these cultural patterns are largely developed by the workers themselves but, increasingly, clever employers realise that it is in their interest to permit them — or even shape them. By allowing some of their workers to enjoy certain freedoms they may promote illusions about their own beneficence and the pleasantness of their particular workplace. The divisions and hierarchies of the sexual world are fostered within the workplace, with the result that the workforce is split. The struggle for the right to express certain forms of heterosexuality at work can be absorbed in such a way that heterosexuality is used as a means of control. But the heterosexuality which is permitted is a very narrow form — one which is male dominated, which divides women into younger "lays" and older "mothers", and which allows no initiatives to women. Gayness — as well as feminism — questions the primacy of this form of heterosexuality and therefore destabilises the control. And in situations where there is no conscious or overt manipulation of the workplace culture by management, the fact that it does appear to have been created by the workers themselves, free of any outside influences, means that there may be even greater resistance to anyone who comes out and thereby calls the culture into question.

Whatever one's job, therefore, if one wishes to come out as gay and to make people understand that this is about more than just fucking, it is necessary to create a new anti-sexist culture there. This cannot be done only by gay people but will involve alliances and friendships with heterosexual people who are oppressed by the dominant pattern of heterosexism — single parents, women who refuse to follow the stereotypical role, the disabled, young people who are expected to engage in domestic labour for which they were not employed, such as making the tea and sweeping the floor, and old people who are treated as objects of pity or fun. By openly asserting another set of assumptions about sexuality it will at least make a challenge to the notion that the world was made for male chauvinists. It will also call into question the nature of the existing workplace cultures and how they are controlled.

Such anti-sexist activity can only be initiated by people at the workplace itself. Much of the trade-union work that has been done by gays over the last few years has been directed at the unions themselves. Gay people who have been politicised in sexual politics in the gay movement have raised the question in their respective unions. Some of the issues have been fairly clear in unions connected with the caring professions, where gay people have been dismissed or threatened with dismissal. Sections of the straight left have been politicised in the process, and any gay teacher or social worker who was sacked would have a better chance of support than several years ago. Several unions, especially white-collar ones such as the Civil and Public Servants Association (CPSA), the National and Local Government Officers' Association (NALGO) and NATFHE have adopted anti-discrimination policies concerning their gay members. These were seen largely as propaganda exercises, but the reluctance on the part of several union executives to publicise them means that even that value is limited. Publicising them would at least encourage gay people who had been victimised to turn to their own union for support; it might also encourage some more closeted gays to come out at work. Failure to publicise them leaves gay people as invisible as ever and subject to the same kind of fears and harassment as we were before the policy was accepted.

Important as this type of work is, one major disadvantage lies in the fact that such struggles must always be conducted on the terms of the labour movement. To get a motion accepted, there must be gays who are good at public speaking, who are respected enough for their other trade-union work to be delegated to district and national meetings, and who are able to engage in the kind of deals and manoeuvres so widely practised by Conference Arrangement Committees. The more you struggle on these terms, the more distant you find yourself becoming from the gay community and the gay movement to which you belong. It is almost as if you need to be competitive, aggressive and traditionally male to win the right not to be like that.

Such activity has its dangers but is not without its advantages. Common cause can be made with other groups concerned with similar issues. This is particularly so in the case of teachers who are working to create materials which are positively anti-sexist and anti-racist. But it is also important in relation to trade-union attitudes to other questions such as fascism, abortion, etc. One of the most spectacular examples of such an alliance being formed was in California in 1978 against Proposition 6, which proposed that any teacher who advocated homosexuality could be subject to dismissal. It was defeated, but only after a well-organised campaign by the gay movement, some feminist groups, the teachers' trade unions and other groups less directly concerned, such as the farmworkers. Such alliances can really only be expected to last for the duration of a campaign around one issue, but they provide an excellent opportunity for gay socialists to stimulate debate about the links between sexual politics and trade unionism, about the need to organise against oppression at work as well as against exploitation, and about the common elements within the diverse struggles of people trying to win control over their own lives.

In formulating past programmes gay socialists often discussed them using the terms and the concepts developed by the early gay movement. The ideas expressed tended to suggest a more rigid categorisation of sexuality than gay socialists would accept now. This problem was highlighted by the very name of the organisation — the Gay Workers' Movement. The movement, though, consisted mainly of students, the unemployed and a small smattering of workers, most of whom were in white-collar professional jobs. There were the occasional engineering, manual or factory workers, but the latter group we called "gay workers", not do was to think about the group we called "gay workers", though we were prepared to base the name of the movement on it. We needed at least to ask ourselves questions about the cultural specificity of the word "gay", which would have led us into the important and as yet undiscussed area of how different groups of people with different class backgrounds see their sexuality. What we needed to do, therefore, was to stand back from our activities and explore the varieties of sexuality which existed in order to formulate a concept and practice of sexuality which went beyond early gay movement essentialism and related more to the needs of the people we were trying to reach.

Many of the ways in which we had learnt to work and the ideas we had about sexual politics arose out of a gay movement where an essentialist notion of gayness became a fixed commodity which could be related to everyone. Moreover, the programme of the gay movement tended to be seen as having a universal appeal — as if everyone would agree with it. However, the related ideas surrounding the family (smashing it), non-monogamy (free love), the importance of short-term relationships, and sex as something pleasurable in itself, were not universal ideals. They arose out of the concerns of a movement, many of whose members believed they had severed their cultural links with their class origins.

Two questions arise out of that programme. First, why are the concerns of the movement, regardless of its background, so important? Secondly, how do gay socialists take those concerns into the left? The underlying importance of the programme lies in its attack on the dominant assumptions of bourgeois ideology. That ideology goes beyond the concerns of a middle-class movement because bourgeois ideology also helps to shape the consciousness of the working class. The left has often been backward on questions of sexual politics, and has rationalised that position by claiming that workers are not ready for a programme which questions the role of the family, personal relationships or traditional sexuality. But if socialism is to mean more than a transfer of power from the ruling class to the working class, then all the apparatus which helps to maintain capitalism has to be attacked and has to be changed. If the premise "the personal is the political" has been accepted as a valid one by the left, then what happens in the economic sphere cannot be seen as the only area of our lives which has to be revolutionised in order to bring about the downfall of capitalism.

How we take our programme into the gay community and into the left as gay socialists is a more difficult question to deal with. For some people the answer is simple: join a party and change the party from within. However, most gay socialists are outside parties because the programme and organisations of parties require both a particular type of discipline and a concept of politics alien to their development within, and commitment to, an autonomous movement. The problem is compounded because the gay subculture is a middle-class phenomenon, and therefore gay socialists cannot organise in the gay community and have the same relationship to class politics as the left in its political organisation. We therefore have to break new ground, continuously, often working in the gay community across class lines because our politics are dealing with levels of consciousness (oppression) as opposed to organising around economic questions (exploitation). Our experience has shown how difficult it is to get the two politics to meet: the politics of exploitation which is concerned with fighting the boss or fighting the state, and the politics of oppression which is concerned with questions of community and lifestyle.

At present there is no organised gay socialist activity which brings groups, working in isolation, together. This can partly be explained by the demise of the GWM and the present state of the gay movement. The collapse of the GWM was mainly due to the problems of trying to organise nationally with a unified programme when the personal needs of those involved often took precedence over the programme. The personal and the political demands of the work involved overwhelmed most people who were not already politically experienced, or who were trying to deal with coming out personally or at work. Making demands on your trade union about gay rights or raising the question in your locality meant you needed a strong, supportive group to be able to turn to. For most people isolation was the norm, and the occasional gay workers' conference could not overcome this.

At the same time, the gay movement of today is less cohesive than three or four years ago. What we are witnessing today is a proliferation of local gay activity and an expansion of gay cultural activities. Of course this is to be welcomed, but rarely do the separate parts of a very loosely defined gay movement ever come together. We are advancing our consciousness and experience, but because of a lack of an organisation, however loosely defined, we are not sharing those advances, nor are we working out strategies about our aims and directions. Such things as switchboards, counselling groups, activists' groups, workers' groups, theatre groups and journal groups carry out their work in isolation. If we want to resist attacks and achieve advances, we need to come together more often than once in a year in Gay Pride Week. At the same time it is more difficult now for gay socialists to organise around current gay activists' practice because that practice has tended to become issue-orientated. In 1977 it was the Gay News Defence Campaign, then the main activity seemed to centre around W. H. Smith, the major newsagents in this country, who refuse to stock *Gay News*, and now a campaign around child sexuality is being developed. The latter campaign, though, does have the importance of presenting difficult questions on the nature of childhood and the development of sexuality. This campaign strikes hard at bourgeois ideology and should be of concern to all socialists. The attempts by all sorts of reactionary groups to define childhood as a state of innocence, which will inevitably turn into heterosexuality at sixteen unless tainted by contact with homosexuals, has to be fought against. Thus the hysterical attacks on paedophiles by the state and the press is an obvious attempt to define homosexuality (if you are a man) as something which just happens when you are twenty-one: if there are any factors which cause a person to be homosexual then they must relate to awful childhood experiences within the family or through exposure to gays and a gay lifestyle.

Obviously, any campaign which attacks these views is important, but it cannot be the sole plank of gay socialists' work; otherwise we will fall into the same trap of the GWM of having a programme which only a tiny élite has the strength to carry through. And if the struggle around childhood sexuality collapses, then gay socialists have to look for another issue — yet again.

In some respects the political tasks which lie ahead for gay socialists are easy to recount. Opposition to any attack on the welfare state, in particular those attacks which redefine a women's role in the home or deny a woman the right to decide how to control her own body are obvious areas of work. At the same time we must not hesitate to stress the effects of Tory policies on the family. As nurseries close, as schools move on to a shift system, as hospital waiting lists grow larger, as old people's homes close, the burden of such work will be shifted back to the home — and women. This, combined with mass redundancies of women workers in the public sector and the introduction of new technology to do office work traditionally done by women, marks a real attempt to restore the nuclear family as a central unit of English society. It is like a prison sentence for women and deals a crushing blow to all who might try to create alternative lifestyles.

It is essential, therefore, to defend the right of all women to work. This clearly involves a defence of the public sector, but also a redefinition of the nature of pay demands. The fact remains that women's pay is still only about two-thirds of men's — and this with an Equal Pay Act. The level of trade-union struggle on equal pay has been very low, largely because women are still seen as dependent. This assumption can also be seen in the fact that many pay demands assume that all full-time workers are male breadwinners with a wife and children to support. Within this context, women are associated with the old myth of pin-money — and inferior rates of pay. All attempts from within the trade-union movement to perpetuate this view must be resisted if heterosexual male domination and women's submission are to be challenged in any meaningful way.

Equally, the struggle for a shorter working week is one which would enable many women responsible for young children to earn a better living and enjoy an independent lifestyle. Failure on these two fronts seems likely to assist the return to the family and the reassertion of traditional masculine and feminine roles.

At the same time there are other areas of work, new programmes and tactics to devise in order to resist activities of the state which are becoming wider and more reactionary with each passing year. This trend started in the early seventies, when the Heath government prosecuted and imprisoned Shrewsbury building workers on a conspiracy charge in an attempt to weaken strike action and trade-union organising among building workers. Today we see these same conspiracy laws being used by the government to prosecute members of the Paedophile Information Exchange (PIE) on a charge of conspiracy to corrupt public morals. Thus just as conspiracy charges were used to weaken the rights of workers, so they are being used to attack the rights of a sexual minority to meet and to organise.

We are also faced with new and old laws being used in order to intimidate both sexual and racial minoritites. Search Under Suspicion (SUS) laws are now used mostly against young blacks, enabling the police to harass and intimidate them on the streets, while lesbians and gay men in pubs, clubs or on the streets and in their newspapers face harassment from the devious use of obstruction laws, buggery laws, blasphemy laws and even a nineteenth-century Licentious Dancing Law. It is also important to remember that these laws and the police interpretation of them are used to define the public presence the state will allow us.

However, what is vital to remember in all the areas of our work is that none of us can afford to ignore our sexual politics and our awareness of oppression, whatever the struggles we are involved in. We must continue to struggle against competitiveness, against aggression and against male chauvinism in the workplace, in the trade unions, in the socialist movement and in all the campaigns of the day. For if we see the struggle against Thatcherism, or indeed any social democratic government which is likely to be elected in a capitalist society, as part of a struggle towards socialism, then we must take with us in our movement all the elements which we hope to see in that new society. Such a linking of the different elements and forms of the politics of exploitation and the politics of oppression is not a luxury — it is a precondition for socialism.

11

Lesbian, Socialist, Feminist

MARGARET JACKSON and PAT MAHONY

In this article we have attempted to give a personal account of the links between the exploration of sexuality and the development of political consciousness which took place over a number of years. We have made no attempt to identify the causes of lesbianism: on the contrary, we start from the premise that a causal theory of lesbianism (weak fathers, castrating mothers, cornflakes for breakfast, etc.) is untenable. All we can do is describe the context in which our lesbianism, marxism and feminism developed, and the struggles on various levels, emotional, sexual and intellectual, that such a development entailed. We can perhaps point to some connections between lived experience and theory, though it should not be assumed that the analysis of experience offered below was necessarily available to us at the time when the experiences were being lived. Rather, our personal experiences began to raise wider questions which led into theory; but it was only the theory that enabled those experiences to be interpreted other than on a purely personal level.

We feel we should explain why this article has two authors and yet is written mainly in the first person singular. The reason is that one of us (Margaret) originally intended to write about herself but found she needed the other (Pat) both to help her interpret her experience, and also because at certain points in our lives our experiences and personal and political growth were so intertwined as to be virtually inseparable. It seemed to make more sense, therefore, to write the account jointly, even though it focuses mainly on one of us. We have decided not to follow the convention of naming those who contributed, wittingly or unwittingly, to the production of this article, but we hope nevertheless that their reading of it will bring its own reward.

The break-up of my first marriage left me feeling devastated: overwhelmed by a sense of rejection, isolation, personal failure, and a terror of living alone in a world best described as a railway siding, i.e. mainly given over to shunting and coupling. Paradoxically, the only obvious escape from loneliness and fear seemed to be to pursue more of the same. Thus there followed a series of affairs, mainly with married men, in some cases the husbands of my best friends, eager for "a bit on the side". Even then I had a sense of being a victim of predatory males, and resented their assumption that my desperation made me legitimately available for their sexual gratification and emotional sustenance (of course, their wives didn't understand them). As a woman who must be "dying for a bit" and therefore an easy lay, I was rendered totally passive, spending solitary evenings waiting for the telephone to ring, grateful for their attentions however transitory and inconsistent, but quite unable to make any reciprocal demands because they were, after all, married, and thus had more important commitments. I was in a double bind: on the one hand I felt used, exploited and degraded, on the other there seemed to be no way of avoiding this if I was to have relationships at all. And all this reinforced my belief, which I had never seriously questioned, that marriage was "the real thing". It never really occured to me that there might be alternative ways of relating to people. I remained more or less untouched by the women's movement, which was only just beginning to make an impact and which I believed to be mainly concerned with economic independence, which I had already achieved.

The reasons why the marriage broke up remained obscure for a long time. My husband simply announced his departure one day and never made any real attempt to explain why he felt it was necessary. It had been obvious to both of us for some time that the relationship was strained, but we both had difficulty in talking about it, and I continued to operate on the assumption that we were merely going through a bad patch which would be sorted out in due course. For a long time after he left I remained convinced he would come back, and when he did not, I oscillated between feeling a helpless victim and blaming myself for not trying hard enough. I did recognise dimly that the strain in the marriage had something to do with my determination not to be a dependent wife; he seemed to resent my financial independence, my commitment to work, and my involvement in activities that did not include him. I, on the other hand, felt that marriage somehow entailed giving up my sexual independence, not so much in the sense of being denied the right to have sexual relationships with other people, as in the sense of being denied the right to say "NO" to my husband. But my terror of either being alone or condemned to the role of concubine so dominated my consciousness that I was unable to give any serious thought to such issues.

Then along came Mr Right no. 2. After a somewhat hasty courtship (one evening, to be precise) he moved in. At first it was blissful, not least because I had at last escaped from the role of the "other woman" and had a proper social life again, albeit with people I hardly knew (they were mainly his friends). Remarkably, I took it for granted that I should cut off from most of my friends and social activities because they were alien to him. Even more remarkably, I accepted as quite unproblematical the role of dutiful daughter: for mainly as a result of parental pressure we got married, and I threw myself energetically into the task of ensuring that this time I would make the marriage work as well as continuing with my teaching career. This time I would be "Super-wife".

Soon afterwards I got a job as lecturer in a college of education, teaching sociology of education. My political position at this time is probably best described as left-liberal. I was aware of the contradictions inherent in schooling under capitalism and intuitively drawn towards a marxist analysis of these contradictions, without fully exploring the political implications of such an analysis. In any case my understanding of marxism remained at an intellectual, academic level, and I made no connections between that and my personal life. My political inertia was bolstered partly by my continuing isolation from the women's movement and partly by Mr Right's growing rejection of marxism in favour of anarchism. In retrospect there was much more to this than merely a conflict in political ideas. My commitment to work and towards a deeper understanding of marxism threatened my dependence on him, and what began to emerge in the marriage was a power struggle on various distinguishable but inter-connected levels: emotional, sexual and intellectual.

Both work and marriage, then, provided the context for the beginnings of a political awareness; but the impetus to get off my backside politically probably came more from my developing friendship with Pat, who had recently joined the teaching staff of the same college. To begin with the friendship was primarily based on shared academic concerns. We both rejected much of the reactionary and pseudo-progressive claptrap that posed as theory of education, although initially our philosophical positions appeared to be poles apart. This solidarity yet tension between us, as well as our relative isolation from the rest of the staff, served to spark off an exchange of ideas which had a sense of urgency and excitement about it, heightened by our spending more and more time together socially, often with students, which for us was a new and positive experience. At the time it was simply enjoyable, going off to the pub after lectures, talking endlessly and getting pissed; but in retrospect it was more significant than merry jaunting, because it raised questions about social relations, both in terms of the meaning and value of friendship, and in terms of challenging the teacher-student hierarchy.

The dynamic of the friendship was given a further twist by the continuing demise of my marriage, although at the time the significance of the friendship was not clearly understood or acknowledged on either side, as is obvious when I admit to the next idiocy, a short-lived and disastrous affair with — yes — yet another married man! Not long afterwards I ended up at Marriage Guidance. The counselling, which was never aimed at patching up my marriage, proved valuable in that, individualistic though it was, it did serve to give me a feeling of personal strength and a greater sense of control over my own life, as well as to a certain extent validating the kind of person I was struggling to be. Mr

Right and I entered upon an uneasy truce. I became fatalistic about what one could expect from relationships with men and began to make links between my situation and that of other women. Many of these connections were forced on me in the context of my friendship with Pat, whose own marriage was floundering in similar ways, for similar reasons, and with similar strategies for survival being employed. The one major difference between our situations was that Pat was a mother, writ large, a situation which I had chosen to avoid, mainly because of its implication for my financial independence.

Our friendship was deepened by our sharing what no longer quite seemed to be purely personal problems. We were both struggling together to understand why, as women, we were in the same boat, but were still far from having even a rudimentary feminist analysis of our personal situations, let alone of the position of women in general. Pat appeared to be more frenzied than usual about her family and personal life, and in describing a new relationship began to adopt what seemed to be a rather odd way of talking, such as "the person says . . .", or "they want me to . . ." — she never referred to "him". This puzzled me, but I was shaken rigid when she finally told me she was having a lesbian relationship. Far from being morally outraged I was shocked because of the lack of fit between Pat and my stereotype of a lesbian. After all, she did not wear a collar and tie or ride a motorbike, or exhibit any of the normal abnormalities associated with lesbianism. Most of all, she did not appear to be predatory. We had even shared a bed on one occasion but she had made no advances — and why not, I asked myself, what was wrong with me?

The outrage, then, though not moral, was fairly complex! I also felt turned on, but would not admit it, even to myself. Instead, predictably, I addressed myself to the theoretical question of my own sexuality. The possibility of my being a lesbian had occurred to me in the past, given the difficulty of sustaining satisfactory relationships with men, but I had (correctly) rejected this pathological explanation, mainly because I did not fit the collar-and-tie image and also, I suppose, because I was reluctant to accept a deviant label. Nor do I remember having had any fantasies or feelings which could be described as specifically lesbian, apart from the "phase" one is supposed to go through during adolescence (the "gym-teacher syndrome"). I was aware of feeling turned on by erotica and soft-porn images of women, but assumed this was because of their forbiddenness rather than because they were women.

However, I now concluded that if it was possible for Pat to be a lesbian, then it was possible for me. She, equally confused by the stereotype, was loudly proclaiming that she was "not a real one". This preoccupation with "real ones" on her part lasted, I might add, well into her fourth affair! Hilarious though this now seems, the very real prospect of losing her children, and, as she believed, her job, brought into focus very sharply and concretely her vulnerability as an isolated lesbian. The strain of all this over a year finally became too much and she left home without the children, believing that she was indeed an unfit mother. During the week that she stayed with me, before she got a flat on her own, we become much closer and I began to ask myself more specific questions about my sexuality in relation to my feelings for her.

Meanwhile a definite development in our political consciousness was taking place. Our college was amalgamating with a larger one and we came into contact with more colleagues who shared our views about education and capitalism and who quite firmly called themselves marxists. We therefore concluded that we too were marxists and had better get into reading Marx, so we decided to try to broaden our understanding by attending some higher degree seminars. Pat and I saw much less of each other socially for a while. She was almost totally absorbed by endeavouring to maintain a relationship with her children while continuing to live apart from them, stuggling to work out a solution which would avoid a lesbian custody case, and trying to prove to herself that any how she was really bisexual, all at the same time as having to cope with a more difficult work situation. I remember feeling a twinge of jealousy when she started a relationship with another woman, yet could not really understand why, given that I was not a lesbian (or was I?). Yet the more I saw of this relationship the more lesbianism appeared to me to be perfectly natural.

My own marriage was grinding on; I felt resigned to it and more or less negative about everything else. Although I knew that there was no future in my marriage I felt incapable of doing anything about it. The bulk of the summer vacation which I spent on my own on the Isle of Wight is a total blank. Pat felt similarly unable to resolve her dilemma: on the one hand she wanted to live alone with the children, on the other she felt unable to cope practically and emotionally with being a single parent, and with the guilt feelings at not having tried hard enough to resolve the difficulties between herself and her husband. She had returned to share the house with him, having ended the sexual relationship with her friend. She came down to the Isle of Wight for a holiday with the children. This was virtually the first time for weeks that we had had any real contact. While she agonised over her oughts and duties I faced myself for the first time with the sexual side of my feelings for her. I felt I had to say something to her about them, but could not bring myself to do so. I felt in total turmoil, but at the same time the strength and elation I experienced, having acknowledged those feelings as real, was very liberating. In the last analysis the recognition of my lesbianism did not disturb me; how to express it, though, was quite another matter.

To cut a short story short, we "sexualised" our friendship. It was not until a few months later that I became aware of a difference between us in terms of the way we viewed our lesbianism. I was out from the start, whereas Pat was out only in those contexts where there was absolutely no possibility of any repercussions on the children. As we discuss below, this issue was to be of fundamental importance in the development of our relationship. Meanwhile, we returned home from the holiday and "confessed all" to Mr Right. At first he went completely to pieces, and the next few months were horrific for all of us. We tried the standard variations on a theme: (1) stay together for the sake of the cat, with the freedom to have other relationships (Mr Right also wanted his share of Pat, a not uncommon phenomenon in such situations, as I have since discovered); (2) stay together as non-sexual partners; (3) split up.

I also went back to Marriage Guidance, but when the counsellor, who appeared to accept my lesbianism quite happily, asked which of us was the man and which the woman, I decided that her helpfulness was over, because whatever else my understanding of marxism and lesbianism meant, I did at least know by that stage that it had to do with challenging conventional power relations. I also felt myself to be much more active in the break-up of my second marriage, and able to interpret it in terms of the constraints imposed by a social institution inscribed within an arena of sexual politics. I was now in a position to understand the emotional battering I had been and was still receiving, and began to make the link between the demands made on me and the general social expectations that a woman's role is primarily defined in terms of emotional and sexual service; and I began to see that the particular strategies my husband used to reduce me to dependence on him were both identical with what was going on in Pat's marriage and also consistent with a growing consciousness of the ways in which men in general maintained power over women.

At last I decided that in order to survive as a person I would have to end my marriage, and this I proceeded to do. For the first time in my life I felt that I no longer needed or wanted the validation of a relationship with a man, and the sense of liberation from the draining effect of such relationships was exhilarating. I was still frightened of living alone, but felt now that it was something I must, and could, come to terms with. I decided that I would find somewhere to live near Pat, so that I could give her practical support with the children, and she could give me much needed emotional support while I adjusted to living on my own. In retrospect, there was a marked contrast between the feeling of insecurity I experienced as a result of my changing material circumstances, and the security I felt in my changed sexual identity. In no sense did I experience this change as traumatic; in fact, as Pat put it, I took to it "like a duck to water". Even though I have still to tackle the issue of telling my parents, there was never really any question of remaining in the closet at work or socially, or of agonising over bisexuality.

The strongest feeling I can remember was one of relief and exuberation at being able to choose *not* to relate sexually to men. It was not that I mysteriously metamorphosed into a different type of sexual being, or suddenly found that I had "really" been a lesbian all the time, but rather that having discovered both the possibility of relating sexually to women, and the fact that lesbian relationships were potentially more satisfying because of the possibility of transcending the female role and creating different kinds of relationships, I no longer had any desire for or need of male approval. It now horrified me to realise that from adolescence to my mid-thirties my ways of relating to people had been almost totally dominated by what I can only call a patriarchal consciousness, so that not only was I denied the possibility of exploring my sexuality or of developing any meaningful (not necessarily sexual) relationships with women, but my relationships with men, even at the level of casual conversation, centred upon my seeking their approval of me as a sexual being. From this point of view I now found it much easier to relate to men as friends, although at the same time my developing feminism made it more difficult, in that I became more sensitive to and less tolerant of their sexism.

Thus I had no difficulty in embracing a lesbian identity; and isolation was never a problem, since almost as soon as I had decided I was a lesbian Pat and I were introduced to a colleague at work who was a member of Lesbian Left, and we began to attend their meetings. As well as gaining a context in which to operate socially we came to understand much more about the specific oppression of lesbians and the oppression of women in all its various forms. Through our reading and our increasing involvement with the women's movement, our own search for an adequate explanation of women's exploitation and oppression led us to explore the various theoretical tendencies within the movement. Classical marxism now seemed unsatisfactory because of its sex-blindness; on the other hand a feminism entirely divorced from marxism seemed idealist and to have little purchase on the possibility of social change. At this point, however, we felt that through the women's movement we were beginning to grasp what marxism might be about, and an understanding of a marxist feminist analysis of social relations in general, as well as its practical bearing on our own lives. Thus for us, lesbianism, feminism and marxism had come together; what still remained to be changed was the way that we were actually living.

At a personal level we began to question issues such as sexual monogamy, what being "a couple" meant in terms of commitments to other people, and the relative value to be placed on sexual as opposed to non-sexual friendships. These were not academic questions, but reflected a growing tension in our relationship. Pat was becoming uneasy about the sexual dimension and its implications while I was experiencing her as restive and emotionally inconsistent, which made me feel very insecure, especially at a time when I was about to embark on living alone. Pat decided that she wanted the sexual relationship to end so that we could concentrate on the "real relationship", which was our friendship. I was very dubious about this but felt I had no choice; after all, wasn't there a rule about a person's right over her own body? It soon emerged that instead of our friendship bursting once again into blossom, precisely the reverse was happening. We became more distant and the relationship even more strained. I had a sense of rejection and a feeling that feminist theory concerning the value of friendship had been used as a rationalisation of something Pat would not or could not express. I also felt that there had been a lack of negotiation in changing the relationship and that I had been rendered totally passive in the situation. In spite of considerable time and energy consumed in trying to sort ourselves out, we both remained painfully confused. Given that there did seem to be theoretical justification both for Pat's unilateral decision as well as for my demand for negotiation, there seemed to be no basis for arriving at any ground rules for determining what counted as correct feminist behaviour.

Eventually we both agreed that our sorting out would have to be done to a certain extent independently. For Pat this involved a decision to remain celibate; for me it involved above all coming to terms with living on my own and laying that particular ghost. I also became involved in various political activities, partly (and I was aware of this at the time) to fill the gap in my emotional life. In spite of a certain degree of bitterness and guilt we continued to see a great deal of each other, being mutually supportive and still struggling to work things out. I gradually began to gain a sense of making progress, whereas Pat's situation was apparently becoming more intolerable. On the one hand she was still married, on the other, since her husband was working away from home, she was virtually living as a single parent. Although her house was always full of friends she still felt in a mess emotionally and realised that the discontinuation of our sexual relationship had done nothing to alleviate this. After four months she decided that celibacy was not the solution and promptly embarked upon an intense relationship with a woman who happened to be a social worker. This choice of a person experienced in sorting out family situations proved, if not by design, then certainly not by pure coincidence, to be just what she needed. For within three months she had moved out with the children and started buying a house with two women from Lesbian Left. She and I had much earlier on in our relationship discussed the possibility of her and the children moving in with me, but we had both been reluctant: I because I was wary of the responsibility and commitment, and she because the imbalance in our material circumstances made her feel vulnerable. She did not want to be in a situation where my goodwill was bound up with our sexual relationship, and was also afraid that such a move would have fatal consequences in terms of the inevitable custody case.

It was in fact in the context of the custody case that Pat's real dilemma began to emerge, and with it a different understanding of the change in our relationship. We believe now that the tension and unease to a large extent stemmed from only partly acknowledged and totally unresolved dilemmas concerning motherhood. First, there was for her an incompatibility between being a lesbian and a mother, given that she was continuing to share a house with the children's father. Secondly, there seemed to be a contradiction between what she felt she both wanted and ought to do as a mother and her belief as a feminist that those wants and oughts had been constructed as part of the ideology of motherhood. The most fundamental issue, in the light of this contradiction, was the question of putting the children first. She felt an inadequate feminist if she did put the children first, and that she was ignoring their real expressions of need if she did not. It was this dilemma, in retrospect, underpinned by the material circumstances of her living situation, which had much to do with the change in our relationship, because the dilemma was not merely lesbianism versus motherhood, but rather a dilemma within motherhood itself, and a confusion about how far motherhood was bourgeois/patriarchal ideology, and how far, even though socially constructed, it was changeable.

What our sexual relationship did was to highlight those dilemmas and confusions, although at the time we were unaware of what was happening. Pat's emotional inconsistency can now be interpreted as an attempt to reconcile her interests as a lesbian with her interests as a mother. On the one hand she was defining the children as the real thing, on the other she wanted a sexual relationship, but felt very guilty about the way in which that defined me as "a bit on the side", so that I was unable to make demands on her, while she made demands on me when and as she could. Her relationship with Anne made this dilemma explicit in a way in which it had not been with anyone else.

This analysis has only become available fifteen months later, in the context of writing this article. One of the reasons it did not seem urgent to analyse it earlier was that our relationship seemed to improve of its own accord. It has continued to develop by virtue of our shared interests at work and the way in which it meets our personal needs, from sheer enjoyment of each other's company, to providing a safe context for anything and everything to be shared, explored and clarified. Probably the most valuable insight I have gained from the development of our relationship so far is that whether it is sexual or not is irrelevant. What seems to emerge most strongly from the account that we have written is that we are both as women attempting to create relationships that are open and honest and not determined by conventional power relations, and that this is one of the major elements drawing us together. The dynamic of the friendship seems to be that we are both free within it to develop independently; but at the same time, given that we share similar class and sex backgrounds and similar political perspectives, that development takes us in broadly the same direction.

To conclude, we will attempt to draw out from our account what we see as some of the implications for our continuing struggles as lesbians, feminists and socialists. In doing so we can only raise issues rather than explore them, though the need to explore them is urgent and forms a crucial aspect of our political perspective and practice. We have both independently been accused by men on the left of having betrayed our socialism and of living in a lesbian feminist ghetto. We have been urged to set aside such bourgeois individualism and to get back to the "real thing", which is fighting the class struggle. While acknowledging our oppression as women and as lesbians, they define our oppression as of secondary importance to the exploitation and oppression of workers under capitalism. This criticism, and the demand to put aside our own particular struggles for the sake of greater cause is precisely what women have been co-opted to do throughout history. Such a notable example of sexism is all the more pernicious in coming from the left.

While not denying the centrality of the class struggle we see it as necessary to give priority to the sexual struggle. First, it is a dimension of social relations which is either ignored or given only token attention by traditional left politics, and in being relegated to secondary status replicates the very same status that women have under capitalism; in other words, to drive the point home, we are being told yet again that it is selfish to put our own needs first, a very old story indeed. Secondly, as history shows, sexual politics do not take care of themselves after the revolution; in some cases precisely the reverse occurs. We suggest that the failure to take the sexual struggle seriously may in fact subvert the revolution. A well-known feminist poster proclaims: "There will be no women's liberation without revolution; there will be no revolution without women's liberation". Traditional and much contemporary left politics ignores the second half of this slogan. If a socialist revolution means anything it means a change in social relations at all levels, not merely at the level of social production. Any political practice which fails to take account of women's double oppression as workers and as women, is a male-defined political practice which has no right to the label "socialist". Furthermore, even to refer to the sexual struggle as a dimension of politics, as we have done above, is to imply that it is in some way secondary; that when we have sorted that particular problem out we will get back to the real thing. Our point is that the sexual struggle is integral to the class struggle, that ultimately neither is "real" if separate from the other; but that as women and as lesbians the sexual struggle must be our starting point.

Finally, what of our specific struggle as lesbians? We hope we have made it clear that we have not become lesbians as a consequence of being "failed" heterosexuals; and, more fundamentally, that lesbianism is not reducible to sexual orientation. It seems to us that our lesbianism has grown out of our attempts to break down male power and to transcend the female role. For us, lesbianism is centrally concerned with challenging and transforming the social relations of patriarchy, and with creating different kinds of relationships which, though they can never be wholly free from constraints, are more meaningful and satisfying. We believe that they have this potential because they are less fragmented and not confined to the straitjacket of expectations that necessarily characterises most heterosexual relationships in present society.

In order to work out alternative ways of relating (with all the attendant problems, such as the relationship between friendship and sex, emotional and sexual non-monogamy, relationships with children and so on), combined with the struggle against male power, it is necessary to find a way of standing outside patriarchal consciousness. It was economic independence from men which provided us with the material basis for doing so; this has enabled us to begin to explore and change relationships and give meaning to feminism in that sense. Now, however, it is our oppression as lesbians that must become the central focus of our struggle. It is not merely capitalism and sexism but also heterosexism that we have to fight. The assumption that heterosexuality is normal, and that one is presumed heterosexual unless one declares otherwise, is one of the most deeply ingrained aspects of patriarchal consciousness. It is not simply a question of asserting the right to be different, for to do so is to do no more than ask "them" to accept "us", which still leaves them with the power to define us as deviant. The point is to challenge and transcend the concept of sexual difference or "otherness" which many of our non-gay feminist and socialist friends seem unable to do. Even with them we sometimes have a sense of either our sexuality not being recognised, or of being regarded as token or "pet queers".

Lesbianism, then, is for us the point of practice for changing patriarchal consciousness. We are not saying that it is possible to do so in other ways, but at the moment there appears to be no way in which men can stand outside it, "Men Against Sexism" notwithstanding. Even gay men are inscribed within it. Not only are many of them misogynists, but their bonding together as men does little to challenge patriarchal consciousness, and some of them appear to share with all males a resistance to understanding feminist consciousness. Our own emphasis on lesbianism as a political practice should not be taken to mean that we devalue, or are not involved in, women's struggles in other areas. This emphasis reflects our own class/sex position. Our starting point was economic dependence, which is not a reality for most women.

In that sense we recognise that our position is one of relative privilege. But we also believe that people have to stuggle from their own class position. Two issues which currently concern the women's movement are its predominant middle-classness and the divisions between those who do or do not identify as lesbians. How to find ways of linking our different struggles, which are all at a fundamental level interdependent, is one of the most difficult and urgent challenges that faces the women's movement, and cannot be avoided if a real socialist feminist alternative is to be found.

POSTSCRIPT
Over a year has elapsed since we wrote this article, and we feel it is important to add briefly that we no longer identify as socialist feminists, as we believe that particular position to be a political dead-end in terms of women's liberation. How we came to this realisation, and how we view sexual politics now, would take many pages to describe, but on re-reading the latter part of this article it now seems clear to us that we were, even at the time of writing, moving in the direction of revolutionary feminism. We only wish it had not taken so long!

12

Two Steps Forward, One Step Back

JOHN SHIERS

*Part 1: Coming Out Six Years On**

There are an enormous number of areas in the experience of being gay which have yet to be explored. Thus it is still possible to find that problems we experience in everyday life continue to be non-issues. The barriers which are built up to avoid raising certain kinds of questions are as great as they ever were. There is a gap between how I believe I ought to live, feel and act as a person committed to a broad socialist-feminist perspective, and how I actually do live, what I feel inside and the things I do as a gay man in this society. Perhaps for the traditional left this is not an issue at all: it is "idealist" to attempt to change your life, better to sublimate all hang-ups in working for the revolution. But once you come to accept that "the personal is political", the way we live as people cannot be ignored any longer. I want, in this article, to write about my experiences not in coming out but in being "out" because I feel, six years after openly defining myself as gay, that a whole new series of issues, which I define as "problems", have emerged so intensely that I have longer and longer periods where I feel totally screwed up inside.

Like many others who came out into GLF, I found the initial experience tremendously liberating. My sexuality, the part of me with which I most strongly identified and most intensely denied, was no longer hidden, no longer even bad: but something positive, good, perhaps even better than the heterosexual, gender-defined norm. I threw myself rapidly into GLF and its ideology because it seemed to relate to my experience, to articulate my oppression. I particularly identified with feminist ideas, because as well as my submerged sexuality, I had always felt inadequate as a male; never found myself able to play the role that most other blokes I met before GLF played. Understanding sexism and the oppression of women seemed like the key which unlocked the prison gates.[1]

GLF thus gave me confidence for the first time in my life: the confidence to be proud of my sexuality. It also gave me an ideology that located my oppressors (capitalism and maleness), and a movement in which I could work for change. While I had previously agreed with socialist goals, I had never been able to cope with the heaviness and severity of members of revolutionary groups I had met and the whole "macho" aura they exuded.

---

*This part was first published as an article in *Gay Left* no. 6.

But years of self-oppression, combined with my childhood experiences, had taken their toll in terms of my self-image and way of relating to others. These things I couldn't explore in GLF — and only dimly recognised at the time in myself. While we constantly talked about "making the personal political", it was always easier to blow up enormous personal conflicts between ourselves than it was to open up about deeply rooted feelings and experiences.

I felt acutely unattractive: hideous even, right through the year that I was a member of Lancaster GLF. I never dared admit this to anyone, yet it was one of the basic underlying feelings that I took with me into every situation when I was with gay people. I found it virtually impossible to envisage that anyone towards whom I was attracted sexually could ever feel the same way towards me. The costs of rejection from people in the group were so great that I only dared risk making any indications to people that I was attracted to them outside of it. That meant at periodic visits to conferences or to London GLF where rejection mattered less since I didn't have to see the person every day (and anyway the people in these contexts were far more bold in telling you if they fancied you than we were in Lancaster!) and at monthly parties above a snack bar in Lancaster (the nearest thing to a commercial scene which existed in that part of the North West).

The political and sexual parts of myself rapidly became totally fragmented: I could unendingly argue about the politics of gay liberation; support new people just coming out and appear "sussed out", but at the same time feel inside totally inadequate at actually having gay relationships. While I overcame the worst feelings of self-disgust, purely because people sometimes did seem interested in me for my body and not just for my mind, I have still in no way gone beyond the fragmentation: in some ways it is worse than ever.

Throughout my time at Lancaster and the following year at York I was scared of what we defined as the "gay ghetto" — gay bars and clubs. In the group we had a very ambiguous attitude towards it. On the one hand, we condemned it because of the money the owners and managers were making out of gay people; for the values that developed in the people who used it and for its sexism, ageism and commercialism. On the other hand, many of us (particularly the men) were fascinated and greatly tempted by it.

It wasn't until I moved to Manchester, the first place I'd lived which actually had any sizeable commercial scene, that I really began to explore it in any serious way. I found that the bars and clubs attracted me and repelled me at the same time. On the one hand it all seemed so exciting, a magic fantasy world where, for an hour or so on a club dance floor, I could simply *be*, transcend all the hassles of the real world. On the other hand it was all so uptight and unpolitical compared with GLF. I felt guilty going down to it:

particularly because I seemed to be going more often than my friends. But I rationalised (of course!) that I was taking GLF ideas into the grass roots from which it needed to build its base. I was there not because I actually needed the company like everyone else but because I could aid the politicisation of the vast mass of gay people!

At some point which I can't recall, I found the reverse was happening. It wasn't me who was changing the gay scene, but the gay scene which was changing me. It happened first in quite subtle ways: I began to be concerned about whether I was wearing "suitable" clothes and whether I was parting my hair in the "right" way. Then my absorption became more self-evident. Should I wear gay badges all the time in pubs and clubs, since they might put people off? Should I talk to anyone around whether or not I was attracted to them, or would they get the "wrong idea" from me being friendly with them? How strongly should I argue with people who said things I considered to be gross?

As the "alternative" gay lifestyle which GLF promised began to wither and decay, so my dependence on the commercial gay scene increased. The ideas that I felt so committed towards became ideals, beliefs which seemed impossible to live out. Gay men were not the potential revolutionaries just waiting for the word of gay liberation to inspire them to political struggle that I had, in my innocence, thought. Gay women I met outside of lesbian groups and uninfluenced by feminist ideas were no more likely to rise up in spontaneous anger against male dominance either. The barriers in communication and lifestyle between "revolutionary" gays and "ordinary" lesbians and gay men seemed more like a brick wall. There was no way that in our role as gay liberationists we could get through. Some people in the face of this had withdrawn totally from the scene in disillusionment. I carried on going to pubs and clubs mostly because I needed the company: it was somewhere to go. I also have the feeling however, that withdrawing can simply mean avoiding confronting the reality which has to be changed. Keeping "pure" ideologically and socially can easily end up as a new form of elitism which judges and despises the way of life of everyone else. The success rate that gay liberationists like me have had simply in keeping our own lifestyle and values together is, however, hardly a model to inspire those who regard it as a cop-out.

What participating on the commercial scene showed me, too, was that however much I have solidarity with the oppression of lesbians, however much I enjoy the friendship of women, I remain a man and as such need the company of other gay men as well as close emotional relationships with women. This really hit home when it became obvious that lesbians were being discriminated against in admission to the two gay clubs in Manchester. One club banned at the time all women unless they looked "feminine" enough to satisfy the whims of the management; the other has a male-only membership and women are only allowed in if accompanied by a member (read man). A number of us protested frequently about this, and some of us made token attempts to change their policies, first by a picket and leafleting outside one of the clubs, then by a petition. But when it came to the crunch none of us, including myself, was prepared to take action which would result in our being expelled from the clubs, or to boycott them as an individual protest. We valued our gay social lives more than the principle of outright opposition to misogynist male managements. The one disco per week which comprises the sole remnant of an alternative gay scene simply did not provide us with sufficient opportunities to mix with other gay men. We could not cut ourselves off from the only places where it is possible to meet and relax with one another. We have completely accepted the terms laid down for us by the rip-off club owners for relating to one another.

The fragmentation between my "political" self and my "sexual" self which began in Lancaster has, of course, been compounded a thousand times over since I have begun to go to the commercial gay scene. I have never resolved my basic self-disgust; consequently I have never let anyone relate sexually to me for more than a few weeks. My sexual and emotional responses are totally disconnected from each other. I have friends, women and men whom I care a lot for and feel close to, and casual sexual encounters with people who then get to be defined as "friends" (and therefore not sexual partners) or who disappear altogether from my life.

Sex becomes a means of affirming to myself that other people can find me attractive, physically can like my body. If I go for more than a month without any sexual encounter, I just feel permanently depressed. I get deep feelings of self-worthlessness. That is how I have come to dabble with cottaging (which is counter-productive because the guilt after the encounter is worse than the depression which leads me to go in the first place) and gay saunas (which are at least in physically comfortable surroundings).

The other side of this inverse narcissism is that I can only sexually relate to people who are socially defined as highly physically attractive. I am relating to their bodies, not to them (which is why I can so often sleep with people with whom I have nothing remotely in common): I would like my body to be like theirs. Through sex I can, for a few moments, "become" the body of someone who is not disgusting as my internal self perceives me to be.

Basically, I would like my sexuality to be integrated into my friendship and emotional relationships. Sex seems to have a symbolic meaning inside my head which gives it little or no connection at all with feelings of emotional commitment. So it becomes almost totally commoditised.

It shocks me how well I can present a public image of being

"sorted out". I can function in daily life, I can participate in the work routine and have close friendships with people, I can belong to "Friend" and help some gays through the first stages of accepting their sexuality. Yet I can't stand being on my own for any length of time. I go through long periods of feeling how meaningless everything is. I reject every attempt anyone makes to have an ongoing sexual relationship with me. My "public" and "private" lives seem totally divorced.

What is worst of all is that I experience discontent yet do not know how to begin to change; and however much I talk to friends about things, analyse the problems, they still remain. Yet I have the feeling that I'm not that peculiar. Many others share similar feelings although their social experiences and contexts are different. Perhaps in writing this article I'm also asking whether it is time to move on in gay liberation thinking. Shouldn't we start examining some of the "internal "factors which generate our oppression; how "the system" gets into our system? How to cope with and change our psychic structures which have been shaped in a sexist capitalist world that is also the world we have to survive in but at the same time work to transform. Where, in brief, we go after we're out.

This article has been highly personal and, at times, painful to write because none of the issues it raises have been resolved. But I think it is important to abstract from the personal and see whether it has anything more general to say about both the first phase of the gay liberation movement and directions towards which we might be moving today.

First, it seems clear to me now that GLF ideology[1] was rife with individualistic assumptions about the potential of individuals to change by their own efforts. It assumed that a lifetime of conditioning could be magically whisked away by one simple act of coming out. While the analysis was of the structural factors which generate oppression, the practice was based on individual self-change as if this were boundless. Changing our lifestyles and challenging ideologically the gender role system is not going to make the revolution. This is no reason not to attempt to make such changes and to challenge sexist ideology, but it is reason to really take account of the deep barriers, both personal and social, which we have to confront, and to examine ways of gradually chipping them down.

Equally there are dimensions of self which are rooted in our underlying psychic structure, largely hidden from our consciousness but powerful in motivating our actions and shaping our feelings. Perhaps one task of gay socialists should not be simply to keep the flame of gay liberation ideas alive but to pioneer new kinds of group which do seek to reach that underlying psychic structure. Maybe it is only from beginning to bring that level to consciousness that the foundations for a revolutionary psychology can be built: one from which we all could benefit.[2]

Secondly, my anxiety has been exacerbated by the lack of any norms to provide me with guidelines as to what kind of personal relations I "should" be working towards. Having rejected the bourgeois norm of the happy heterosexist couple, what kinds and quality of relationships are the goal of gay liberation? In GLF there seemed to be a vague belief in the "eroticisation of everyday life", of sex no longer being a "special" act done in "special" places with "special" people, but merely an extension of a general sensuality which would be part of all relationships. I have never met anyone who has achieved this goal. Few of us have even begun to break down our stereotypes despite mouthing attacks on "ageism", "sexual objectification" etc. The male gay scene offers the possibility of sex disconnected in any meaningful way from emotional relationships. This route is the route which has been traditionally taken by probably the majority of gay men who have got as far as meeting others socially at all, but still at the back of their minds (and mine) there is usually a strong desire for an intense one-to-one relationship.

Could we not be working out more clearly the kinds of social/sexual relations which advance the development of a gay liberationist consciousness and way of life, and which are merely the result of a brutalisation of our lives under capitalism, a reduction of others to objects for consumption? I don't mean that this should be done in a moralistic way of laying down new "you should's" and "you shouldn't's": there was too much of that in GLF. But through thought, discussion and sharing of experience, and probing of the internal and external forces which keep us committed to lifestyles we feel discontent about, new possibilities may emerge. At the moment, I am particularly vulnerable to whatever norms get to be thrown up in the social groups of which I am a member. Since I, like many others, have come to depend on the gay scene, I am particularly likely to be influenced by the norms which emerge "within the walls" of the scene itself.

Thirdly, we grossly underestimated in GLF the capacity of capitalist enterprises to colonise gay men. We tried to avoid confronting the gay scene altogether, hoping that some mass conversion would turn out all its participants from the bars and into our ranks. But the reality is that they can provide better facilities than we could in a material sense, more regular meeting places and more exciting discos. Socially we could not compete and little attempt was made in GLF to welcome people who did not already have a fairly clearly defined left-wing stance.

In many small towns up and down the country the bar is, literally, all that there is for gays in the area (apart of course for the public conveniences which become cottages for gay men). Since commercial facilities are obviously going to be the main places where gay men and probably lesbians, too, are going to meet for a long time to come, gay liberationists in the gay movement ought to be starting to press organisations like CHE and NOOL to organise effective campaigns to prevent at the very least sexual or racial or class discrimination in access to these facilities. How this is to be done in local areas and nationally I don't know, but surely we should immediately put it on the agenda both as a serious gay issue and for action.[3] Maybe rip-off, misogynist gay capitalists do determine many of the places we meet, but why should they have everything their own way?[4]

Fourthly, a lot more attention needs to be paid to the provision of decent alternative social facilities in areas large enough to sustain gay groups. The total inadequacy of gay commercial facilities as genuine centres of gay community can be seen by briefly looking round at the groups of people who are absent from them, not by those who are present. Places like the Birmingham Community Centre perhaps pave the way for what could exist in a lot more areas. The problem is centrally to do with who does the work to get alternative facilities together. How much time is it reasonable to expect individuals to give up in organising social events? When they are provided without the hassle by private enterprise, it is tempting to give up the laborious process of hiring rooms and equipment for discos; making sure gay centres are adequately staffed, etc. When the collective anger that partly gave rise to GLF dissipated, did the desire to create a radically different form of community life dissipate, too? I would like to see local gay groups more concerned about the kinds of community they wish to build in their areas and the kind of facilities the members feel they need, just as much as I want to see them working to prevent discrimination in commercial facilities.

I hope this article has not given the impression that here is poor, weak, innocent John Shiers who has got sucked into a nasty, horrible gay world which is fucking him up. I actively sustain my lifestyle: I am not like a pinball being pushed around without any power to stop the cycle. I choose to use commercial gay facilities; I consent to the one-night stands; I also have a fairly satisfying and enjoyable social life quite independent from all of this. Yet my choices are not "free": I have needs which gnaw away under the surface and which gay bars, clubs and sex do provide temporary relief for. But it is temporary: the underlying issues remain and I have no idea how to begin to go about fully understanding them, let alone sorting them out in such a way as to give me a constant feeling of personal integration.

Part of me says "Be realistic: realise that personal integration is an illusion in this society. Accept yourself as you are because it's not that terrible". Yet I can't totally accept that. Another part of me says, "NO — struggle against your fragmentation", for it is the awareness of fragmentation that sustains emotionally and not just intellectually my socialist commitment. And perhaps after all that is the chief gain, six years on.

Part 2: Moving into the 1980s

I wrote the article above, two years ago, out of desperation. I felt totally isolated and utterly empty inside. I found myself feeling things that I could not really communicate to others and doing things which seemed at variance with my political values as a gay liberationist. I desperately needed to say to people with whom I felt some kind of collective solidarity: "Look, this is where I'm at, I don't particularly want to stay here, but it's me at this point and I want to make some sense of it."

Two years later I feel a lot less out on a limb. The response to the article was largely one of empathy and support. Many people told me that they too, were experiencing the same kind of gaps between their ideology and their lifestyle, and had the same fear of openly discussing it. I no longer felt some kind of freak. Today, there is a lot less of that dreadful moral judgementalism, which acted as such a powerful agent of moral control, around. To that extent, we have moved forward.

But within the developing gay male subculture generally it hardly need be said that there is still the same wall of silence over how people feel about their lives as gay men, that there has always been. Pain and anxiety about our lifestyles continue, by and large, to be individualised and therefore experienced as a personal problem. While gay men may sometimes joke about urges to be pissed on or sucked off through holes in cottage walls or their penchant for cloned macho men/young dolly-looking teenage lads, all this remains part of our "secret lives", of the things which we do not feel it is respectable to make public, guilty secrets which can only be confided to very close friends who are probably into the same kind of thing or something quite similar anyway, while we know that, at least in "reasonable", "liberal" circles, we are tolerated for being gay, we also implicitly realise that the tolerance only really extends to us living lifestyles which ape as closely as possible straight people's fantasies about their idealised heterosexual norm.[5]

In other words, if we are good boys, who are prepared, perhaps after an initial coming out fling, to settle down with a nice man in quasi-marital bliss, then we may be tolerated (provided that we are reasonably discreet, particularly in front of the children; do not scream in the street at night or wake up the neighbours with distasteful rows about who forgot to buy the KY) as an uncomfortable but essentially harmless departure from the norm. The problem with this scenario seems to be that most gay men, as they become relatively more comfortable in their sexuality, either are not able or do not want to live as their heterosexual opposite numbers claim to live. Herein lies a further complication. For not only are we having to discover for ourselves, largely in isolation from others and certainly without any support from the mainstream culture, what our emotional and sexual needs are. But also, if we do openly declare and discuss our sexual lives or our sexual fantasies, we at the same time open ourselves up to a further round of heterosexist labelling devices and moral judgements about our "disordered" sexuality and the poverty of our "condition". Since there is no equal self-analysis forthcoming in mainstream heterosexual culture about how they really do feel about their relationships, fantasies and "deviations", the short-term result of gay men affirming our sexual desires openly could be the increased persecution of all elements of our subculture which seriously undermine their fantasies about how they (and we) ought to live.[6]

A recent *News of the World* "exposé" on the Cellar in Charing Cross Arches, where the reporter witnessed the "vilest" things happening that he had found in twenty-seven years of reporting (that is, men, dressed in leather, having sex with one another individually and in groups) is but the tip of the iceberg. The vast increase in police activity around cottages, the systematic and continuous crushing of any saunas and clubs which allow sex to take place on the premises, are other indicators of this. If we have to be queer, they are going to make very sure that it either takes place "in the privacy" of our own homes or it will not take place at all.

Because in the gay male movement we have put so little emphasis on understanding and interpreting our actual sexual desires as we experience them in the present, we are ill-equipped to tackle the threat we now face. Our sexual desires are largely uncharted territory, yet it is exactly in these uncharted territories that gay men up and down the country are facing the main brunt of the growing climate of sexual repression and backlash.

I believe that this is not coincidental. For however fragmented and contradictory our lifestyles are, however insecure most of us feel about them, and however unsatisfactory are the contexts within which we encounter one another, gay men's capacity to have casual genital sexual relations with one another does pose a challenge to the heterosexual moral order and thus to patriarchal sexuality, where power defines the sexual relationships made by men and women. Gay men encounter one another as reciprocally acknowledged equals, and the ease with which sex can happen between us reflects this. Our challenge, however, lies dormant for as long as we continue to play along with the double life which the culture forces us to live and squeeze our sexual lives into a twilight world acknowledged barely to one another let alone to the outside world. Equally important is the virtual impossibility of fully recognising or even beginning to work through the contradictions that we experience in living out our sexual and emotional lives when the right to organise our social and sexual relations with one another as we choose is denied us.

If we are to begin to build an effective political movement for gay liberation in the 1980s, then we have to take the growing gay male subculture seriously, both as a place which many of us need and also for the particular contradictions which result from the way we relate to one another in it. I still feel the same commitment to making the links between gay liberation, feminism and socialism that I did in the days of the Gay Liberation Front, but I feel now that the processes through which those links will be made in practice as opposed to in theory are a lot more complex than I did then. Unless, however, those of us who believe the links must be made are prepared to affirm as gay men what we are most oppressed for (our sexuality), then any acceptance either by the feminist movement or the socialist movement will be on their terms not ours. This does not mean that gay men do not have to change a lot too: we can be as oppressive to women as straight men are, and class inequality is hardly a major issue for discussion on the gay scene. But it does imply that gay men are specifically oppressed for their sexuality and that it is we who must resolve the contradictions which our lifestyles throw up, not the moral judgements of those on the outside.

I want to go on to look in a little more depth at some of the key areas which concerned me in the first article, using the kind of framework which I have just outlined as a basis for understanding them. From London to Berlin, from San Francisco to Amsterdam, the gay male community is characterised, wherever large numbers of us can get together, by its overt sexuality. If it is clear that you fancy someone and they fancy you, then sex is assured to be OK, almost regardless of the place it happens in. Gay men develop highly sophisticated codes of signifying sexual attraction to one another and even what particular sexual interests we may have. Sex is a constant subject of discussion amongst gay male friends; cruising is an important leisure-time pursuit. Even when ongoing sexual relationships are formed, these are rarely monogamous for very long.

This obviously sets in motion a whole variety of contradictions and internal conflicts. Casual sex is only OK with certain bodies and not others; we feel the need to constantly present and preserve an image which we hope will turn on those who we want to fancy us; those of us who are still young or fairly young often fear growing old, and it seems that many who are old wish to be young. People can also get very hurt if there is ambiguity about whether a particular partner is simply wanting sex or is really looking for a relationship. It can be hard to form emotionally committed sexual relationships even if and when people decide they want to.

The motives for having casual sex are therefore not surprisingly manifold,[7] but so are the motives for desperately searching or clinging to an idealised monogamous union with one person. The difference is that one is regarded as socially unacceptable and psychologically deficient, particularly if it is people of the same sex or if it is heterosexual women who are initiating casual relations, while the other is exactly what we are all brought up to believe we should be living out, with the opposite sex and in clearly demarcated roles between women and men. The equality of gay male "promiscuity" makes its meaning entirely different from heterosexual male promiscuity in the mainstream culture because we are not seeking to assert our dominance and control over another, who we have been taught to believe is subordinate to us, through making a sexual conquest.[8] It is very different, too, from the pattern of relating which lesbian feminists are developing, and it is tempting for gay men who identify with the feminist movement to define our sexuality in a negative way in contrast to theirs. Some feminists have also been highly critical of the way in which they see gay men apparently aping straight male sexual patterns.

I think this response is a mistaken one, but if gay men are not prepared to talk about how we do actually experience our sexuality, it is not surprising that women who have experienced men's sexual advances as an imposition on them all their lives define our sexual behaviour through heterosexual categories. We as gay men need to affirm the positive elements which we experience in the gay subculture without glossing over the contradictions or denying the validity of the pain experienced by gay men whose sexual needs are not reflected in the subculture's values. We need to feel confident enough to defend our right to define our own sexuality, which originates in the specific oppression which we have suffered in society. In so doing we are not only asserting what our own needs are, but we are also challenging the lack of open discussion about how sex is experienced and desired in the mainstream culture, its privatisation as a deeply personal "intimate" act between two people of no consequence to anyone else. The "radical kernel" in our sexual lifestyles may we be that we are debunking the mystique which surrounds sex and placing it where it had to be placed if we are ever to begin to move towards a less genitally fixated, more sensual society, that of a fun activity we have with others who also feel like having it with us.

It is only with the dawning of such changed attitudes towards sexuality that it will be possible to get "beyond" the point we are at. Gay male promiscuity is the reverse side of the coin from compulsive monogamy and the attempt to fixate all our sexual and emotional needs in one person. Both ultimately need to be transcended, but you do not transcend deeply internalised ways of being because you think you ought to do so. We have to establish the material precondition for this in terms of a society where people are not forced into male and female roles or subject to a viciously anti-gay socialisation process. This inevitably requires political struggle for both women and gay men, around our right to define our own sexuality for ourselves.

As a distinctively gay male lifestyle is beginning to emerge, so it seems that the barriers between lesbians and gay men are also increasingly being put up. The expansion in commercial facilities has been largely for gay men over the past decade. Clubs seem to have become more restrictive of access to lesbians as more have opened up. While there are a small number of women-only commercial clubs in London and one or two mainly women's clubs out of London, by and large lesbians face the option of having to socialise in largely male-defined social facilities or to form their own alternatives. The discrimination which gay women who want to go to commercial clubs face from many club managements has only served to distance them still further from gay men. For a number of lesbians feminists it confirms their strong suspicion that really gay men are just as antagonistic to independent, strong women as heterosexual men are. It has led to considerable conflict between men in the gay movement and lesbian feminists in areas like Manchester, where despite the expansion in the numbers of women coming out as gay, there are still not enough women to generate a fully alternative lesbian scene in a way which is possible in London.

The relationship between gay men and lesbians is, to me, a very complex matter. The gay liberation movement has identified strongly with feminism and sought theoretically to connect gay male oppression with women's oppression through an analysis of the gender role system and enforced heterosexuality. The "gay rights" type activists (the bulk of CHE for instance) have sought to emphasise the common situation which both women and men are in as gay people in a hostile heterosexual society. Yet the relationship between lesbians and gay men has been a stormy one in all groups, whether "liberationist" or "reformist", where women and men have attempted to work together. Lesbians find the way gay men behave with them is too sexist to make joint action easy; men react defensively and sometimes with hostility. As lesbians have increasingly chosen to work in women-only organisations, because they see their priority as being with other women, the issues posed by this have tended to be shelved by gay men rather than worked through.

On the gay male scene, gay men do not necessarily see any connection between themselves and lesbians. When gay men, for example, bring women friends to clubs, these friends are usually heterosexual, not gay. While many gay men build up close personal relationships with a number of heterosexual women, this happens much more rarely with gay women. There seems to be mutual suspicion on both sides about the lifestyle of the other. In social situations gay men collectively tend to create highly sexually tense atmospheres because they see them as potential sexual situations, too. This can be both off-putting and oppressive to lesbians who just want a relaxed place to drink and dance with friends. From the perspective of a large number of gay men, cruising becomes more difficult in clubs where there are lots of lesbians around, who are not interested in men at all. In my original article I saw discrimination against the admission of lesbians in gay clubs as a product simply of misogynist clubowners. Now I think its source lies in more than this: it lies in the insecurity gay men experience about their lifestyle and the consequent desire to close off places where they socialise from anyone who they consider might be hostile to it. It has been my experience that quite a number of gay men perceive lesbians to be as hostile towards them as heterosexual men, and thus want to keep gay women out of "their" clubs as much as they want to keep straight men out.

Is this misogyny? For some men, a minority, I think it is. But I do not believe this is true of the majority of gay men who seem to relate very well with many heterosexual women. But it clearly is a lack of awareness on our part, collectively, as gay men, about the privileges we still receive in society because we are men. I frankly do not know how, in the immediate situation, things are going to change. But I am convinced that to the extent that gay men feel able to be more open about our lifestyles and more militant in demanding our right to live as we choose, the fears that many of us currently have about sharing our social situations with lesbians will dissolve. This does not mean that lesbians will want to relate any more closely to us, but it does mean that enough of our defensive values will have been removed for us to look a lot more sensitively at the position of women who are gay than most of us do at the moment. For gay men the connection with feminism is obviously a lot less direct than it is for women; but the connection is clearly there, and it is through our greater politicisation as a community that more gay men are going to make the connection in reality. That, hopefully, is where the gay movement comes in.

The gay movement is going to be as vital to any further changes in the situation of gay people in the future as it has been in fostering what changes there have been to date. The gay male movement emerges in Britain, after a decade of its existence, lacking any clear sense of direction. On the one hand, lesbians have by and large chosen to stay out of mixed gay organisations and to work in feminist groups with other women; on the other hand the number of gay men who define their sexuality in political categories is very small. The commercial gay scene provides facilities which attract far more people than any alternatives which gay groups set up. It is also increasingly clear that the forces of reaction are marshalling themselves and there is a considerable danger that we may lose some of the small gains we have already made.

The gay organisations which over the years have proved to be the most successful and durable have been the gay information centres and counselling groups such as Friend and Icebreakers. This aspect of the provision of practical support for people coming out and trying to find their feet is obviously going to expand as supportive places for people experiencing difficulties and problems right through their lives. Once we can explode the myth of the perfectly adjusted person who only needs to find the "right" relationship for everything to be hunkydory, we will have come a long way!

But I feel that if the gay movement is to have a dynamic and living relationship with the gay subculture, one of its most important roles has to be understanding and interpreting our collective experience, making public what otherwise would remain private, affirming with pride our sexual lifestyles and challenging by our actions patriarchal sexuality which makes genital sex into an act of power instead of an act of fun. From the assertion of our right to define our own sexuality comes the demand that we should be able to develop our own facilities to relate to one another as we choose. It is from this basis that the commercial exploitation of our needs by gay businessmen will be undermined. Hopefully, too, we would also be in a better position to work through the unresolved conflicts which we sometimes express in our sexual relations with one another and to examine fantasies critically rather than being forced either to repress them or to act them out in a shadowy world of semi-illicitness.

The danger we constantly face in the commercial scene and in the contexts we at present create for ourselves at the margins of society, is getting stuck where we are at now, being permanently thankful for the small degree of cushioning it provides us from the hostile heterosexual world, losing or never even gaining the desire to fight the dominant anti-gay culture which we seek temporary relief from. I am convinced, however, that it would be a big mistake for whatever gay male organisations which emerge in the 1980s to revert to the old Gay Liberation Front position of attempting to set themselves apart from gay men on the gay scene. The "ghetto" will be broken when we manage to create a society which ceases to drive us into it, not by a moralistic rejection of the "unpolitical", "unright-on" attitudes of "gay scene" men. The only consequence of such a politics would be to isolate still further the gay movement from most gay men and incapacitate ourselves from effective defence against external attack.

For if the intensification of class and race conflict does continue to lead to increasing state repression, we are going to have to be better organised to meet the challenge. The bulk of the left is likely to respond to economic and social crisis in a fairly traditional manner and to make a return to the more narrowly based economism of its origins. To avoid being squeezed out of the political arena altogether, both the gay movement and the women's movement are going to have to spotlight the oppression we experience all the more vigorously. We need to show why sexism and heterosexual dominance are key issues to tackle in the process of building a political movement which really begins to involve rather than exclude large numbers of people who have previously remained passive or drifted towards the right. If the gay movement does not stand out and state that taking seriously sexual anxieties and discontents is a serious political issue, who else will? Certainly not Arthur Scargill or Ernest Mandel.

A combined strategy of going on the offensive in the sense of affirming more openly the lifestyles which we are in the process of developing, and on the defensive in the sense that we must be prepared to defend what existing rights and facilities we have achieved, seems to be the key task that confronts us at the moment. Potentially, I am convinced that gay men as gay men have a very important role to play alongside feminists in the reconstruction of the left and the broadening of its horizons into a genuine movement which liberates and grips people's imaginations about the possibilities of how life could be lived, freed from the constraints in patriarchal capitalist society.

The "feel" of the beginning of the 1980s is very different from the "feel" of the early 1970s. We are only just beginning, personally and politically, to find our bearings in this changed situation. My experience is of having moved into defining myself as part of an oppressed group from the inside rather than being a gay outsider attempting to mobilise other gay people, fundamentally different from me, to challenge their oppression. Quite a number of gay male liberationists up and down the country have been gradually making this same transition. In the transitional stage that marked my original article, I was still trying to make sense of this shift of identification. Now I feel much more positive about it, but the problems posed for working as a gay liberationist and anti-patriarchal socialist remain. I hope that in the 1980s we can, collectively, begin to confront and tackle some of these problems.

NOTES AND REFERENCES

1. My new ideology went something like this. Men oppress women by their "maleness", by "machismo". Male dominance is structured into all the institutions of society, into our whole culture and way of life and into our most intimate personal relations. Heterosexual relations are the linchpin which holds together the gender-role system. The rejection of heterosexuality is thus a revolutionary act, particularly for women, but probably also for men, because it provides them with the possibility of developing non-gender defined ways of relating both to themselves and to women. GLF meant more than being simply a campaigning organisation; it was a way of life which, alongside the women's movement, was to revolutionise personal relationships. Through the transformation of the "personal", the consciousness of the necessity to transform the capitalist economic system would also develop, since capitalism was built round sustaining the power, wealth

and status of a small number of white, economically exploitative men. The rest of us were conned by the subtle kinds of divisions which translated capitalist authority relations into all social relations. This could be blown wide open by women — gay and straight — and gay men collectively rejecting male power. The result would be the rejection of all authority relations in capitalist society, since they are built round the "first" authority relation — the power of the man.

2. I think it is important not just to develop a psychological theory: but also techniques of therapy. Even if (a big if) a revamped Freud does have a contribution to make to understanding the human psyche under patriarchy (as Keith Birch was suggesting in "Politics and Ideology", *Gay Left* no. 5), how can we go about beginning to liberate ourselves from our pasts? By psychoanalysis?

3. An illustration of the lack of importance which this issue at present merits can be seen in the refusal of *Gay News* to publish either of the articles we sent it about our activities in relation to the two, sexist, Manchester clubs. Any campaign would also have to be properly co-ordinated. There were simply too few people involved in ours and little enthusiasm from lesbians themselves to participate. They either were not interested in going to the clubs or thought that it was impossible to change the clubs' policies anyway. The majority of gay men we talked to, while agreeing with us that discrimination against lesbians was bad, were worried about getting on bad terms with the management of the clubs. Such is the power of club managements in their quasi-monopolistic position in all parts of the country outside London.

4. There is also an important political point to bear in mind in such a campaign: that in opposing discrimination in clubs, what is being opposed is the right of men to restrict women's access to social facilities. If women (or any other group at present in the process of defining an autonomous identity for themselves from their dominators) choose to set up their own clubs and restrict access to them from men, this I consider to be quite acceptable. To refuse to support male-only gay clubs but to support the right of women-only clubs is a recognition of the specific oppression women experience from men. If this view is generally accepted, it makes the terms of such a campaign an important issue to discuss, particularly in organisations composed mainly or entirely of men, such as CHE.

5. For a report which absolutely epitomises this patronising, oppressive form of liberal tolerance, see the recently published Church of England Working Party's paper on homosexuality.

6. I emphasise that I am referring here to mainstream heterosexual culture, not to the very open and honest exploration by many feminists of how women's sexuality has been controlled and defined by men and what the consequences of this have been for women.

7. I know from my own experiences how unclear I often am about why I am seeking out casual sex. It can be because I feel bored, lonely, low in self-image or depressed. It can also be just for the fun of it. I am also pretty clear now that I block off emotional commitment from sexual

relationships because I am scared of the consequences of such commitment, and that relates further back to a score of unresolved conflicts which I continue to experience emotionally between my mother and myself. Wouldn't Freud have a field day!

8. As least gay-defined gay men are not. The fact that there are men around who try to relate to gay men in the ways they have learnt they should relate to women does not negate this point. These men remain heterosexual male-defined, but run into a lot of difficulties because most gay men will not stand being treated as highly sexist men treat women.

13

Horrific Practices: How lesbians were presented in the newspapers of 1978

SUSAN HEMMINGS

Lesbians are not accustomed to seeing much about themselves on television or in the papers. We make regular appearances on the problem pages of women's and girls' magazines ("I think I might have lesbian tendencies." "Don't worry. It's normal to have strong feelings of friendship for another woman, but it definitely isn't sexual."), and we turn up occasionally in the *Sunday People*: My Wife Ran Off With Sex Change Doctor. But apart from that, we are studiously ignored. Even those who are widely known for their well-meaning tolerance, and who genuinely try to be helpful, seem to be under the impression that we simply do not exist: "We must recognize the fact that love, whether it be between a man and woman, or man and man, can achieve a pure and glorious relationship if it is expressed with restraint and discipline." (Bishop of Southwark, June 1979.)

Against this background of sensationalism and silence, 1978 emerged as a freak year (or year of the freaks?), in which lesbians managed, like it or not, to hog headline after headline. Hardly had one story run its course than another would begin. The three major stories, intertwining and overlapping throughout the year, were: the sexuality of Maureen Colquhoun, then Member of Parliament for the Labour Party; lesbians becoming mothers through artificial insemination; and the feminist schoolteacher who tried to teach her class to question sex-role stereotyping.

Each of these "stories", for that is what the media reduce us to, had profound effects on the private lives of the women concerned. It harmed all of them. It changed them from being relatively trusting, though not naïve, women into people who would never again give openly of their personal lives and their ideas to the straight press, or even to the straight world in general. And it harmed all other lesbians who were not in the direct line of fire, but knew how to read the smoke. Women in politics and other areas of public life went on disguising their sexuality. Lesbian mothers, some of whom were actually beginning to fight openly for custody of their children, were regalvanised into anxiety, as their families again began to abuse them, and their children again stopped inviting school friends home. And gay teachers, always under the threat of exposure and suspension, felt even less safe in the classroom, especially at a time when education cuts were taking jobs, particularly women's, away from anyone who was the slightest bit unconventional.

For every time the press hounds lesbians, it makes us all stop in our tracks. We are all familiar with the argument that the public "has the right to know", as if all the papers did was to disseminate information which, somehow, we as lesbians have been wilfully withholding from them. The information which the papers chose to give that year lifted no veils, and only served to mask us further. Usually we think that information is liberating. But we can see from these stories, and the way they were presented, that their particular purpose was to confine and ghettoise us, to instil fear into us. When we fought back, and said what we thought about such representations, we were accused of being "loudmouthed" and "bullies". Apparently the public only wants the information which Fleet Street can provide, and it is a public which editors presume to be totally heterosexual.

During the course of the artificial insemination "scandal" (the one which, as a lesbian mother, I was most personally touched by) many of us simply could not go into newsagents, launderettes or any public place without hearing anti-lesbian abuse, that is, from members of the public who assumed us to be part of them and their mentality. It is no exaggeration to say that even our nights were invaded by the kinds of fearsome dreams that many of us had suffered during demonstrations at Grunwick's and against the National Front, dreams where fascists were in power. It is important to emphasise the "human" side of it all (as the papers themselves so often smugly assert) — because we should all remember that such newspaper copy is entirely wrought out of our pain. A sneak reporter, or a portentous editor, can, in the name of responsible journalism, make our lives unbearable, reduce some of us to a state of virtual house arrest . . . and it can all be explained away as our fault for being lesbians in the first place. "Well," as I was told during the AID scandal, "you *chose* to live that life, so you've got to face the consequences."

Here, then, are accounts of the three stories about lesbians in the papers of 1978, reconstructed from press cuttings of the time.

THE PUBLIC FIGURE: MAUREEN COLQUHOUN

Maureen Colquhoun's story began well before 1978, although it came to its major political crisis then. And it has not ended yet, for although she lost her seat in the general swing to the right in the last general election, she will be standing again at the next, and no doubt the issue of her sexuality will be thoroughly done over again then.

It was in 1976 that she first "confirmed that her twenty-six-year marriage has broken up and she is now living with a girl friend." They did not at first directly label her as a lesbian, but preferred to impute it through the presumed sexuality of her "girl friend", Barbara Todd, whom they described as "regional director of the magazine *Sappho.* The publication describes itself as 'the only lesbian magazine in Europe' and its headings say 'Gay women read *Sappho'*" (*Daily Express*, 24 April 1976).

Meanwhile the *Daily Mail* approached the subject via its gossip column, with the statutory photo of the street name at which the couple now lived. As a result of this piece, their children, relatives and friends were continually pestered in the street and on the telephone. Maureen took the *Mail* to the Press Council for invasion of privacy, but lost on the grounds that the public has a right to know. Lesbianism is news, so if you want to stay out of it give it up or stay invisible.

It was against a sustained attack on her sexuality that she then pursued her already difficult political career. By the middle of the following year, things were beginning to come to a head within her local constituency party. Besides the usual round of complaints for missed surgeries and making speeches not reflecting local party lines, she had made a particularly serious error by suggesting that Enoch Powell, a rightist on the move even futher right, was not a racist. Subsequent events have incontrovertibly shown her to be wrong, and even at the time, many people were shocked at her misjudgement, whatever its context.   A major function of the constituency party and its committees is to engage in discussion with the MP, argue out points of debate and action. Indeed, her comments about Powell were discussed there. But it was the issue of her lesbianism which enabled the group on the executive committee particularly dissatisfied with her to organise against her. They began to make remarks about her "passing herself off as a married woman" and "living a lie" (reported later in *Labour Weekly*, 27 January 1978).

So by the new year of 1978, Maureen had effectively been sacked by the general management committee of Park Ward in her constituency, and was awaiting the decision of the Labour Party's national executive on the matter. They ruled in her favour, saying that the local party had not given sufficient notice of their motion to dismiss her. Dr Heaney, who as a strong anti-abortionist had been the most vocally opposed to Maureen's feminism, and now to her lesbianism, was shocked at the criticism of his local party. "This action of dismissing our decision on a technicality has really got up the noses of many people in Northampton. It is treating us like idiots. People here have a tradition of independence. They do not take kindly to being pushed around. We shall go through the whole dismissal procedure all over again, dotting every 'i' and crossing every 't' . . ."

By now her lesbianism had been public property for over two years. In December 1976 she had swiped a car park attendant when he dropped the exit barrier on her new car, and columnists like William Hickey were still referring to this incident eighteen months later, along with a reference to the invitation she and Barbara had sent out to their housewarming party (to which he was presumably not invited) showing "two intertwined females". But after she won her appeal to the national executive, what she was mainly in the news for were any remarks she might make on her own or on anyone else's sexuality. She had by now given up any attempt to be reticent or ambiguous about her sexuality. Since the press had allowed her no choice, it became senseless to remain in the closet. When challenged, as she constantly was, she would reply that many MP's were homosexuals, and that many others committed marital and extra-marital indiscretions. Statements of such obvious truth set the *Sun* screaming. They dubbed her "Maureen the Mouth", as if she had scaled Big Ben and broadcast the horrific news to a cringing and disbelieving nation. "Ordinary voters are not yet ready for an anything goes society. Wouldn't it be better if she simply shut up?"

So having goaded her more or less without remission for two years, the papers now decided she was boring, because she was always going on about being gay. And in particular they got upset about this use of the word "gay", because apparently they were being deprived of a lovely and useful little word. (After all they had donated us "queer", "lezzy", and several others, so they could not see why we appropriated others.) Veronica Papworth (*Daily Express*) put it succinctly: "'I'm gay and I'm proud of it,' said that much publicised left-wing MP and car park (sic) basher. Far be it from me to comment on her private life — no matter how public she chooses to make it. All I question is 'gaiety' in this context. Good grief, I'm gay, I'm gay as a lark. But may I no longer say so? On the other hand, pictured all over the papers fiercely defending her sexuality, the lady in question exudes as little gaiety as Guy the Gorilla."

Another columnist who, you understand, is not interested in Maureen's private life, is Jean Rook. "If Ms Colquhoun has, at 49, had a lovely torrid change of love life, that's her business. I wish she'd stop making it mine. I wouldn't want to live with her. So whatever she's found, she should hug it to herself. And not bore the pants off me by gossiping about it" (*Daily Express*, 5 April 1978). This time Maureen demanded the right to reply. After all, just who had she gossipped about it to? On what occasions had she tried to make her life any affair of Jean Rook's? A week later the *Express* published her reply. (We have since seen this established as a Fleet Street tradition. First you queerbash, and then you let the oppressed have a few words, while boasting that you are bastions of the democratic tradition, of discussion and free speech: both the *Evening News* and the *Guardian* which, like the *Express* on the above occasion, got noisily occupied by protesting homosexuals after publishing offensive pieces, graciously allowed those whose lives they had denigrated to have a column or two.) The debate was then continued in the letters page — who is right, Jean or Maureen? Some did support Maureen, but most were in this vein: "The Creator gave us two sexes with mutual attraction between them to ensure perpetuity of the species, and men and women who seek to pervert this divine plan must surely bore the Creator himself." Even God is bored with us? I had never encountered the bored Lord theory before, but come to think of it, it could explain his propensity for natural disasters.

Interest in her sexuality was very widespread during those months. Women's magazines were competing for her story. By now she had an active support group, and they felt what was needed was material which presented lesbianism as just another way of life which "ordinary" women could see as a parallel to their own. So Maureen agreed to be interviewed by a *Woman's Own* journalist who wrote a sympathetic/romantic presentation of her relationship, from the point where she and Barbara fell in love, the problems of telling her family and her husband, to setting up in the new home. Her lesbianism was now being packaged and sold via its apparent similarities to heterosexuality — love is the same the world over. The article played down their courage, her threatened career, the harassment of their children (who were just "upset" like any separating couple's children are). She came across as the typical emotional woman we are all supposed to be — except that she is a little unusual in her sex life "In some ways being a self-confessed lesbian has ruined my political career. I still feel rotten about what I did to Keith. But when you are in love — and I'm passionately in love with Babs — nothing else matters" (*Woman's Own*, 16 September 1978). But far from not mattering, her political life was taking up more commitment and energy than ever before. Here, in the context of the women's magazine, her whole sense of struggle was inverted — what does it matter if I'm finished politically so long as I have Babs? The journalist who wrote this piece meant to be supportive, and to counterbalance the stuff coming from Jean Rook and so on, by showing that lesbians are essentially just like "real" women. The only way she could reach this equation was by romanticising us. Indeed, many gay people, especially gay men, were making similar pleas at the time — look, we only want the right to fall in love with each other, just like you. Such sentiments made the basis for the Campaign for Homosexual Equality's education pack which was being produced around this time. It will not work.

During the two years and more that Maureen was under such intense pressure to present her sexuality first in one way and then another, she evidently changed her politics a great deal. She became steadily more vocal as a feminist in parliamentary debates, often the only woman there who would make an uncompromising statement from a feminist perspective, and who would draw out such a perspective when others preferred to lie low and not irritate the men. Gradually she sorted out a more coherent pattern for herself, one not dependent on romantic explanations alone, but one that tried to link together her commitments as a socialist, a feminist, and a lesbian who had suffered more painful public exposure than any other in recent years. "Of all the hurly-burly of the last months, what grieves you the most?" "The lack of socialism in the local labour party." "I get the impression that you are a party politician first and a lesbian second. Am I right?" "I was. But I think I'm rapidly becoming a lesbian first and a party politician second" (interview in *Gay News*, October 1978).

LESBIANS AS MOTHERS: THE AID AFFAIR

Further evidence that neither the Creator nor the papers were bored with us in 1978 was the extraordinary AID (artificial insemination by donor) scandal. Though what exactly was scandalous depended upon your politics. Was it the amazing fact that there are women who want to get pregnant without getting screwed? Or was it the incomparable deceit of a group of journalists who, instead of asking for information which was freely available, lied and cheated themselves into a position where they could make a miserable exposé?

Two journalists on the look-out for scoop copy decided that the public ought to be informed about the methods some lesbians were using to get pregnant. In a way the story contained two very popular press themes — sexual deviants (that is us) and the dreaded test tube babies. It was bound to be a big headline catcher. The female journalist subsequently went along to Sappho, the London based lesbian group (which also publishes the magazine). She took with her a woman friend, and together they posed as a lesbian couple wanting a child. Sappho put them in touch with the doctor at that time helping lesbians to become pregnant via AID. Gradually piecing their story together, they also asked to be put in touch with other lesbian parents who'd had AID children, and Sappho obligingly did so. The lesbian parents concerned were kind and supportive. The journalists now had all the names, and some photos deceitfully taken: they sprung their final trap, arriving at the Sappho office, this time with the male journalist, demanding photos of the office and of office workers. The story was due to appear within two days. Sappho did all it could to get injunctions against publication, demanding that at least the names of the lesbian parents should not be used, nor their pictures. This had some minor effect, but in the first week of January the double-page spread appeared with huge headlines: "Dr Strangelove: The *Evening News* today reveals the extraordinary and disturbing case of the London doctor who is helping lesbian couples to have babies."

In fact, the whole piece was slanted towards the "medical ethics" side of it, making the hapless doctor the main target, as if they did not quite have the courage to attack lesbians head on. Even lesbians are a little sacred, when they are mothers. However deviant a woman is, no one can deny her potential motherhood. Baby snatchers, after all, get light sentences, on account of their unsurmountable biology. The *Evening News* certainly was not going to fling the first rock.

The relationship of fallen women (like prostitutes, feminists, lesbians or women who want to go out to work, or who have to) with their children has always been a popular newspaper topic. The question of who is fit to be a mother is raised daily, often on the letters pages, where nurseries are often depicted as hell-holes for rejected children who will grow up hollow delinquents. What the papers really love is when we all give up our silly ways and return home to the children: the prostitute who falls in love, sets up a proper home, and gets her baby back out of care; the feminist who now sees the error of her ways because she's found a non-sexist man and they've got a lovely little baby; the working mother who . . . well, there's no jobs for her any more, and think how the nation will benefit from those contented children. But as for lesbians, we are a hopeless case. There is no way we can clean up our act and make ourselves acceptable (except perhaps through behaviour therapy back to heterosexuality). Wanting to have babies and even stay home with them does not bring *us* societal approval. It horrifies everyone. We refuse to behave like real women, and yet we have the cheek to want babies. Getting pregnant is only the beginning. Using AID (tampering with nature) is bad enough, but bringing up the baby . . . What horrors lie ahead for it?

Once the press began to ponder the fuller implications of all this, the "medical" ethics were submerged under rising panic at the notion that babies could be brought up in a manless (horror) world. Everybody knows that what makes healthy, loving people is a mummy *and* a daddy, and that is why the Western world today is full of such super people. Children brought up in a manless environment could only turn out to be . . . what? Now there may be some lesbians who keep their children shut in cellars to expunge from their environment any reference to men. But most of us have noticed that of all the information that daily enters our homes, men feature most predominantly. Indeed a visiting child from another culture might think, from watching our TV and reading our papers, that *only* men really existed. And when we take our children out on the streets, no doubt our children notice who is driving the buses and almost all of the cars, and who is walking about with the clipboard in Sainsbury's. Our children see men daily, and talk with them. They have men among their relatives. We even know lesbians who have men coming to visit them . . . and sometimes even living with them. The press, however, behaves as if this were all classified information.

What they were all on about during the general hysteria which followed the *Evening News* exposé was that the presence of the strong male father-figure is essential in the control of the growing child's developing sexuality. In other words, a child without a male model might grow up to be . . . well, a male model. A butch daddy is an insurance policy against queerness in the family, as all of us who've grown up gay know.

As a result of this fixation on the family's need for a male, the general assumption in the press at this time about lesbian couples was that they came in butch-femme pairs, as if we had to imitate heterosexuals to make ourselves into pseudo-parents. (The arrogance of heterosexuals in assuming everything we do is patterned on themselves passes all understanding.) That week in January paper after paper put out cartoons on the butch-femme theme. *Punch, The Observer* and *The Guardian* were among those who had drawings of two women, one in a apron, one in tweeds smoking a pipe, discussing the future of an infant in a cot. The idea that two women might specifically want to rear children as much as possible outside conventional sex-roles, totally eluded every journalist, "respectable" or otherwise, who wrote then or later on the topic. Reproduction and childrearing could only be perceived as heterosexual activities, bringing with them the whole hetero-sexist package . . . links which feminists and lesbians have been pointing out for a very long time.

Meanwhile groups of feminists invaded the *Evening News* and demanded the right to reply, which they received. The Sappho women also took the paper to the Press Council, where, in a particularly shameful judgment, considering the unnecessary and corrupt methods of journalism used and the bitter pain it caused to the lesbian parents, they were told that the *News* had acted justifiably and in the public interest.

It is true that a paper like *The Guardian* would probably never use such tacky methods to get a story. Could we then look to it to cover the matter fairly, if not favourably? The next week showed that their working methods, though subtler, were no less sensationalising and manipulative, though perhaps less visible to the eyes of those who have not much considered how stories are pieced together by journalists working to deadlines. Here they had a hot issue, which they needed to spin out a bit while seeming to be engaged in reasoned debate. Such news pieces are constructed by interspersing "factual" bits with quotes from "experts". Obviously, such experts do not come rushing in to the newsdesk with their opinions handily written down. They have to be either quoted saying their thing in a speech, or you have to phone them up and ask a few leading questions. In the first category, we had *The Guardian* quoting a well-known rightist (who campaigns for the return of capital and corporal punishment): "Dr Rhodes Boyson, MP for Brent North, called it an horrific practice" (*The Guardian*, 7 January 1978). As you see, lesbian motherhood so threatens society, I am pleased to say, that it raised questions in parliament. Now, since *The Guardian* might be expected to pride itself on balance, the journalist could have contacted another MP of less bias, or indeed Maureen Colquhoun, who at that time was being paraded as a lesbian *cause célèbre*. But instead of making any such efforts to find the middle ground (let alone anyone the least bit radical) he went steadily down his list of right-wing experts, predictable for their constant intolerance towards feminists' ideas. "Dr Mia Kellmer Pringle, director of the National Children's Bureau, also said she was concerned. Children of lesbians, she said, would suffer from having no father, which could lead to a confusion of the children's sexual identity." And just to cover the subject in depth, he then hauled in someone who really knows about wombs and babies: "Mr Ray Booth, honorary secretary of the Royal College of Obstetricians and Gynaecology, said, 'I personally find this extremely bizarre. If sex donors knew that their sperm was going to lesbians, one can't help wondering if they would think it was a good thing.'" And so, overnight, My Ray Booth swells the ranks of queerbashers, seeing his perhaps formerly repressed intolerance validated in a great national newspaper. A spokesperson is born.

Gradually more and more experts were lined up in the "better" papers to give us their theories, which all turned out more or less to feature anxieties about sperm abuse and fatherless boys. (As usual girl children got no special mention.) At last it began to dawn on men that boys might be brought up to be radically *different* from them, away from their controlling influence, and that, perhaps even worse, men's sperm can be frozen and used after they are dead, even after they are *all* dead. The terror these ideas created in their minds made them yell with panic, as well it might. Lesbian motherhood was indeed a plot to subvert the whole planet ... even though most of us hadn't planned for it to have quite that impact.

How was this terror to be abated? How was faith to be restored in the impregnability of heterosexism? We now entered the third phase of the debate. *The Observer* began it this time by featuring a lesbian AID couple with a school-aged lad (of course) who really seemed, well, awfully normal, short hair, nice manners and all that. Then followed article after article telling the world what nice, bright kids we all had, and that, as far as could be seen, they were all completely normal down below. Polly Toynbee of *The Guardian* raised the question, what *are* the qualifications for parenthood? Mental deficients and psychotics, she said, don't have to take tests before they are allowed babies, so why should lesbians? Her juxtapositions were rather a giveaway, but she did ask a telling question — what is the basic objection to us being parents, when other people make such a mess of it all the time? So far, it is straights who have produced the gays, and sane people who made all the loonies.

In order to prove that lesbians are OK as mothers she then went on to refer to various bits of research that are being done on us and our children. A researcher says, "So far we haven't found any children who appear to have been harmed by being brought up by lesbian mothers." Harmed? What were they looking for — stunted growth, nervous tics? "There seems to be no harmful effect on the children's psychosexual development." Ah! Polly Toynbee then goes on to relate how one lesbian couple (whose psychosexual development is presumably not part of the research) are now sleeping apart, so as not to "harm" the children. The main aim of this article was to reassure the reader of the children's incipient (and intact) heterosexuality, and the lesbian mothers' motherly decency in letting them be normal.

A few days later, *The Sunday Times* took up the same theme, in its Behaviour section, this time featuring American research. "Richard Green has examined twenty-one children aged between five and fourteen. He found them all distressingly normal. All-American boys and girls, choosing the games and toys and dress expected of their sex." If only they really did find this distressing. ... But the next bit definitely is: "Those old enough to report sexual fantasies were exclusively heterosexual." You can even, apparently, pry into children's inner sexual lives — if you're a heterosexual developmental psychologist. This research gives the lie to the belief widely adhered to that little children are asexual. It proves that most people believe all children, far from having no sex lives, are all basically practising (but infantile) heterosexuals, who could be "ruined" by contact with homosexuals.

Again, the conclusion of this article was that growing up in a lesbian household did not "harm" children. (It discounted, of course, the visits from the psychologists.) This sort of research will pretty soon find its way into the mausoleum crammed with comparisons between men and women's brain sizes, and black and white people's intelligence scores. One might think that reputable newspapers could pick it out a mile off.

Gossip columnists, of course, have no pretensions about the scientific. This makes their work less obscured by the aura of tolerance and respectability which we have to peer through to detect the prejudices in the work of the liberal feature writer. Jean Rook, who a few months later would be professing to be bored stiff with lesbians, was really horrified by the idea of us having babies. She devoted her column, that week in January, to explain the full facts about lesbian couples. She said that behind the cosy cat-loving exterior we are all active sex perverts. Every night, after the children are tucked up in bed, we drop all pretensions to normality. One of us gradually takes on the mentality of a man, and then we both creep up to bed and ... do it ... within hearing distance of the innocent children. (Presumably she imagines one of us yelling, "Oh, Harry, you're the champ." We are, she said, unstable, role-playing hysterics. Like her male cartoonist counterparts, she is incapable of imagining any form of sexual activity (or any relationship) which does not have people pretending to be men (and who in her book invariably are men) while others play out the role of women.

It was left to the *Morning Star* to give the only straightforward account of the original sordid incident — the sneak reporters, and the pain it caused the lesbians involved. But their reporter was also quick to emphasise the harmlessness of lesbian motherhood. "The only way lesbian's children differ is that they do not cling to one mother but go to both quite happily." Most of us would not go along with the assertion that this is the only way our children differ. The assumption is , of course, that we ourselves do not want our children to be different, but I will now blow the gaff. We do. We are not crazy about the world as it is, and we'd like our boys not to grow up into bomber pilots or our girls into animated aprons. All-American boys and girls leave us rather cold. So it does have rather more to it than just extending the mothering by adding another mommie.

The article then continued to get itself well and truly bogged down in leftist liberalism. Obviously it did not want to take *too* radical a line with its already hard-pressed readership, and after all, aren't gay rights already part of the Communist Party's overall commitment? Well, aren't they? "Many sincere people have genuine reservations about homosexuality and its implications but are willing to admit their ignorance and possible prejudice." So you can have reservations, and only possibly be prejudiced. "They would be glad to discuss the matter in an atmosphere of friendship, tolerance, and trust. The hope for such a discussion has taken a severe battering during the last fortnight of media sensationalism."

She was right, of course. Sincere (but ignorant and prejudiced) folk were henceforth refused when they proffered invitations to lesbian mothers to talk about their experiences (although, to my knowledge, local branches of the Communist Party were not among those sending out such invitations). Lesbians asked by the press at this late stage, several weeks after the initial *Evening News* article, now pointblank refused to co-operate. And twelve months later, when the British Medical Association's ethical committee was still trying to get doctors banned from carrying out AID, lesbians approached by journalists on the subject ("We'll write a sympathetic piece") remained silent. Meanwhile we go on getting pregnant in a variety of ways, and our children get on with their lives, waiting for the days of "friendship, tolerance and trust" to reach their classrooms.

FEMINISM IN SCHOOL: HOUNDING A TEACHER

It has gradually become apparent, during the stories about Maureen Colquhoun and then the lesbian mothers, that it was not just the issue of sexuality that was causing the rumpus, but that the whole area of sexual politics was, however clumsily and hysterically, being opened out. Maureen was not just a lesbian, but was persistently campaigning for both gay and women's rights, in the middle of parliament. Lesbian mothers were not just deviants, but were evidently engineering ways around nature itself, having both sex and children without the interference of men.

The fact that these women were lesbian made them into ready and legitimate targets for public criticism and disgust. Had they been *just* women's libbers, they might have been trivialised and scorned, but there would not have been the same rhetoric of outrage from the right, nor the same sense of investigative tolerance from the left.

But in this third story, the situation is reversed. This time the sexual politics of a teacher are focused upon, and her sexuality, though imputed, is not so directly under attack. Through hints and nudges, the press reports suggest that anyone who wants to teach children these things (namely that sex roles can be questioned) must be a dangerous pervert. Again, such a deduction allows the papers to lay into the teacher with such viciousness that she almost loses her job.

It began when Sally Shave, a deputy headteacher in a country primary school, wrote a piece for *Spare Rib* magazine, enumerating ten ways to fight sexism in the classroom, for example, use of non-sexist books, getting girls to take up boys' sports and so on. In fact, her list simply described what hundreds of feminist teachers try to do all the time, things which her own education authority, when goaded to take action against her, said they'd been doing for twenty-five years ... though we might find it hard to believe that.

Shortly before publication of Sally's piece in September 1978, *Spare Rib* press-released all education journalists, as this whole issue of the magazine was to be specially about schools. One such journalist, on the *Daily Express*, was particularly interested in her piece, and rang the magazine for her phone number, saying he wanted to do a sympathetic piece. He was not given the number, but was sent a full copy of the article, and he promised to send a draft of his own article to the magazine before publication.

He did not do this. Instead he began his ring-around-the-experts routine, which as usual meant the right-wing spokespeople. He rang, of course, the most retrogressive of the teachers' unions, whose comments, naturally, were that her ideas were shameful and disgusting. Thus he constructed a vicious and inflammatory article.

It appeared under a double-page headline, "Boys Will Be Boys", because of course we all know by now it is boys they are worried about. (Apparently sex-role stereotyping is so fragile that unless we are a hundred per cent vigilant against the activities of lesbians, feminists and the like, malehood will crumble). Besides the article itself, the main editorial of the day was also on Sally. "If Sally Shave, who is responsible for little children, does not mind their growing up neither men nor women, the sooner she turns her talents to working a capstan lathe or a manicurist's scissors, the better." The grammar doesn't disguise the sentiment: don't make our boys into poofters.

The day that was published, Sally was as usual in school. Before morning lessons got underway, an irate father came storming into the school , the *Express* under his arm, saying Sally was turning his daughter into an atheist. He'd always known, he said, that there was something strange about Sally, because she rode a man's bike. And he intended to lead a petition among the parents to get her sacked.

A small group of parents, along with some of the school's governors, then set about making her life as difficult as they could. The head teacher of this relatively progressive Church school at first took a fairly supportive line. He supposed she had the right to publish her opinions, though he didn't think much of *Spare Rib*. Still, he argued, unsuccessfully trying to calm his opponents, it's a "special interest" magazine, just read by a handful of feminists harmlessly dotted about the country . . . very low circulation. But the governors pressed him. Didn't he realise what she was doing? It was unnatural, it was perverted, and worst of all, it undermined discipline. Girls in her class were allowed, even encouraged, to wear trousers. And Sally, too, wore jeans all the time.

The head then asked Sally to attend a special governors' meeting to discuss the circulation of an apology to parents, and he reminded her it would be best to wear a skirt, or at least a smart pair of trousers. She came to the meeting dressed as usual. The head just couldn't see why she would not compromise. He later explained to her that she was perhaps unwise to go so openly to the local pub with her "friends" and that, although he wasn't prejudiced, the village was not ready for people of her sort.

Up to this stage in her life, Sally had defined herself as "not a banner waver", but was now being brought to the realisation that these people, who defined themselves as practising Christians, saw her as one whether she liked it or not, and were shouting out loud what she had so far been considerably discreet about — her sexuality. Meanwhile the papers went on with the story, but not one of the reporters now to take up the matter could distinguish between gender and sex-roles, and not one appeared to have the slightest grasp of the concept of sexism.

Two days after the *Express* article, Angela Ince wrote in the *Evening News*: "Parents can't help smiling fondly when they watch their daughters taking half an hour to decide which cardigan goes best with the dress she is planning to wear tomorrow. Or their small son putting on the muddy torn trousers he took off the night before because 'they're the comfortable ones'." Apparently, biology dictates even what we should wear, to the extent that showing irritation with a dithery girl or a filthy boy would be interfering with nature. While such ideas are fairly basic to everyday journalism, what then followed was a much more serious imputation, especially at a period of high teacher unemployment, as it virtually asked her employers to sack her: "You only have to think how worried you'd be if it was the other way around (i.e. *dithery boy and dirty girl*) to realise what pernicious rubbish Sally Shave is talking. And to wonder why Hertfordshire education authorities allow her to practise her half-baked theories."

But this was not the end of the pernicious rubbish and half-baked theories poured out about Sally. The following weekend, the *Sunday Express* plunged in with a piece so unbelievably garbled that you could laugh aloud in your incredulity — unless you were Sally, back in the Hertfordshire village, fighting for your job and your sanity. "Those teachers who as reported last week are trying to blur the distinction between boys and girls have a lot to learn. The trouble with these fanatical reformers like these non-sexist nuts is that they throw out the baby with the bath water and in their fervour to sweep away everything that is bad about discrimination, they sweep away everything that is good too. Equal opportunity is one thing because it offers choice. Being bulldozed into total sameness is quite another. If the non-sexist lot had their way, girls would be made to feel inadequate if they follow their age-old instincts to attract a mate, set up home, have babies and devote their life to looking after all three. This is not imposed upon them. It is as natural in girls as in a plant or a robin." This is, of course, of tremendous interest to feminist botanists. And at least, for once, it shows anxiety about girls, rather than boys . . . though the writer doesn't think lesbianism will result, only feelings of deprivation from housework.

Finally, Sally's story appeared in the local Hertfordshire paper, but she and *Spare Rib* had already sent them a warning letter, reminding them not to libel her professionally. As a result, a fairly palliative but front-page piece appeared, which concentrated on assuring parents that the boys taught by Sally were turning out unharmed. The girls got no mention. The headmaster was quoted at length, reminding readers that it was his boys, some of whom were in Sally's class, who'd recently won the local football tournament. What better masculinising accreditation could there be than that?

And so the story died, having lasted about five weeks in that 1978 autumn. Meanwhile Sally stayed on at the school, trying, unsuccessfully, for several other posts, and like the other women in this chapter, cautious about ever sharing her ideas openly again.

CONCLUSIONS

We felt at the time, and we are certain now with hindsight, that by 1978 the tentative tolerance shown towards gays was being withdrawn. Indeed, it had been so tentative that most of us had hardly noticed it in any practical sense, especially those trying to be "out" *and* hold jobs, or those of us bringing up children. The focus of the right, then very much on the rise, might have been primarily classist and racist, but there was also a fast growing reaction against feminism, and against those gays engaging, in whatever ways, in the struggle against sexism and sex role stereotyping. And even on the left, as we have seen here, there was a thin layer of benign patronage hardly disguised as real contempt for gay and feminist politics, as any of us knows who has raised those issues through the unions, or who has tried to carry their banner in among the union ones on mass demonstrations.

1978 was not a backlash year for lesbians, for there had never been any real let-up of hostility towards us. What happened was more of a bubbling to the surface of attitudes we were already well acquainted with, but had perhaps been slightly lulled into feeling were in abeyance. After all, it was 1978. But it was rising anxieties about the *implications* of feminist ideas and practice, in these three particular incidents, which led to these public manifestations of disgust with our sexuality, implications which both the right and left stood appalled by. Given that entrepreneurial rightism was rapidly making its way back into government at the time, homophobic and misogynist views were finding validation alongside anti-unionism, hardening of attitudes towards the poor and the welfare state, and newly rampant racism.

The newly respectable racist line was that we would be nice to the ones who were (unfortunately) here already, but we didn't want any more. This was rapidly becoming institutionalised in new nationality and immigration legislation. (Such legislation also contains discriminatory clauses to keep out homosexuals.) And in the anti-lesbian stories of 1978, we have clear evidence of the same "OK, that's enough" policy — they know they can't do much about those of us who are here now, but they want to be sure we don't make any more, as lesbian politicians, mothers and teachers. At times of rising economic and ideological crisis, tolerance is only extended towards the scapegoated groups if they promise to shut up, limit their numbers and integrate.

1978 marked the end of an era in gay rights, one in which, temporarily, public pillorying of homosexual men had somewhat abated in the wake of the "sexual revolution", while public mention of lesbians continued to be taboo. But now in retrospect we can see how it was that lesbian bashers leapt through these oddly intertwined restrictions, giving prominent space to attacks that were soon to take a more materialist shape under the openly rightist state of the following year.

Throughout 1979 we were to see massive cuts in public spending, and withdrawal of paid work from the mass of women, as well as closure of nurseries and extensive pro-family propaganda. In such a climate, those who seriously challenge women's subservience to men, and men's dictates on what sexuality consists of, are bound to find themselves targets of abuse and public punishment. Perhaps the strangest factor of all in these stories was that none of the women directly concerned had actually planned or intended to make such a conscious challenge — it was dragged from them by the people who feared it most, people who had suspected, rightly, for a long time, that there were inextricable and revolutionary links between lesbianism and feminism.

Note: Some of the material in this chapter is closely based on work already published in *Spare Rib.* Many thanks to Maureen Colquhoun and to Sally Shave, and to all lesbian mothers, for going through it all again.

14

The Politics of Gay Culture

DEREK COHEN and RICHARD DYER

There are few moments of our lives when we are not assailed by myriad forms of popular and select culture in our society. Much of this is deemed superficial or a mere distraction, but whether it be television, theatre, music or advertising, culture at once shapes our identity, tells us about the world, gives us a certain set of values and entertains us. The purpose of this article is to examine gay culture and its politics.

Before doing this however we want briefly to consider a prior question — what are the *politics* of culture? All too often this phrase, familiar enough in recent years on the left, simply means drawing up a balance sheet as to how right-on such and such a work of art is. But this still leaves culture inert — an expression that we approve of (or not) from our political perspective, but not something that actually does political work in the world, alongside leafleting, demonstrating, lobbying, picketing and so on. Yet while culture cannot, as some cultural workers fondly hope, by itself change the world, as part of a programme of political work it has certain key functions to perform. To begin with, it has a role that necessarily precedes any self-conscious political movement. Works of art express, define and mould experience and ideas, and in the process make them visible and available. They thus enable people to recognise experience as shared and to confront definitions of that experience. This represents the starting point for a forging of *identity* grounded in where people are situated in society, in whatever strata. This sense of social identity, of belonging to a group, is a prerequisite for any political activity proper, even when that identity is not recognised as political. This role for culture has perhaps a special relevance for gay people, because we are "hidden" and "invisible". For many of us, reading about, say, David and Jonathan, or seeing *The Killing of Sister George,* is one of the few ways of identifying other homosexually inclined persons. Without that moment of identification, no other political practice is possible.

Secondly, culture is part of that more conscious process of making sense of the world that all political movements are involved in. This process is the social group's production of *knowledge* about itself and its situation. Cultural production is more orientated to the affective, sensuous and experimental, whereas theory and research are more concerned with the analysis of situation, conjuncture, strategy and tactics — but both are forms of knowledge. Traditionally, analytic work is upgraded relative to cultural production, usually because the latter is considered to produce less useful knowledge. We do not need to detail here how crippling this restriction of knowledge to the analytical and cerebral has been — for our purposes, it is enough to insist on the role of culture in a group's total political intelligence.

Thirdly, all cultural production is some form of *propaganda*. We should not flinch at this word. While in practice much propaganda is simplistic and manipulative, it is not defined by these qualities. Rather propaganda is *committed* culture, which recognises its own committedness, and enjoins the audience to share its commitment. Political work is unthinkable without it. (All culture is committed, but most makes out that it is uncommitted. To be committed to non-commitment is at best fence-sitting and at worst acceding to the status quo.) Finally, related to but distinct from propaganda, culture is in general pleasurable. We tend to ignore *pleasure* as part of the business of politics — at our peril. At a minimum pleasure clearly allied to politics keeps us going, recharges our batteries. More positively, the pleasure of culture gives us a glimpse of where we are going and helps us to enjoy the struggle of getting there.

We shall be using these four concepts of the politics of culture — identity, knowledge, propaganda and pleasure — in the rest of this article. We begin by suggesting some working definitions of culture, and their particular relevance to homosexuality. In the next section, we look at what we term "traditional" (predominantly male) gay culture and then in the following section consider contemporary "radical" gay culture. In the final section we look at the relationship between these two modes of gay culture and what each has to learn from the other.

The distinction between "traditional" and "radical" gay cultural modes, though conceptually and historically valid, also springs from our two different experiences. This difference can best be indicated by the contrast in how we come out as gay — one of us by learning and adopting camp behaviour and taste before the advent of the gay liberation movement, the other coming out straight into the gay movement and the already altered gay world. For this reason, in the section on "traditional" gay culture (largely written by Richard Dyer) and "radical" gay culture (largely written by Derek Cohen), we draw on our respective personal experiences of growing up and coming out into these different cultural situations. As the area we are dealing with needs considerable research to move beyond the tentative ideas put forward here, we hope these personal accounts may serve as testimony for more sustained work in the future.

Any full definition of the word culture has to go beyond the arts to the products and practices of what Raymond Williams calls "a whole way of life". What this means in terms of homosexuality — the gay subcultures and their relation to other aspects of the social formation — is discussed elsewhere in this book, and we are therefore deliberately confining ourselves to that area more or less loosely referred to as "the arts". These tend to be those things that are either produced (e.g. sculpture) or performed (e.g. dance), rather than experienced or transmitted (e.g. ways of talking).

The philosophical problems of defining such an area need not delay us here. We imagine everyone will know the kinds of thing we are talking about. We would however want to make two qualifications. First, we want to use the word "culture" to avoid the snob connotations of the word "art". Second, it is clear that culture in the narrow sense in which we are using it nevertheless depends upon and is part of culture in the wider sense of "a whole way of life". Specifically in relation to gays and culture, and gay culture, what particular artefacts and performances mean, how they feel, depends upon how they are situated within the gay subculture(s). Drag acts depend for their appreciation upon an understanding of the semi-closeted gay atmosphere of many of the pubs and clubs where they are performed, and the ambiguous relationships of the men in the audience to the man/pseudo-woman on the stage. Many lesbian singers refer to aspects of gay life in their songs, and the powerful resonances come from the way they are touching on the lives of women in the audience.

In trying to do a review of gay culture it becomes apparent that there are other divisions within society which overlay gay people. The differences between lesbian and gay male culture reflect the different positions of women and men in society. Gay men have, for all their oppression, gained practically all the advantages of men generally. Men's work is valued above the work of women, even when that work is identical (men are chefs, women just cooks) and this is also true of cultural production. Men have always had greater access to culture, both as producers, where their greater material assets have enabled them to have a greater access to resources, and as consumers, as far as the working class is concerned, with men having more leisure time as compared with the all-consuming domestic labour of women. Thus while we may be able to identify, through history, homosexual tendencies in artists, sculptors, writers etc., these are nearly always men. Lesbian culture has suffered from the same invisibility as women's culture generally, and is emerging within that framework.

Class is another largely determining factor in culture. If we use definitions of culture which preclude those things which are at the same time associated with work, which concentrate on the fine arts, theatre, opera, ballet etc., working-class culture becomes invisible. Once we extend into work-associated culture, we find many examples of working-class culture, from barge-painting to ornamentation in architecture to street cries and drinking songs. We know about the historical development of culture by what lasts, and by and large what is made to last is élite culture. Gays seeking their roots are bound to use élite cultures as part of their so-called heritage, and the lack of working-class culture in this heritage reinforces the tendency to upwards mobility among gay men.

TRADITIONAL GAY MALE CULTURE

If one turns to the centre pages of *Gay News*, one finds the "culture" section. Anyone unfamiliar with the gay scene might be forgiven for finding this section puzzling in some regards. It's obvious enough why there should be reviews of plays, books and films that deal with homosexuality in their subject matter, or else are known to have been produced by gay people. But why all these other reviews, page after page of reviews of classical records, ballet, cabaret artists etc.? Although it is certainly the case that gays have no more instinct for culture than any other group in society *Gay News* moved swiftly and unerringly to this broad coverage in its pages, as indeed have other gay publications. Such publishing ventures grew out of the tastes of a metropolitan male gay milieu — *Gay News* and the rest helped to solidify and define this culture as gay culture itself, and hence to reinforce in a certain measure the notion that this culture, very narrowly rooted in social terms, was what gays "spontaneously" turned to.

In literature, the characteristic mode of gay cultural production has been that of the minor literati — e.g. Christopher Isherwood, Robin Maugham, J. R. Ackerley. That is, gay men working within established middle-class literary modes, and writing very "well" within them, but always restricting their literary ambitions to the small-scale and exquisite.

The arts of opera, ballet, certain painters and sculptors and antiques, have for so long been thought of as gay preserves that, for instance, Noel Coward could make a risqué reference in his adaptation of Cole Porter's song "Let's Do It" by singing "Nice young men who sell antiques/Do it". These arts have, like that of the minor literati, an ambiguous place in bourgeois high culture. Recognised as Art, and subsidised as such, there is still a strong current of opinion that does not quite take them seriously as Art — not compared to the kind of non-musical theatre subsidised by the Arts Council or the kinds of art hung and displayed in national and municipal galleries. Ballet — with its association with women as well a gay men — has suffered particularly from this ambiguity.

Not all traditional gay male culture is highbrow, however. Show business traditions especially cabaret and musicals (stage and screen), are part of the canon. Among the most characteristic icons here are the flamboyant/tragic singers such as Judy Garland, Diana Ross *et al.* (compare the reperoire of Craig Douglas in the film *Outrageous!*). Central here are drag and camp, the most well-known and obvious aspects of traditional gay male culture in its showbiz inflection. Finally, somewhere between highbrow Art and showbiz come the areas of "taste", such as couture, coiffure, interior decoration and so on.

Before proceeding, it is worth stressing that this set of cultural artefacts and practices is not identical with the work of gay artists and cultural workers. On the contrary, some of the above may have been produced by non-homosexual women and men, while much culture produced by gay men clearly stands outside, or in an ambivalent relationship to, the gay subcultural mainstream under discussion here. The many gay male ballet dancers and choreographers do not seem to have made many inroads on the heterosexual assumptions of most ballet scenarios and forms of movement. Traditional gay culture essentially refers to a distinct way of reading and enjoying culture, and hence involves both gay and non-gay products.

For me, growing up gay and getting into this sort of culture felt like the same process, namely the process of establishing an identity. It was summed up for me in the word "queer". Being queer meant being homosexual, but also being different. It is easy to see how easily I formed an equation between this and being interested in culture. In an all-boys school in the late fifties and early sixties, culture was as peculiar, as "other", as being queer. To begin with, the connection between culture and queerness was spatial — culture seemed to be a place where you were allowed to be queer. This is partly because I had picked up on the folklore about cultural milieux being full of, or tolerating, queers. Ballet and hairdressing above all, but coteries of painters and writers, for instance, were supposed to be very queer. At a minimum, the world of culture just seemed to be a place you could go if you were queer.

My sense that this was a place for me was confirmed by three people. One was a teacher at school, whose shelves were full of books like *Mr Norris Changes Trains* and *Death in Venice,* books which he lent me and I read avidly as I have never read books since for their revelations of decadence. But the real point was that they were Penguin Modern Classics — they were Art, not just books. This teacher also implied a knowledge of gay cultural circles and when he got married (an event which rather confused me) I went to the wedding party and met a poet, a composer, an actor, all queer. The culture-queerness connection was made, and it was confirmed by the first man who ever picked me up. He took me home to a flat in Chelsea full of books and paintings. He and his flatmate discussed cultural matters that meant nothing to me, but impressed me. Eventually I asked him what he did for a living. "I'm a writer," he replied. "What sort of things do you write?" I asked. "Novels." "What sort?" "Surrealist." (Again, not just books.) "What's that mean?" "Do you know Kafka?" "Ye-es." "Well, it's like that." Thirdly, my first real friend who was gay had been in the theatre, although he now runs a coffee bar. In a way, Michael was different because what he was really into was showbiz, but the point was that he was from the world of culture. All queers were in those days.

Culture was the place to go — and a way out. The attraction of culture, to begin with, was just that it was an apparently liberal, tolerant milieu, where you could be queer. That much I had picked up from gossip and the mass media, as well as my few encounters with other queers. (The gossip included the usual dirt on Shakespeare, Wilde, Tchaikovsky, Gielgud and the rest; but I also remember eagerly reading Freud's book on Leonardo da Vinci, without any knowledge of psychoanalysis, while on a school trip to Italy.) Homosexuality was also the subject-matter of a fair amount of literature, to an extent that was not true of the kind of films I had access to, or of television. (I remember the curious sense of pride I felt when in my first term at university the lecturer started on about Gide's characters.) There was no place else that I could identify as "riddled with it", no place that seemed at least to accord queerness recognition.

Culture was also attractive in ways that went beyond the fact that its practitioners and subject-matter were queer, but ways which were still crucially related to queerness. Culture was beautiful, sensuous, fun. This is true anyway, as is people's use of it as escape. My involvement in culture certainly included enjoyment and escape, but the kind of culture I got into accorded more precisely with what I thought about being queer. I was into high culture. Actually, I found this quite an effort — I was really into the *idea* of high culture, while in practice preferring Michael's showbiz. I didn't come from an artistic or even particularly cultured background, and although I got myself into "serious" music and literature, I never had any spontaneous response to painting and sculpture. But nevertheless I thought of myself as someone capable of appreciating high culture. I would sit painfully through Antonioni films and assure everyone of how "beautiful" they were. I was keen on things being beautiful.

All this was connected to being queer; indeed, it was part of being queer. Queerness brought with it artistic sensitivity — it gave you the capacity to appeciate and respond to culture. It was a compensation for having been born or made queer; it was a positive to set beside the negative of being queer, with which it was inextricably bound up. Being into beauty was also part and parcel of the mechanism of self-oppression, because I defined my cultural sensitivity as a compensatory *product* of being queer. It also made you doubly "different" — queer and cultured. And how splendid to be different! Even if you were awful.

This sense of being different certainly locked me into ways of thinking about myself — as queer, as cultured — which reinforced my self-oppression, for further reasons that I will explore in a moment. But it did have relatively positive consequences, too. It made me feel myself as "outside" the mainstream in fundamental ways — and this does give you a kind of knowledge of the mainstream you cannot have if you are immersed in it. I do not necessarily mean a truer perspective, so much as an awareness of the mainstream as a mainstream, and not just the way everything and everybody inevitably are; in other words, it denaturalises normality. This knowledge is the foundation of camp, to which I took like a duck to water, since camp is so much about the exaggeration and send-up of normality. Camp's roots in showbiz also gave it a vitality that saved it from the rather anaemic qualities of some of the high gay culture. Feeling different also gave me identity, a real sense of queers as a social group — an advantage later on when I got into the gay movement, although actually a rather problematical concept, since homosexuality is so much more fluid an aspect of human beings than class, gender or race.

One other thing needs to be said about the attractions of the artistic=-queer=different equation — its snobbism. At best, being different and proud of it gave me a defence against the blandishments of the middle-class, masculine society around me — who wants to be like *that*? But because it involved getting into high culture, at least notionally, it meant getting into bourgeois culture, and of the most apolitical sort. This was ultimately the problem for me and perhaps why I never took this gay route out all the way. I loathed the middle classes in a way that only those brought up by them can; and culture is curiously placed in relation to them, despised and honoured at the same time. I found too that gay men who were really into high culture could be extraordinarily reactionary and snobbish. I do not want to give the impression that I was a worked-out, right-on socialist from the cradle; but I did "care about" the poor and the starving, about war and privilege. I could not sort it all out — being into culture and against privilege — but I was never able to hold both things together, and in the process high art lost out, somewhat.

Culture was not just an attractive place to go, it also seemed the right place. I have already mentioned that artistic sensitivity seemed to be part of what being queer was all about. It gave one a sense of beauty, a sense of being outside — and a sense of pain. The kind of poetry I liked at the time was full of the melancholy recognition of the awfulness of the world. A. E. Housman was the perfect poet for me to come across (introduced to me by a closet gay French teacher who kept quoting him in lessons) with its melancholy allusions to being queer, along with other sad things. "Melancholy" was one of my favourite words; I felt it summed up my condition, for it caught — and here is the real trap — that peculiar mixture of pain and beauty that I took to be the "condition" of homosexuality. In other words, artistic melancholy, part of being queer, reconciled me and even bound me to that very definition of homosexuality encapsulated in the word queer.

But the rightness of being cultured and hence queer, or vice-versa, went further into an area I still have not disentangled. Somehow to me cultural sensitivity was "feminine"; and being queer was not being a man — that was why the two went together.

This obviously involves a particular conception of male homosexuality (and of course of femininity); it also involves a particular conception of culture, precisely by linking it to femininity. It stresses culture as concerned with social manners and domesticity (not work, or Big Subjects); culture is "expressive", not useful or instrumental; culture is affective, sensuous, even passionate, but not intelligent or, perhaps, finally serious. This way of seeing culture — which means attending especially to certain kinds of culture — raises theoretical and empirical questions and political ones. The former require elaboration and research, to come to grips with how culture is placed in relation to gender in this society. The political questions are contradictory. It is clear that, as I experienced it then, the equation of artistic queerness with femininity downgraded both femininity and me. I negate myself by identifying with women (hence refusing my biological sex), and then put myself down by internalising the definition of female qualities as inferior — for the values I was brought up with were those of work, instrumentality and seriousness, values I still feel the pull of. Yet, with the women's and gay movements, it became possible to turn these values on their heads while preserving that art-gayness-femininity link. Only now one was asserting the inherent seriousness of "small" subjects (in the slogan, "the personal is political"), identifying the repressiveness of a life so focused on instrumentality and seriousness, so afraid of or unable to handle emotion and sensuality.

The traditional gay male culture was never knowingly political, and fully effective political movements have to be self-conscious movements. Nevertheless, this traditional culture did and does have political significance. It provided a space and, however maimed, a definition/recognition of homosexuality, and thus constituted one homosexual identity. There is real knowledge there, too. Directly, traditional gay culture has the capacity to see the constructedness of gender identities, to feel the sensuousness of role play and sexual behaviour, to respond to sensuousness and fun. We can also gain knowledge from it (if we pose the right questions of it) about how self-oppression works, the relation between culture and gender and so on. Finally, and not opportunistically, the fact is that many gay men are into this form of culture, for better or worse, and thus it is in a manner part of the constituency of gay politics. It is one of the languages in which propaganda can speak; it is one of the grounds in which the pleasure of politics can be rooted. Whatever its limitations, we have to work with it in order to move beyond it.

RADICAL GAY CULTURE

The same period which saw the emergence of a self-defining, self-asserting "gay" identity, as opposed to a furtive or concealed "homosexual" one, also saw the beginnings of attempts to bring together the isolated experiences of lesbians and gay men that had for so long been separated. Visual, written and performance arts were seen as channels through which those who had "come out" and who had some positive things to say about their experiences as homosexuals could communicate to others, whether they were gay or not.

This self-conscious culture differs from the traditional one, even when this is on rare occasions affirming of homosexuality, in its ability to look critically at our experiences without being condemning, to be self-aware rather than descriptive from the outside. The reason for this lies, most obviously, in the fact that the (homo)sexuality of the artists is an integral, rather than incidental or hidden aspect of the work. In the film *Word is Out* many of the lesbians and gay men who spoke about their experiences talked of the role-playing that used to go on between gay couples, and as a viewer I felt that these gay people were not putting down those experiences, but speaking from a more self-aware, less constrained position. The lesbian theatre group *Hormone Imbalance*'s satire of lesbian stereotypes extended well beyond their name (a reference to a supposed cause of lesbianism) to a chilling song by Lottie and Ada called "You don't know what it's like to be revolting" portraying the very worst fears of what lesbians are like: predatory, deranged, "dildo users, child abusers...". The Brixton Faeries' play about the Jeremy Thorpe case, *Minehead Revisited*, was created not out of a sense of revelling in the misfortunes of someone famous, but because the case was having consequences in the daily lives of the actors. The company felt able to respond to the Thorpe affair, where gay activists felt caught between wanting to condemn Thorpe's tactics whilst not consequently putting down his homosexuality. Lesbian and gay male singers can assert that it's not enough just to come out, even to be a conventional commercially successful out gay rock star like Tom Robinson. One must, like Ova (a lesbian duo), challenge the very concepts of being successful in terms that are defined by male heterosexual values. Rather than try to compile some sort of list of alternative gay cultures, it seems more useful to look first at what marks off radical gay culture from non-radical treatments of homosexuality, and secondly to look at ways in which gays have tried to exploit cultural production and consumption in a political way.

Whereas much conventional handling of homosexuality in the arts works by introducing gay characters or images into an otherwise heterosexual milieu, radical gay culture defines its own situation. A lesbian or gay character in a TV play (or even soap opera series) does not constitute gay culture. We are presented there as objects to be consumed. Radical gay culture sees our *experiences* as being central. In a paradoxical sense, as one of the essentials of our experience as gays is our alienation from society, any culture which attempts in some "liberal" way to include us fails to portray our experiences accurately. That very assimilation, as if we were the same as everyone else but different in one minor way, shows a preoccupation with the surfaces, with the physicality of our homosexuality, and not the dynamics of our interaction with the rest of society. For if it were to recognise that interaction for what it is, an oppressive one, it would also have to recognise its own role in that oppression.

Even where an appreciation of the experience of being outside is allowed, it is compartmentalised, almost sanitised. This week a gay character, next week a black one. For example, the kind of fuss that attended the presentation of a television play about men (*Coming Out*) reveals just the separation that we are challenging. We will know that we are gaining ground when serious presentation of our oppression on TV is such a commonplace that it coheres with the rest of the characterisations and presentations. At that time such productions could only make sense if the forces we fight against were also presented seriously and accurately. However commercially motivated, arts do not present and endorse material that is critical of their own practice, including their contributions to gay oppression.

Radical gay culture can play a key role in the development of a gay indentity. When I started coming out one of the handicaps I had to overcome was having only a stereotypical view of what gays were like and how they lived. Thus I was quite fortunate that at that time the original "Homosexual Acts" season started at the Almost Free Theatre in London. Those plays presented a number of scenarios of gay men's lives. They served a number of functions for me. Firstly they were informative, conveying the dynamics of gay men's lives — jealousy, seduction, loneliness, comradeship etc. While talking to other gay men might have given me some ideas about how they lived and conducted their relationships, unless I knew some of them quite well (which I didn't) I would not have gained much deep insight into the joys and conflicts of being gay and relating to other gay men. Those plays provided me with that privileged view of some (fictional) lives.

That season of plays also provided a focus for meeting other gay people. A season that was so blatant in its declaration of the subject of the plays was bound to attract a high proportion of gays, and there was a chance to feel, for that period at least, that there was something of a shared positive experience among the audience. The characters in some of the plays enjoined us to share their good feelings and their bad ones. As I remember, some of the plays involved sequences where the characters addressed either the audience as a whole or supposed members of it. Homosexuality was not something being examined in a test tube, separate from reality, but as an experience shared by the characters and the audience. In addition, the season was something I could take my non-gay friends to, an entertainment where, for once, *I* was on home ground.

The close link between performers and audience meant not just that culture was close to me, but also that I was close to culture. The easier access to these performers meant that I could bask, ever so slightly, in the glow of their fame.

This is not to idealise the season; all the actors denied that they were gay, and some parts of the plays were extremely self-oppressive. The achievement and the power was in having a season called "Homosexual Acts" — the word was on the streets not in the form of political sloganeering or snide media abuse, but as an integral part of entertainment.

When gay people define their own artistic environments, as opposed to slotting in to traditional ones, they can move beyond art which is purely description from the outside. An exhibit at a gay photographic exhibition contrasted a collage of photographs of naked men from porn magazines with a picture of a line of naked gay men arm in arm at a gay men's weekend. We could note more than the difference in posture, and reflect on the contradictions in our own lives as gay men between the objectification we often promote of other men's bodies, and the pleasure we can experience in just being with other gay men in a close physical situation. The basic acceptance of homosexuality which permeates radical gay culture allows us to question ourselves and be challenged by that culture into new ways of thinking. For gays in small towns who cannot support many of their own gay cultural events, the visit of a gay theatre group or musicians, for example, can provide a focus for the start of further development of local activities. The small scale of much gay culture, arising partly out of financial necessity, enables it to be mobile and to counter the concentration of good events in the big cities.

Because radical gay culture is rooted in both a radical tradition and a cultural one, it can challenge us to reconsider the notions we have accepted of homosexuality (our own), politics and entertainment as being separate elements in our lives. Pleasure, propaganda and the personal can be combined in one experience.

THE CONTEMPORARY SCENE

In order to make our point at all, we have had to pose the traditional and radical gay cultures as being utterly separate. They are distinguishable phenomena, but we need now to look at inter-relations, overlaps and blurred edges, especially in the contemporary scene.

For a start, the very terms "traditional" and "radical" need qualifying. The traditional culture is not necessarily reactionary (as its opposition to radical might seem to imply) — it has simply been around longer and is not defined by its self-conscious political orientation. The traditional culture could be very radical, whether in terms of artistic innovation (e.g. Diaghilev, Eisenstein), political affiliation (e.g. Oscar Wilde, André Gide, Christopher Isherwood) or simply in being blatantly homosexual (e.g. Quentin

Crisp, many drag acts). Equally, "radical" as a term covers a multitude of differences. There is radicalism that links sexual politics to other kinds of politics (e.g. Tom Robinson, lesbian left revue) and radicalism that confines itself to the assertion and development of gay identities (e.g. *Word is Out, The Front Runner*). There is radicalism that remains aesthetically conservative (e.g. *Outrageous!, Bent*) and another that is formally innovative (Virginia Woolf, Joe Orton). There is radicalism whose style and tone derive basically from other, not gay, forms of radical culture production (e.g. *The Dear Love of Comrades,* Barbie Norden), and radicalism that is deeply and/or ambivalently involved in traditional gay cultural forms (*As Time Goes By*, the Brixton Faeries, *Nighthawks*).

These overlaps in the meanings of the terms "traditional" and "radical" tally with the actual inter-relations between the two streams, since the emergence of the radical culture with the development of gay liberation politics in the seventies. We will consider briefly here the use of the traditional culture by the radical, the impact of radical gay politics on the traditional culture, and the emergence of a third stream of gay culture.

As has already been noted, much radical gay culture has drawn on the traditional culture for its imagery. This can be traced back to cultural production before the advent of gay liberation, for instance in the "underground" films of Andy Warhol, Kenneth Anger, Jack Smith, Ron Rice and others. While by no means socialist, nor informed by gay liberation ideas (how could they be?), such films were rooted both in gay male imagery and lifestyles and in the concerns of avant-garde film-making, and the latter acted back on the former in different ways so that these films were not simply another example of gay culture but in a kind of dialogue with it, now ironic, now critical, now celebratory. It is this creative tension between the traditional and the radical forms that characterises some of the most interesting contemporary work. Gay Sweatshop's men's company from *Mister X* to *As Time Goes By* remained ambivalently — but also productively — locked into certain traditions of theatrical and cinematic camp. Jan Oxenburg's film *Comedy in Six Unnatural Acts* draws on a whole range of references, from camp, the lesbian subculture and the mass media in an exploration of the definitions and understandings of that social category, the lesbian. Such examples are not only using a language many gay people can feel is their own, but are also working on it, examining it, helping us to reflect on it.

Not all the radical gay culture is informed by this, nor would we want it to be. Oxenburg notwithstanding, it does seem that lesbian radical culture in particular has developed in a rather different direction to gay male radical culture. Lesbian radical culture is a component of feminist culture, and particularly the adaptation of the confessional novel (e.g. *Rubyfruit Jungle,* Marge Piercy) and contemporary folk songs (e.g. Holly Near, Chris Williamson) that characterises much feminist cultural production. These two forms lend themselves to a feminist inflection — the novel is one of the few art forms to which women have always had relatively greater access and which is to a large degree defined by a socially developed approach to the personal and the individual (as feminism is); contemporary folk song not only had women stars from early on (Joan Baez, Judy Collins, Joni Mitchell) and deploys readily available artistic means (voice and simple guitar) but is associated with the peace movement and its receptivity to "feminine" ideas (hippy lifestyle, flower power etc.). One can even present this difference between lesbian and gay male radical culture as a polarisation of sensibilities — the emphasis on self-reflexivity and artifice in working on camp, as opposed to the stress on authenticity (the hallmark of the confessional novel) and naturalness (the folk song ethos) in feminist culture. While this would ignore key overlap figures, it is a real difference of tendency between the two.

The radical gay cultures relate in different ways to the traditional — now working on it, now ignoring it and finding a more valid reference point in progressive and alternative cultural modes outside the gay world. The kind of politics that informs this radical gay culture has also had an impact on the continued life of the traditional culture. It has even given the traditional culture a new confidence in itself. *Gay News, After Dark, Mandate, Q, Blueboy* and other such publications continue to find opera, old Hollywood and so on their most salient cultural reference points, but this goes along with a degree of campaigning (or at any rate complaint) and an acknowledgement that the readership is homosexual (though *After Dark* is still uneasy about this). Unlike the Brixton Faeries or *Comedy in Six Unnatural Acts,* this new confidence rarely extends to taking a critical distance from the traditional culture — it merely asserts the homosexual connection where previously it was implicit: it seldom asks why this connection is there, or what it means.

Between the growth of the radical gay cultures and the renewal of the traditional, and perhaps as a result of them, there has been the emergence of a gay mainstream culture, operating in neither the alternative modes of the radical culture nor the subcultural languages of the traditional. This mainstream culture signals the presence of gay expression in the wider general culture of the society, and it takes three forms in particular. First, there is the increased and confident use of straight artistic forms for gay content — the detective novel (e.g. Joseph Hansen), the sentimental/romantic novel (e.g. *The Front Runner,* Gordon Merrick), the thriller movie (*Dog Day Afternoon,* the TV movie *The Ice Palace*). These of course are no longer necessarily gay culture, in the sense of being produced directly out of a gay experience or perspective. Their value is hard to assess too — they do insist on the humanity of gay people, on the possibility of having gays as heroes or at any rate people you can identify with — but the price is often the avoidance of the gay liberation politics of experimentation with gender identities and lifestyles, and of a wider vision of social and sexual transformation. It is hard to know whether we can move beyond the immediate value the mainstream culture offers of helping us to feel good about ourselves and see ourselves as having a social role, or whether this very quality does not precisely block off more completely the wider perspective.

Secondly, television programmes such as *Rock Follies* and *Soap*, themselves relatively experimental in terms of television, have been able to include gay characters whose lives have been treated with the same seriousness (of lack of it) as the other characters, while at the same time always holding on to the specificities of being gay. Because these programmes have developed new forms of narrative and characterisation they are more easily able to sidestep the usual unquestioned heterosexist assumptions of what is good family entertainment.

The other mainstream development has to be disco culture. Although not always visibly gay — even Sylvester and Village People need not be perceived in that light — it has established not only a form of social recreation but an aesthetic that is unthinkable apart from notions of gay culture. It draws heavily on black music and dance, and on white (heterosexual) popular song, but equally it is informed by the theatricalism, sensuality and fun of traditional male gay culture and something of the rethinking of sexuality occasioned by the sexual politics of the seventies (though it is not yet clear whether "liberation", or its patriarchal capitalist version "permissiveness", is what disco ultimately asserts).

There is a sense in which all these developments — the radical gay cultures, the continuing traditional male gay culture and the new mainstream forms — are politically significant and even to a degree to be welcomed. At a minimum they further help establish homosexual identities, which we can work with, or if need be against, politically. They are all identifiably homosexual, while at the same time offering a variety of ways of socially expressing and communicating their different roots, and they provide us with a wider knowledge of how it feels — how it *can* feel — to be queer, lesbian, homosexual, gay, and hence a wider field for investigation of how people live out and make sense of their sexuality. It is important to listen to this variety of gay cultural voices, and not to think that the one we individually use most comfortably is *the* voice of gay culture. We must listen for the knowledge of each other and of social definitions that they contain; and we must use the voices, in propaganda, to widen the constituency of gay and sexual politics. We must acknowledge the different pleasures that each form offers, and hence embrace their manifold political potential. This is not to say that anything goes, that anything which comes vaguely under the banner of gay culture is fine and wonderful. Rather we would want to say that within the distinctions between the broad *kinds* of gay culture that we have outlined, there is politically effective and politically ineffective, reactionary and revolutionary cultural production. But at the most general level each has much to learn from the other — the political vision and daring of the radical culture and the mass appeal of the mainstream, the awareness of artifice of the traditional culture and the commitment to authenticity of the radical. It is starting within these terms, taking each mode at its strongest point, that a socialist gay culture is constructed.

15

Here, who are you calling a lesbian? Some thoughts on lesbians in literature

ALISON HENNEGAN

Some ten years ago I embarked — with more enthusiasm than prudence — upon a Ph.D. thesis ringingly entitled *Literature and the Homosexual Cult, 1890-1920.* Blowing the dust off it now and turning its (unfinished) pages — occasionally with a frisson of unexpected pleasure at a neatly turned phrase, more often with a shudder of embarrassment at a resoundingly empty one — what strikes me most is how many of its basic questions remain unanswered. Invited some months ago by the *Gay Left* collective to "write us something on the lesbian in literature", I recognised uneasily even as I accepted that some of those questions would have to be asked again with little reason to suppose that, this time, the answers would be any easier to find.

First, and always, who is she, this lesbian in literature? And do we mean the lesbian *in* it, or the lesbian who writes it? Or both? Will I know her when I see her? Will she look like me, feel and think like me? What did she know herself as? "*How*" did she know herself, how express herself? Does she count as a "real" lesbian if she has been created by a male author, or by a heterosexual woman? Could she recognise herself from today's descriptions of· her?

The process of discovering or deciding who lesbians were and what lesbianism is or has been is very similar to all the other "uncoverings" with which feminist history concerns itself. It presents the same problems. Briefly, that there are too few facts; that there are the Right Facts selected and presented by the Wrong People; and that there are Wrong Facts (that is, not facts at all), misguidedly presented for the best of reasons by the (almost) Right People.

So, this lesbian. Who and what is she?

She has been many things, and most of them created by men. It is rare indeed that we can turn to an Aphra Behn and listen to a woman's voice telling us in ardent, guilt-free verse what it was like to love and make love to women in the last years of the seventeenth century. We are more likely to hear that we are a manifestation of Beautiful Evil, loved and feared by generations of writers and artists throughout Western Europe from Baudelaire to Balzac, Moreau to Beardsley. Or that we are the daemonic evil which so haunted Strindberg that he returned to the attack again and again because a beautiful red-haired actress who "stole" his wife became a symbol for him and many others of all that was degenerate and obscene in late nineteenth-century Europe. For men like him we are cruel, rapacious, sexually insatiable but emotionally cold, and cleverer than any woman has a right to be: we are, in fact, the complete and fearful opposite of everything which marks the Real Woman.

Sometimes we are the objects of passionate admiration for men who prefer their women tough (but ultimately vanquishable) — and that's as true of Diderot's nuns (*La Religieuse,* 1780) as it is of Ian Fleming's lesbian interrogators (*From Russia With Love*), as true of De Sade's sapphic tormentors as it is of George Macbeth's secret agent, Cadbury (*The Seven Witches*, 1978). And sometimes we are the object of compassionate affection from men who feel that their sexuality, like ours, is "flawed". So Swinburne, "marred" by his need of flagellation, produces lovingly his doomed creation, *Lesbia Brandon* (written between 1864 and 1867, but not published until 1952), setting her in symbolic landscapes of sterile beauty amid heat and light which parch rather than nourish and consigning her to a series of abortive relationships which bring only pain and humiliation.

On the rare occasions when we are happy it is only because we have been transported to a different century, as when Pierre Louÿs takes us to ancient Greece in *Aphrodite* (1896) or the *Chansons de Bilitis* (1894) and makes us represent the grace and easy sensuality of pre-Christian morality. It is, needless to say, ancient Greece seen through the eyes of very worldly Parisians for whom a little dash of lesbianism added spice to a jaded world.) And sometimes we are happy because we are truly in Utopia (or "no place"), as we are when Théophile Gautier makes one of us the hero of *Mademoiselle du Maupin* (1835), setting her down somewhere, somewhen, in the woods and *châteaux* of a fairy-tale, pre-revolution France with more than a touch of the Forest of Arden about it. There he leaves her to weave her irresistible spells over women and men alike, crediting her and us with all the magic of the androgyne.

For men uncertain of their own heterosexuality, we are disquieting and to be attacked as Henry James attacks us in *The Bostonians* (1886), heaping his ponderous doubts upon the head of Olive Chancellor, a feminist and strong-minded. She represents, for James, the dangerous ascendancy of the feminine in public life, with its inalienable qualities of "nervous, hysterical, chattering, canting", its "false delicacy and exaggerated solicitudes and coddled sensibilities" leading inevitably to "the reign of mediocrity". Condemned so roundly, is it consolation to find that for those men who welcomed the new feminism we were the vanguard heralding the new age, our dilemmas and anguished battles watched with sympathy? (I still find George Gissing's 1893 novel, *The Odd Women,* remarkable for its support from an unexpected quarter.)

Often where we might have looked for support we find only attack. We learn the hard way that defenders of sexual freedom are often only really interested in male freedoms. We realise ruefully, for example, that to D. H. Lawrence we are part of the spiritual corruption against which he inveighs. Our lesbianism is an eternal affront to him and he can never forgive it. With undisguised pleasure he kills one half of the lesbian couple in *The Fox* to clear the male's path to the woman who is "rightfully" his and ends the novella in a swirl of purple praise glorifying The Male Principle. (And somehow, even though I know, thanks to Emile Delavenay's 1971 *D. H. Lawrence and Edward Carpenter* and Paul Delaney's 1979 *D. H. Lawrence's Nightmare,* that Lawrence had his own pressing difficulties with homosexuality, I find it difficult to forgive him.) Mercifully he usually stops short of murder, and is content with the jibes and sneers at lesbianism which characterise *The Rainbow* (1915). (When, by the way, will somebody tackle the fascinating subject of the love-hate relationship between Lawrence and Katherine Mansfield, recognising that the major tensions sprang from the unwillingness of each of them to recognise their homosexuality?)

Not everybody jibes and sneers. Many a heterosexual male author looks with Tender Pity (or something like that) at two victims of male lust briefly seeking peace and solace in each other's arms. (Zola's numerous studies of lesbian liaisons often came dangerously close to that — *Nana* (1880) and *Pot-Bouille* (1883), for example.) And always there seems to be the implicit thought that if man's brutality to women can have such charming side effects, who would seek to check it?

Some male authors, it's true, love us as themselves, for the simple reason that we *are* themselves — or the men they love. (Yes, that *is* what I said: I'm thinking, for instance, of Proust's Albertine and all those enchanting girls who fill the budding groves of *A La Recherche du Temps Perdu,* every one of them, if Proust's biographer, George Painter, is to be believed, in origin an enchanting youth.)

And still we can be more. Murderous, as in classics, Balzac's *La Fille Aux Yeux d'Or* (1835) or as in pulp, such as innumerable detective novels. That's especially true of those by Dorothy Sayers. Remember Miss Climpson's strictures in *Strong Poison* and the salutarily horrible murderess in *Unnnatural Death?* Certainly Miss Sayers seems to have had it in for us, possibly because she was a fag-hag, as evidenced by her creation of Lord Peter Wimsey. (Alternatively, and the theory I prefer, she was herself homosexual and created Wimsey as an alter ego.) Or we can provide the material for High Comedy, as with Compton Mackenzie's *romans à clef* based on the expatriate lesbian colonies in Capri and Anacapri (*Extraordinary Women,* 1928, and *Vestal*

Fire, 1927). From E. F. Benson's 1920s six-volume saga of English shabby-genteel life come the bitcheries and bêtises of Lucia and Mapp and "dear Irene", fresh from the Slade and ensconced in happy domesticity with her six-foot-tall parlour maid who doubles as model when her mistress does Studies From the Life. This is comedy with the added sting which one has come to expect from a gay brother.

But what we are most often, of course, is a frisky interlude in a pornographic tale, the soft-focus lull before the storm of the hero's revived sexual powers bursts upon us. And now that more women are feeling able to take sexual initiatives, we're seeing the growth of women writers who use lesbians in the same way. Is Erica Jong's account of a lesbian relationship in *How To Save Your Own Life* (1977), for instance, very much more than a ritual and now obligatory encounter with a makeshift before she returns to the Real Thing? Perhaps that's unfair: let us rather say that for women whose sexual emotions are centred upon men, other women can never be more than a temporary refuge, an occasional pleasure. Even Colette — deeply though it hurts to say so when I love her so much — often seems to see lesbian relationships in that light.

Is there, indeed, any reason why we should expect that women authors will have recognised lesbians more clearly, depicted them more objectively than male writers have done? Certainly we owe some of the most unpleasant lesbians in fiction to women's pens. Clare Hartill (note the name), the central character of Clemence Dane's 1917 novel, *Regiment of Women,* is a monster of egotism: callous, manipulative, incapable of giving or receiving love, she uses her profession of schoolteacher first to ensnare then to reject her besotted pupils. Not only does she cause the suicide of one girl upon whose emotions she has played expertly: she also brings to breakdown a devoted young teacher, Alwynne, who all but misses her true destiny of man, marriage and maternity, such is the strength of Clare's almost irresistible attractions. Only the intervention of Alwynne's aunt (good but not clever) averts disaster. Clare (clever but not good) is incredulously defeated. The fictional Clare, by the way, bears a remarkably strong resemblance to a woman whose case history is cited as A Terrible Warning To Parents in *Sex And The Young,* 1926, written by that intransigently anti-lesbian proponent of birth control, Marie Stopes; and there are also Clare Hartills in abundance to be found in many of the non-fiction works of the period which claim to document the lesbian temperament. Such a confusion of life and art raises some pertinent questions. Objective fact or beastly anti-gay propaganda? Clemence Dane (or Winifred Ashton, to give her her real name) clearly had something to work out of her system, for her 1919 novel, *Legend,* again involved a spoilt, capricious woman, the centre of an unhealthy circle of hero-worshipping women. Even more influential was Geraldine, the swarthy, broad-shouldered lesbian of Rosamond Lehmann's once notorious novel, *Dusty Answer* (1927), who spreads chaos by wrestling in Ash Court and prowling the corridors during her weekend visits to Girton. (Ah, it wasn't like that in my day, nor, as a Fellow in her seventies confided to me, in hers, either.)

And the anti-lesbian tradition in fiction was already an old one. Eliza Lynn Linton, best-seller of an earlier generation, had made interminable attacks, notably in her 1880 novel, *The Rebel of the Family*, in which, unfortunately for her, Bell Blount, the lesbian anti-hero, is amongst the most attractive characters in the book. For fifty years Mrs Linton fought a spirited battle against women's suffrage and all attempts to change the established sexual order. Such are life's ironies that we need not be surprised to learn that the emotional centre of her own life lay in her passionate friendships with younger and usually beautiful women.

Certainly those women who felt that their own lives were vulnerably unusual or unrepresentative had reason to attack loudly and clearly the more conspicuous "unnaturalness" of homosexual women. (One thinks of George Eliot's anxieties about the hordes of adoring young women who surrounded her and her distinctly chary attitude to the older, more self-aware and probably lesbian Edith Simcox who for ten years regarded Eliot as "my Darling and my God". Eliot had fought one vast battle with mid-Victorian society over her failure to marry the man she lived with. A second struggle was too much. K. A. Mackenzie charts the vagaries of the two women's friendship in *Edith Simcox and George Eliot,* Oxford, 1961.)

George Eliot's are not the only vested interests we have to reckon with in our attempt to find the lesbian in literature. Accounts by contemporaries and the endeavours of critics and biographers (past or present) ought to help us. Often they don't. Too many have good reason for ignoring or obscuring lesbianism in their subjects. And autobiographies, consciously or not, help to confuse us. And we confuse ourselves by taking our own prejudices and assumptions to such scanty evidence as there is. We may not be naïve enough to cry, "Oh, but she *can't* have been. She was married." But we may say, "Oh, but she can't have been. She was *happily* married," as, indeed, were both Vita Sackville-West and the Princesse Edmond de Polignac — to their homosexual husbands. We may spend so much time listening to Marie Corelli's claims that she wants a husband that we fail to notice that the endless best-sellers which made her fortune from the 1880s to the eve of the First World War contain headily voluptuous and keenly-felt descriptions of languorous female beauty and rather cursory accounts of male attractions. Having once noticed it, we find ourselves attaching rather more weight to the otherwise easily overlooked but devoted friendship which she shared with her companion, Bertha Vyer. And here we tend to find ourselves caught in a double bind. On the one hand we are impatient with the idea that relationships matter only when they are sexualised. We know all too well that bonds between women have been ignored, trivialised and ridden over roughshod precisely because they were "only" friendships. On the other hand, we know equally firmly that those of our unions which are sexual will also be trivialised or dismissed because lesbian sex isn't "real" sex. Paradoxically we find ourselves equally bound to assert the importance both of sex and of no sex.

Recognising the paradox helps us, for example, to sympathise with the plight of poor Edith Somerville when confronted with Dame Ethel Smyth in particularly rumbustious mood. Edith Somerville and her cousin Violet Martin had enjoyed an unusually close personal and professional union. Writing as "Somerville and Ross" they co-authored extremely popular novels and short stories, mainly set in Ireland based on the lives of the Anglo-Irish ascendancy to which they themselves belonged. Their stories of "An Irish R.M. [Resident Magistrate]" (first published in 1899) are indubitably the best-known, but their output included historical novels and semi-autobiographical accounts of an art student's life in Paris and London. When Violet ("Ross") died in 1915, pre-deceasing Edith by some thirty-three years, Edith continued to write and, claiming that she was in spiritual communication with Violet, insisted that both their names should continue to appear on the title pages of new books. After a spirited tussle her publishers — Longmans — yielded gracefully. Clearly a woman to be reckoned with. But she was no match for Ethel Smyth, who fell in love with her, and whisked her off on what was to have been a honeymoon tour of Sicily, only to become distinctly huffy (and really rather rude) when she discovered that Edith was sexually completely inexperienced and had no idea of what was expected of her. Once it was explained, Edith remained (politely) unconvinced and firmly unco-operative. She was clearly distressed to realise that the life she had led so idyllically with Violet Martin was, in Ethel's eyes, open to only one interpretation.

But then Ethel Smyth was always unusual in her robust acceptance of her homosexuality. Forcibly she raised conscious-nesses in all directions as she swept into, through and out of the lives of women as diverse as Mary Benson (the mother of E. F. Benson who caricatured Ethel as "Edith Staines" in his 1893 novel, *Dodo*), Mrs Pankhurst and Virginia Woolf. Unlike Dame Ethel, most people have sought to disguise either their own homosexuality or other people's. Perhaps the protected person is too precious to be allowed to suffer "taint". Think how long it has taken for Virginia Woolf's lesbianism to be acknowledged. Or perhaps, it is argued, important causes which she led will be undermined if her possible homosexuality is disclosed. Think of all the little flurries of panic each time Christabel Pankhurst's sexuality is questioned and all the sighs of relief when David Mitchell's recent biography came out on the side of the angels and declared firmly that she was not, repeat *not,* a lesbian. Oh for the refreshing and all too rare candour of the octogenarian suffragette who said in a recent television interview that if anyone had ever *asked* her, of course she would have *told* them she was a lesbian but, frankly, it had never occurred to her than anybody could be so *stupid* as not to realise.

Yet even when we're not lying through our teeth or being wilfully stupid, we may often be excused for not realising, and as we go further back into literary history, the excuses grow. There are the women writing under men's names, the women writing as male characters, the women living and dressing as men. There are, too, good sound, commonsensical reasons for all those things, and these are the ones we usually hear. In an age predisposed to dismiss women's writing it makes sense to use a man's name, and once you've done that you might as well write of men's experiences. If you want to see the world, you're safer in men's clothes. But is that really all there is to say of Emily Brontë's love poems addressed to women? Is there really no more to Eliza Lynn Linton's "fictional" *Autobiography of Christopher Kirkland* (1885), with its careful analyses of love relationships with women which bear a marked resemblance to her own experiences with women? Does that explain the cross-dressing of George Sand and of the animal painter and diarist, Rosa Bonheur?

Sometimes, as with Bonheur, our incredulity is justified by secondary evidence. The official story says that she needed to wear men's clothes to attend, without fear of insult or assault, the sales of livestock and the assemblies of horse-copers where she found her subjects. For that reason and that reason alone the Paris Prefect's office gave her the permit she needed for male attire. As it happens, however, we also know from another source that Bonheur submitted an account of herself as "a contrasexual" (lesbian) to Magnus Hirschfeld's Institute of Sexology in Berlin. Here hunch is validated by fact. But so often hunches remain just that. And indeed the camouflage is often excellent. George Sand, after all, had *two* men to her credit: Alfred de Musset and Chopin. The fact that both men were less than a hundred percent heterosexual is neither her nor there. They were men and she was a woman and, in theory at any rate, that means heterosexuality. It was a relief, nevertheless, when recently published researches showed us that what we had always known by the pricking of our thumbs was true: that she had had numerous sexual relationships with women, including the Adah Isaacs Meneken whom Swinburne loved so hopelessly.

I say "it was a relief" to know, because for many of us there is a great need to establish a sense of continuity with the past, to affirm for ourselves that we are part of it rather than an aberration from it. The need for some sense of a shared past is so great that some of the best modern writing on lesbian themes has been devoted to recreating one. It may come in the guise of non-fiction works such as Elizabeth Mavor's *The Ladies of Llangollen* (1971), which relives the fifty-year "marriage" that united Lady Eleanor Butler and Miss Sarah Ponsonby from the time of their elopement in 1778 until the death of Lady Eleanor in 1828. More often it comes in the form of novels and short stories.

Few will take on as much as Radclyffe Hall attempted in her short story, *Miss Ogilvy Finds Herself* (1926), which is particularly interesting for its fictional use of contemporary theories about the genesis of homosexuality. She wrote the piece as a trial run for certain of the themes which she later intended to expand in *The Well of Loneliness* (1928), defined by her as "a serious study in congenital sexual inversion". The quasi-scientific language, familiar to us from Ulrichs, Carpenter, Havelock Ellis and other predominantly nineteenth-century sexual theorists, gives us the clue. Miss Ogilvy, a misfit with no apportioned part to play in the modern, ruthlessly heterosexual world, has had her one brief hour of glory during the First World War. There her "masculine" qualities of quick judgement, leadership and physical courage made her (like Stephen Gordon later in *The Well of Loneliness*) a valued member of a front-line ambulance unit: desperate ills demand desperate remedies, and in a period of "unnatural" chaos, "unnatural" women such as Miss Ogilvy can be gratefully accommodated.

But Europe's return to "normality" leaves Miss Ogilvy once more a redundant and embarrassing anomaly, chafing at her uselessness, humiliated by her pitiable irrelevance and wretchedly aware that the qualities which made her valuable in war now make her risible and more than a little indecent to "ordinary" people. Using a mixture of fantasy, time-travel and retrospective reincarnation, Radclyffe Hall takes her character back to a prehistoric world where she discovers that she — and her sexual temperament — are a vital link in the chain of human evolution. Despite some deplorable and unintentionally ludicrous passages — including a "me Tarzan, you Jane" episode when the metamorphosed Miss Ogilvy first meets her female soulmate — we can see ideas thronging in from all sides to feed and shape this short story. Edward Carpenter's *The Intermediate Sex* (1908) and *Intermediate Types Among Primitive Folk* (1914) are there, as is the pre-destinarian belief of many nineteenth-century sexologists in "the *real* homosexual", plus, of course, a strong dose of the contemporary concern with matters psychical (Radclyffe Hall and her lover, Una Troubridge, were for many years hard-working members of the Society for Psychical Research).

Locating itself more precisely in history, Isabel Miller's *Patience and Sarah* (1969) recreates the pioneering battle for autonomy and freedom fought by one of America's early nineteenth-century primitive painters and her lover. "To Miss Willson and Miss Brundidge, who, quite a while ago, lived something like it, this book is lovingly dedicated" reads the author's prefatory inscription. "Lived something like it" is the key to a work which fulfils abundantly one of literature's functions — to create, through the extending power of the imagination, characters and events which convince us of their psychological truth and value. It is also the key to our often quietly desperate need to know, or to believe we know, that we ourselves are simply following on, sexually and emotionally, rather than blazing trails.

Closer to home, Barbara Hanrahan's *The Albatross Muff* (1977) takes the grimmest basic facts of Victorian women's lives — loveless marriages of convenience, unrecognised syphilitic infection, death in childbed — and sets them against a softening but basically powerless background of intensely erotic female love relationships. She avoids an over-simplifying polarisation whereby male sexuality equals Evil and female sexuality equals Good. Instead she is at pains to show that no Alternative (in this case, lesbian love relationships) can fully escape the flaws and cruelties of the Norm (male-centred sexuality) from which it flees. Those women in the book who theoretically condemn male power while continuing to accept their sense of personal worth from the men who confer it can form only half-hearted and ultimately treacherous links with other women. Inevitably, the woman most betrayed is Edith, the only "real" lesbian amongst them.

Past and present fuse in Michèle Roberts's first novel, *A Piece of the Night* (1978). Here she uses a love relationship (broken eventually by marriage) between two late Victorian women as the sub-plot which runs round and through her main and very modernly lesbian characters. Her account of the older women's relationship is elusive, fragmented, tantalisingly incomplete. Necessarily so. How can it be otherwise when so many of the concepts and values which meant most to them are all but lost to us? How can it be otherwise when half the language in which we define and explain ourselves today was uncoined then? Take away from us the words "role-model", "gender identity", "stereotype", and then see how far we get in our attempts to understand Radclyffe Hall's lifelong pursuit of gentlemanliness, Colette's fascination with the hermaphroditic, George Eliot's fears of her imperfect womanliness and Vernon Lee's battle to accept and express the "man" in her.

Conversely, take ourselves back into a world of pre-Freudian biography, letters, journals, poetry and novels and we find ourselves floundering. There, women "fall in love" with each other, "lose their hearts" to each other and accept a "marriage" relation between them. We struggle with the perfervid "sentimental friendships" which express themselves in language of deepest purple, with echoes of *The Song of Songs* and the Ceremony for the Solemnisation of Matrimony. "Those whom God has joined together let no man put asunder", writes one half of "Michael Field", the aunt-and-niece writing team made up of Katherine Bradley (1846 - 1914) and Edith Cooper (1861 - 1913); Florence Nightingale writes almost daily to her "Goddess-baby"

(Miss Rachel Williams, one of her nurses) and to her "Dearest ever Dearest", Miss Pringle, her "pearl". We watch as women "mother" each other with a degree of erotic passion which would leave Oedipus gasping. "I have my love close to me. . . . Looking across at Sim's little bed I realise she is a goddess, hidden in her hair — Venus. Yet I cannot reach her. . . . I grow wilder for pleasure and madder against the ugly Mädchen [the nurse]" writes Edith Cooper from her German hospital bed when scarlet fever and hospital decorum conspire to keep her briefly from Katherine. We grow accustomed to finding the phrase "maternal affections" used to describe physically passionate relationships. Little wonder that in Radclyffe Hall's magnificent and quite unjustly neglected novel, *The Unlit Lamp* (published in 1921 but set in late Victorian England onwards), the luckless Joan Ogden should be ardently courted by her mother and conscientiously mothered by Elizabeth, her (chaste) lover.

It's not only the difference in language which jolts us. We also find ourselves looking at the lovingly entwined and sensuously preoccupied female couples in the photographs which Clementina, Lady Hawarden, dared to exhibit in the 1860s. (See for yourself in Graham Ovenden's *Clementina, Lady Hawarden,* 1974.) And, as we look at the 1916 *Life and Letters of Maggie Benson* (written by Arthur Benson, brother of E. F., son of Mary) we find ourselves wondering how many of today's biographies would dare to include the photograph in which Nettie Gourlay stands behind Maggie, her chin resting soulfully on Maggie's shoulder, her eyes closed in some undefined, but definitely guessable, near-ecstatic state. How did they get away with it?

Perhaps, you say, there was nothing to get away with? Perhaps. When we are very young and gullible we believe those critics and social historians who tell us breezily that linguistic conventions change; that sentiments which seem to us extravagant were once part of common currency; that verbal and physical expressions of affection — often intense — between people of the same sex were then freely given and received. That, in short, we have suffered Freud and thereby lost our innocence. As we grow older, read more and think harder we know those critics lied. We realise that our pre-Freudians suffered quite as much from anguished introspection over the wayward nature of their affections as any aspiring analysand might do. We discover how upset the reviewer in *The Times* became over Tennyson's "unhealthy" passionate grief for Arthur Hallam whom *In Memoriam* (1850) commemorates. We learn that the guardians of children's literature deplored the "un-English" degree of osculation (too many kisses) amongst the schoolboys of Dean Farrar's *Eric, or Little by Little* (1858). We discover that the mid-Victorian resurgence of classical Greek studies was attacked in some quarters because critics believed that eager students were drawn less by the great texts' promise of literary perfection than by the hope of homosexual passion. We recognise, in fact, that it was a century bedevilled by sexual uncertainty and doubt.

So how, then, did the Maggie Bensons and the Nettie Gourlays survive? Partly, perhaps, by taking advantage of the period's own contradictions. Theirs, after all, was an age in which, according to Acton's notorious dictum, "decent women have no sexual feelings". Or, to put it another way, provided you know that you're a decent woman, whatever you're feeling can't be sexual. All very reminiscent of the tireless campaigner against masturbation who, so Havelock Ellis enchantingly tells us, was appalled to discover late in life that the pleasantly soothing practices with which she lulled herself to sleep each night were part of the very evil she condemned. (This poignant anecdote comes in the introduction to the section on auto-eroticism in volume 1 of *Studies in the Psychology of Sex,* revised edition of 1920.) Possibly by such redeeming ignorance many lesbians escaped the weight of guilt which knowledge would have brought. But others almost certainly found themselves intolerably burdened by the menacing half-knowledge conveyed by the period's vague talk of "morbid sentimentality" and "neurasthenically intense" relations between girls and women. Some suicides in particular arouse our suspicions: Amy Levy, the young poet and protégée of Wilde who killed herself in the late 1880s; Charlotte Mew who took her own life in 1928. And it's impossible to know now to what extent Maggie Benson's own eventual descent into "madness" was linked with her struggle to reconcile her homosexuality with her Christianity. No easy task for the daughter of an Archbishop of Canterbury.

And when we tire or despair of goading the past into yielding up its secrets, there is always the future which, in terms of literature, we are free to do with as we will. Already lesbians have claimed large chunks of it, as in Marge Piercy's *Woman on the Edge of Time* (1976) or Zoë Fairbairns's *Benefits* (1979), where lesbians provide the force which spearheads radical political change in an ailing twenty-first-century Britain. Positive images, created by women who are themselves openly lesbian or genuinely at one with lesbians: and not before time, either. But, as Marge Piercy herself said in a recent *Gay News* interview, we don't want "comics for lesbians", nor do we want another set of equally distorting albeit vainglorious clichés to replace the fiercely hostile ones fashioned by our enemies.

So now, some pages and several hundred years from my original starting point, I find myself asking: this lesbian in literature — who will she be?

Note: This article first appeared in *Gay Left* no. 9.

16

Gay Activism

STEPHEN GEE

The Gay Liberation Movement's attempts to redefine homosexuality in a positive way have come under increasing attack in the last few years. The shock to the heterosexual system has manifested itself particularly in a moral panic around its children. The old pernicious myth of the homosexual as child molester has been the theme of a number of reactionary campaigns in the West; Anita Bryant's "Save Our Children" campaign, designed to remove state ordinances protecting employment rights of gays, was successful in several states. Recently the Briggs proposition attempted to witch-hunt gays out of California schools. It failed, but generated the atmosphere which led to the murder of an elected local government officer, San Francisco's openly gay supervisor, Harvey Milk. In Canada the gay newspaper *Body Politic* was prosecuted by the state for an article called "Men Loving Boys Loving Men". (*Body Politic* was acquitted, but the state is now appealing against the decision.) The prosecution counsel in the *Gay News* trial (1977) used articles on paedophilia as evidence of the paper's corrupt nature, and W. H. Smith banned *Gay News* from their stores in February 1978 for its paedophilic content. (Paedophilic content in *Gay News* was in fact limited to a contact address for PIE and the occasional sympathetic article.) PIE itself was the victim of a hysterical campaign initiated by the *Daily Mirror* in August 1977, and as a consequence a public meeting held by PIE the following month was besieged by the National Front and British Movement thugs. People attending the meeting fled afterwards in terror of their lives. The fascist violence of that night was applauded the next day in the papers as the righteous "Fury of the Mothers".

The attack on AID (Artificial Insemination by Donor) for lesbian parents by the *Evening News* in February 1978 is part of the same panic over childhood, as was the hurried and unopposed passage of the Townsend/Whitehouse Child Pornography Bill. Finally the campaign against PIE has culminated in 1979 in the prosecution of PIE organisers by the state for Conspiracy to Corrupt Public Morals.

In so far as these attacks have affected the civil rights of homosexuals in general we have mobilised fairly successfully in our own defence. In so far as there is a specific attack on paedophiles we have neither been sufficiently supportive nor have we challenged the dominant ideology of childhood and child sexuality which informs this attack. What constitutes this partial success for gay adults and this failure to support paedophiles is to some extent revealed in the struggles of the last two years. As someone closely involved I will try to recount and interpret those struggles in some detail.

The mood of the Summer of 1977, in the aftermath of Bryant and Whitehouse, was summed up for me by Ian McKay of the American gay theatre group Hot Peaches who, in laid-back tones of the drag queen who's seen it all before, said "it seems we're entering a new era of oppression — like did we ever get out of the last one?" To judge from the serene non-reaction of existing gay organisations to the *Gay News* conviction, we had indeed emerged from our oppression, never more to be harassed, sneered at or queerbashed again. A new group took the initiative. It consisted at first of gay men who had attended the trial and grew into a coalition of gay groups in London. A demonstration was immediately organised in support of *Gay News.*

This demonstration and the one which followed it, a protest at the murder of Peter Benyon outside the Rainbow Club in North London, articulated a new mood of resistance. In the first instance a huge banner displayed the faces of Bryant, Whitehouse and Hitler with the slogan "Homosexuals Fight Back". The route of the march through Chelsea and Earls Court aimed to capture the attention of the gay community in the area. Among the speakers at the rally was Nicolas Walter of the National Secular Society. Mr Walter readily welcomed the gay community into its own struggle for opinion free from religious constraints.

The second demonstration, which went through Wood Green in North London, addressed itself to a working-class community. In a message of support, the local Labour Council identified the Benyon incident as part of the growth of Nazi-like violence against minorities. (Wood Green had earlier that year been the victim of an NF march.) As the message acknowledged, we were clearly not alone in suffering setbacks with the general move to the right in Britain and elsewhere. These demonstrations were the first to rebuild support within our own oppressed group, and to seek allies outside the movement.

This strategy was developed at a meeting in Birmingham in the Autumn at which the National *Gay News* Defence Committee was formed. The *Gay News* case was seen as a focus for the wider attacks on gay people, and central to the campaign was a resolution around which people could work in their unions, parties and gay groups. The single-issue nature of the campaign commanded a broad centre-to-left political support, enabling people to work together in a newly united way. The climax of the campaign was a national demonstration just before *Gay News* appealed. Both the large numbers of people and the non-gay groups on that march were unprecedented. The range of speakers in Trafalgar Square, from the gay and women's movements, the left and other civil liberties groups, reflected the broad alliance we had begun to create. The appearance of the Tom Robinson Band also reflected the new cultural power our politics now had.

In the afterglow of this demonstration the Gay Activists' Alliance was formed, and the politics which had emerged in the National *Gay News* Defence Committee became explicit in GAA's founding statement: "To co-ordinate at a national level the fight against the increasing number of attacks against homosexuals and homosexuality. We see our struggle as part of that of other oppressed people and therefore seek the active participation of the maximum number of gay and non-gay organisations in this aim."

GAA groups were formed around the country. For a year a campaign was sustained against W. H. Smith, anti-fascist literature was produced and in Manchester the GAA focused national attention on the Chief Constable, James Anderton, who had invoked the city's "Licentious Dancing" laws against gay clubs.

The politics of GAA are not explicitly socialist. In identifying itself with other oppressed groups it resembles early GLF, or rather it has maintained that principle of GLF politics. GAA has none of the millenarianism of GLF. It is faced with the reality that capitalism has, to an extent, accommodated coming out. There is now a sizeable gay subculture, much less closeted than before, although threatened. GAA therefore sees its goals in a more limited way; it is trying to preserve gains already made rather than build an alternative.

GAA is so structured that local groups can relay information and call upon support swiftly. A newsletter published after every national meeting and a telephone tree are the main means of communication. It has proved to be very effective. For example, when Brighton gays were attacked by the National Front at a film show and by the Brighton *Evening Argus* in the same week (January 1979), we were able to back up the response of local people in Brighton with a phone-in to the *Argus* from all over the country.

During the first year there was an acutely felt need to organise, but no single issue comparable to the *Gay News* trial around which to organise. An attempt to remedy this was made at the Birmingham GAA conference in February 1979. A new campaign on the law and sexuality was proposed. It was to work against all laws affecting lesbians and gay men, including the age of consent, importuning, gross indecency, child custody and police harassment. Its aim was to encourage the growing resistance to and awareness of particular laws amongst gay people. Lobbying MPs, etc., would be much less of a priority than working through trades unions and with other allies. With the arrival of the Thatcher government even the Campaign for Homosexual Equality had doubts about the prospects for law reform —

Michael Steed, a former CHE chairperson, suggested a campaign of "civil disobedience" at their last conference. How that would work is not immediately clear, especially as gays in this country are not as geographically concentrated as in the United States. It is consonant, however, with the GAA idea of resistance, and suggests possibilities of the two groups working together on this.

On its own GAA has so far encountered considerable difficulties in launching this campaign, both in terms of "taking positions" on such a wide-ranging campaign and in terms of the way we have been conducting our politics. These are, of course, only superficially separate difficulties, and are a recurrent problem for liberation groups which have posited the political as the personal.

Let us take one of the positions which gave difficulty — the age of consent. No one at first argued strongly for parity with heterosexuals. Recognising the problems we would be faced with by arguing for no age of consent, however, we tried to find ways of using the concept of "no crime without a victim". The International Marxist Group gay commission, a group which worked in GAA later, put forward a kind of interim position of parity. The whole question is unresolved and is likely to remain so as long as the current political climate persists — characterised as it is by general panic about childhood and, more specifically, by the state's prosecution of PIE.

In addition to political demands and positions, a lot of thought went into how we could build on the trust and support of people who came up against the law. Historically there had been an uneasiness, even hostility, between activists and the gay scene, and there was no contact between activists and isolated gays — for example, men trapped by the police in cottaging or cruising situations. We therefore decided to approach existing counselling organisations and work towards a conference. We arrived at the following declaration:

> The GAA will work with other organisations and build practical support on a personal basis for all lesbians and gay men who find themselves up against the law because of their sexuality.

This represented a clear realisation that our politics should take responsibility for the feelings and vulnerability of individuals concerned. This inward support-building aspect of the campaign complemented the outward political demands: it was in a sense an expression of the concept "the personal is political", and a development and growth, at least in organisational terms, in the gay movement.

This development is arrested, however, for a number of reasons which are also personal/political. Externally there is the shift to the right in Britain's social and political climate, which has led to a general decline in confidence and activity on the left; the hysteria surrounding paedophilia and child sexuality have had a particularly immobilising effect on the gay movement. Internally there are a number of problems which were identified and discussed in the newsletter and conferences after Birmingham. The main problem — how decisions could be truly democratic when participation was so uneven — was not new. Articulate people had dominated discussion, unaware of the growing alienation of those unable to contribute, through lack of either knowledge or political experience. At the Birmingham conference, the tendency to push for political clarity in articulate intellectual terms and the demands the campaign was making on people's understanding created divisions. The discussion within GAA about this had been prefigured in a trenchant criticism of the concept of gay activism by the early Gay Liberation Front:

> Gay activists are not apologetic about their homosexuality, so they can be more militant and defiant. But they refuse to think politically. Gay activism is generally for men, often hostile to women. It wants rights for gay people as they are; it does not challenge butch or femme stereotypes or examine ways of relating.

One of the women at the Birmingham meeting certainly detected some hostility. She characterised the division between the articulate and the silent as a competitive separating of "the men from the boys". Developing this, she compared the urgency of getting a campaign off the ground, immediately and at all costs, to the need of male-dominated left-wing parties to produce leaders and trot out party lines. Other people resented the fact that the activist urgency of conferences meant that no reflective discussion could take place. The impasse presented us with the dilemma of either accepting that some people (the dominant and articulate) have native talent, therefore recognising a hierarchy, or acknowledging that political and communicative skills are learnt through experience. The latter implied sharing and devolving those skills, and we had not yet attempted this. A general inhibition against taking responsibility for each other in this way was identified by one criticism in the newsletter: "we all suffer from blindness, self-interest and distortions of behaviour due to our conditioning as women and men — and for men there is the added complication of operating under unexamined rules of competitiveness for attention, power and sex, which can neither be wished nor moralised away."

Another weakness of GAA is a lack of a sense of our own history. Like many recent groups it imagined itself to be the first of its kind, and so avoided a useful learning process. If GAA was renewing any early GLF demands, "Out of the closets and into the streets" was one of them, inasmuch as one simple aim of GAA was to be visible. Gay visibility and pride have recently become expressed more in cultural political terms than in activist terms. The 1979 Gay Pride Week celebrations demonstrated this and suggested that cultural events are the most powerful ways of communicating our experience. If specific political activism is dwindling at the present time, gay culture is growing very fast.

Apart from a more openly gay male popular subculture, with figures like Tom Robinson, Village People and disco in general, there has been an explosion in the number of women's and gay theatre groups and bands. About 115 events of this sort were on the Gay Pride London programme. This is of course politically important. Gay culture does not consist of apolitical works of art; it is part of our productive consciousness as gay women and men. Precisely how distinct from the main culture that culture is or can be needs examining. Is it possible, for example, to produce gay rhythms or forms, as the American blacks did with the Blues?

First we need to affirm that gay people have had an immense influence on the dominant culture in the past. Most expressions of their homosexuality, however, were mediated in covert ways (gay love poems passed as straight). Gayness might be suggested by the use of camp as in Oscar Wilde, or in the dark fatalistic metaphors of horror films (*Daughters of Darkness*).

Our reclaimed gay culture is now using the correct pronouns and transforming innuendo and suggestion into affirmation. (And the best horror films these days are about the nuclear family.) All of the recently formed groups and bands as well as individual performers have their roots in the gay and feminist movements. These groups work collectively and non-commercially, and their primary audience is a gay one. Their material goes beyond agitprop or political theatre, though none of them claim to have discovered a "gay form" or a "theatre of homosexuality".

For gays to attempt to search for such cultural essences would be, I think, to regard ourselves as having the same unifying characteristics as an ethnic group. Since we come from different classes and racial backgrounds, and given that the sexuality of men and women is learned very differently, the expressions of homosexuality in this society are implicitly various; we construct a political and cultural identity from this. It is a paradox that we sow it within the category of homosexual and lesbian — originally meant to contain and control us. The transformation in meaning of the pink triangle is the simple and most vivid expression of this paradox.

If making a homosexual culture is necessarily complex, then constructing a gay political unity is equally so. It cannot be done by any one single organisation. We should continue to work at making alliances between women and gay men and other oppressed groups. Alliances rather than tight organisational structures are a way of keeping the autonomy we have assumed over the past decade. We need alliances because we face a period of resistance to attacks with little chance of any extension of civil rights.

Indications of what this alliance can be have been vividly seen in the *Gay News* Defence Committee and, in anti-racist struggle, the political and cultural developments of Rock Against Racism and the Anti-Nazi League. What we need now is something more enduring than any of these forerunners. The attack on PIE is possibly only the beginning of a general undermining of sexual rights and freedoms; it is the state fortifying itself in a battle for the possession and dispossession of children, women and homosexuals. Are we ready?

17

Right to Rebel

AMBER HOLLIBAUGH

Part One

I came from a small town in California (Carmichael). I hated it and wanted out, but not into marriage. I heard about the Civil Rights movement, was exhilarated by it and wanted to get involved. This was 1964. I was naïve in my outrage at the Southern community's reaction to Civil Rights, but that naïve anger is as good a way into struggle as any. I felt that we all had to do something otherwise nothing would change.

I discovered a real sense of community through that involvement: people were trying to kill us, which brings you together! The Black community in the South had already built networks of care and concern, and by being involved on the margins of that we whites learned that survival was a matter of taking responsibility for each other.

We worked hard and organised, but there were problems, especially for a white woman in a Black community. So many racial myths centre on that and I began to feel that we put the Black community in even more danger because of that heterosexual racism. We brought down the wrath of god: we were staying with Black families, frequently lovers of Black men, and certainly their friends, which was horrific in the eyes of the surrounding white community. The violence was incredible, people trying to shoot you all the time, houses you were staying in getting firebombed. The last straw for me was that the man of the family I was staying with refused to sit down to supper if I was there: he said that he couldn't sit at the same table as white folks, it wasn't done. I freaked: this man would come in from working fourteen hours working on some white man's plantation, and he couldn't eat his meal in peace. My being there was doing him no good at all.

So I left Mississippi, went up to New York and worked with the Student Non-Violent Co-ordinating Committee there until Whites were expelled as the Black movement grew into a consciousness of its own need for autonomy and the ideas of Black Power began to grow. That was extremely painful, a traumatic experience where I was forced to confront the fact of being white. Up until then I'd sort of thought that if we could just come to love each other it would be OK. But now people that I loved were telling me to fuck off, that it was no good me spending six months in the South —

they had to be there all the time. I was white and could pull out of the struggle at any time.

Most Blacks had started out as naïve as me, but the toll of the struggle was a growing cynicism, a defensiveness that chimed with the growth of a new Black nationalism. I didn't understand that, many of us failed to understand it at all and grew embittered. Those who survived that experience remained politicised, and I was hooked. In the society I'd come from I'd been taught that nothing mattered, nothing was worth fighting for, but through that struggle I'd come to know people who believed in something, and who were prepared to act on that belief: the right of people to be equal . . . which was an extraordinary thought in a racist society. The struggle gave me so much, and even though I didn't know where to go I couldn't give up political involvement.

Then for the first time, whites rebelled in the sixties. In Berkeley, Ca., sparked by the struggle for SNCC to have the right to raise money on the university campus, the free speech movement was born. It escalated rapidly, involving straight students from all backgrounds and was fuelled by the resentments of being in an alienating university. The ideas of the beat movement fed into it too, and soon the anti-war movement spun out of that explosion.

Again my first involvement in the free speech and anti-war movements was from a naïve perspective. I thought killing was wrong, but was horrified when people tried to stop troop trains. But within the movement politics was serious: people had theories, could articulate strategies and tactics, and were often explicitly marxist. I started to learn about class, found out what imperialism was, and felt a real commitment to building a movement that would control our government, which lied to us, killed people in our name without taking the trouble to ask us what we thought. It was an exciting time, in which I began for the first time to understand what was happening.

But I was also working-class: I wasn't a college drop-out, and my parents weren't supporting me. I had to work but kept losing jobs because I was a red, a commie, and McCarthyism hadn't run its course. So I began to work as a hooker, and led this weird double life. . . . Over here I was political, over there I sold my body. Slowly I began to understand the power of men over women too.

Someone in the CP had explained to me that you didn't have to get married . . . a shocking idea to me, because I thought you only didn't get married if no one asked you. The idea slowly dawned, though, that I could be an independent woman. But then there was the whole deal about how women were supposed to relate to men in the left. I was a hooker for living but I was also prostituting myself to the men in the left, for power and for education. The way you got both in the left then, if you were like me not so articulate, a poor farm kid, was by sleeping with the men who had them. You fucked for a book. They didn't even go with me: I wasn't some guy's girlfriend, just some guy's fuck. And there was a push in the left then on all women to sleep around. Those straight men got a lot! Part of the "new world" we were building was men and women together: you were free with your body unrepressed — basically you had to sleep with anyone who asked you. Otherwise you were called frigid, peculiar, or got kicked out of the movement.

Then there was the division of labour within the movement. Men argued and debated with each other, theorised, and women went out and organised: we went door-to-door and asked housewives what they thought of the war: "Hi, you don't know me but I'd like to talk to you about the war in Vietnam." The reason women were so good later at organising our own communities was because we'd learned the skills in the sixties, while the men were arguing with each other. Slowly I grew to hate men, even while I had to sleep with them, all of them, communally etc. I didn't want any part of it but I didn't know how to get out of it. So I went through with it, and it's a dull meaningless memory now. I was lucky. Some women were destroyed.

Eventually I got pregnant by a draft dodger. I got an abortion but got so sick that I had to leave with him and go up to Canada, where we got married so that we could stay together and he could look after me. That was one of the bitterest times. I became all the things I never wanted to be. I'd lost my connection with the left, and I was trying to be married. I managed it for nine months, and was miserable. But you couldn't talk about it with anyone. I had no sexual knowledge. I kept asking myself "What's wrong with me?" I couldn't make it with men: I could fuck for money, but I could have no emotional life with men. I didn't know myself to be a dyke. I was just barren.

So I left my husband, organised a strike at McGill University in Toronto, and began to reclaim my political self. This was about the time (1966) that women's caucuses first began in the left. I didn't want to know. I'd made a decision that I would never sleep with a man again: I was going for power, for leadership. *I* was going to be a heavy. While I was married I'd read Marx, Engels, Lenin, the lot. I came out of that at least a thinker if not an intellectual: I was as smart as any man on the left, and by God, I was going for the big time. And then these women started caucuses!

I didn't want to go to them, but I was persuaded, even though I was not impressed. I hated being a woman, which was a lot of what stopped me from seeing I was a lesbian. I hated what women did: I hated their dependence, their tears. The biggest compliment to me was that I thought like a man. Talking with women made me feel bad, and I didn't want to identify with them. I wanted to identify around men's appreciation of my "masculine" part.

Through the caucuses I began to think about my own contradictions: outside organisations I was a nice person, but inside I was a killer. Then at a conference I was one of eight women who gave a paper on Juliet Mitchell's "Women: the Longest

Revolution". At the end of an eight-hour conversation with one of the other women — pow! I left the room with her and we were together for five years. I fell in love, and moved in with her. I came out then, and before the women's movement that's how a lot of women came out. We didn't say we were gay, we said we were in love. We said that women were forming new relationships and we were a part of that. Women came first.

Slowly many women, leftists and socialists, came to the realisation that we had to leave the left to create a women's movement. It was painful for me. I'd fallen in love with a woman but I had to leave the left. It was my revolution but here I was organising women, with no relation to marxism seemingly or to any other struggles (the anti-war movement was at its height). I felt alone and only being with this woman made it possible. During that period I had to face my own self-hatred, my own oppression of women, but through that I could open up to the possibility of women in my life. Only the strength of the beginning of feminism was enough to confront women as tough as me with how misshapen we'd become: we were committed to the left but we were cold. The brand of socialism we had was not enough. It didn't change anyone.

We had to face what women had become. I'd fought for power and now I realised that it was useless. I was torn. Did we have the right to organise separately? Mitchell's article was crucial, it gave us a theory. And the love of a woman was crucial too, a love not based on power. Lesbianism is about that.

This woman didn't want me for the power I had, for my status, but for who I was. And she didn't lie about the rotten qualities I had too. There was a quality of honesty which I'd never known before, and which women had in their gift. Heterosexuality was all about lies, if you were honest in a relationship you lost the relationship. Both of us could be honest, not have to play games. She'd been wounded, had only been tolerated in the left by men because she was brilliant. Tolerated, never liked, and I loved her. Neither of us had had someone love us who'd seen us as we were. I began to open up to being soft in a relationship, she didn't hold it against me. Being caring, nurturing, sensual, was not something I finished up having to pay for. We made a commitment to each other for life.

But, but. Our relationship was in the closet. The women's movement had begun by now (1967) but it hated lesbians. We were suspected and we had to keep the illusion of separate bedrooms. The women's movement despite its militancy was terrified of sexuality. Everyone was being dykebaited.

We weren't gay, not even to each other. We talked about being in love: what it meant for women to love each other, and we talked about celibacy — we were real big on that! Our relationship was classically closet. An enormous emotional intensity, a primary commitment and very little sexuality. You can't have it in isolation. But what we need from another woman was not primarily sexual: ultimately it was a validation of our femaleness, only secondarily sexual, primarily emotional.

It was a rich time, discovering what it was to be women, in our relationship and as part of a wider movement. We wrote papers, organised conferences, and went through the rage from what men had done to us. It wasn't hard to be without men, e.g. SDS leaders who spread clap through the women's community. We were exploring an internal women's life that had been invalidated before. Sometimes we discovered how damaged we'd been and there was a sadness for parts of yourself that couldn't be brought back to life. We feared that men were so damaged that relations with them were impossible. Radical feminism had emerged by now, but in Canada we maintained an unapologetic marxism which, however, was not protective of the male left. We kept race and class consciousness whilst developing our feminism.

But as dykes . . . we couldn't be out. The first glimmers of understanding what it was to be in the closet came through the very success of creating a women's culture. We were women together, but I couldn't be with the woman I loved in the way I wanted to be. We'd be invited to parties, but most of the women were straight, and you were meant to dance with men. I wouldn't and stayed in the kitchen and got nasty. Any man could walk up to her and say "Hey honey, you wanna fuck" and walk off with her, but if I looked at her with any emotion people treated me as though I was an animal. So we stopped going to parties! We didn't have what you might call a political consciousness of the situation!

Our relationship got more neurotic: we couldn't talk to anyone about it. I finally had begun to realise that I was gay. I read (surreptitiously) "The Ladder", from The Daughters of Bilitis. Finally I said, "We're lesbians, we live together, it's obscene that we should have to hide." Her reply was that no, never, she was not a lesbian, being a lesbian destroys you. If you have to come out you do it alone. This was heavy. To be out as gay meant I lost the woman I loved. To keep her I couldn't be who I was. It was intolerable. The few lesbians in the Toronto movement had discovered each other, quietly, "I won't tell on you if you don't tell on me" style, and in 1970 we decided to do a forum on lesbianism and feminism. In it we were all going to come out. I was to come out first, since I was part of the leadership, with the hope that it would somehow calm people down enough for the rest. (My girlfriend of course was freaking out: if I came out then who was she?) So we did it. I came out, and nobody else did. Oh, they admitted to fantasising about women and so on. . . . These were stone dykes! Freak out. Within three weeks my girlfriend and I had split, I left Canada, the women's movement. . . . For what? To be a lesbian, and I knew nothing from lesbian.

It was the pits. I'd left the left for the women's movement, now I was leaving that for a lesbian movement that I wasn't sure existed. I was back in the States, with the craziness of the early seventies, Weathermen and so on. And I'd lost the woman I still loved. Our relationship had been so important, even if it wasn't gay. To be gay you have to be able to look at your partner, know what you're doing and be glad. We couldn't do that. We weren't proud enough to call ourselves lesbian.

I was confused, I had a political commitment before I had a real understanding. I had to go through all the vulnerability of discovering lesbianism whilst still being a politico. And I'd lost the woman who'd been my political partner as well as my lover. It was like being deaf and dumb.

I'd maintained some involvement with mainstream left politics, working with the Black Panther Party and doing draft-counselling, but it wasn't an easy glide back into the US. I was a lesbian and I didn't want to face it: lesbianism was harder for me to accept than anything in my life. There's something very lonely about gay self-acceptance — or leastwise there was in that period. Coming out — we were defiant, proud, angry — we wore a lot of lavender, but the self-hate is so deep that it takes you years to work through it, and there's no social movement that removes you from that pain. You love the same sex which is horrible in heterosexual society. No one can make that easier. For me it's taken years. I hated being gay: I knew I couldn't change it. I knew I wasn't straight, I was gay, but I didn't like it. Hell, I don't like being oppressed. Being gay is not something that you learn. At least if you're black you're raised in a culture that explains to you what racism is and how to deal with it. If you're gay, first they try to tell you that it's really not true, then they spend years trying to change you. You just have to hate yourself more than straight folks do. Everything that comes at you tells you it's sick, wrong, perverted, demented. You never get reinforced. And what's this puny little movement. Circle-dancing deals with all this? That every straight man wants to kill me because I'm a dyke. Nothing deals with this.

I wasn't happy. I felt outside the lesbian movement: I was working-class. I wasn't comfortable with middle-class assumptions that gay was good. I felt that gay was right, I was defiant but I had an enormous amount of self-hate. I was socially conscious, I felt I had a right to be gay, but in bed, alone at night I did not like being a lesbian. I kept saying "I can't help it", and felt that I was going to be alone, without a stable relationship. Even being a communist you feel normal, being a lesbian though . . . through and through you're abnormal, or that's what they tell you and what you believe.

I left Boston, came to San Francisco. I knew if I was going to find an answer it was going to be here. San Francisco has a diversity: there are working-class lesbian bars, something I'd not known. There are so many different ways here to work out who you are within the definition "gay". There are all races, ages, types of lesbian, and there's a strong women's movement here too. I was also coming home. And I've been here seven years. San Francisco allows you to be a whole lot of things without hating yourself. I feel that I've worked through that self-hatred. I've accepted my lesbianism and also feel that I have some control: my lesbianism isn't some alien thing apart from me. I feel I've reconnected to who I am as a marxist, a lesbian and a feminist. Ultimately "the revolution will have come when I go to a party and be all the things I am". Contradictions are there but I feel I am more whole. San Francisco gives that to many gay people. It gives you a community to work through who you are and who you want to be.

Part Two

When I came to San Francisco in 1972, the lesbian community was pretty submerged. It thrived in the space between the gay male community and the Black community. But there was a space: San Francisco had always had large communities of Black, Chinese, and Latino peoples, a thriving women's movement and a large left focused more around working-class struggles than around the war.

The gay male community centred on Polk Street was seedy, flashy and almost a parody. The Castro was a quiet, residential district. I was removed from it, having a more or less separatist position, although feminism in that form was beginning to fall apart from class contradictions, and I was beginning to feel uncomfortable with that brand of feminism. My lovers were coming out of the bar, not from the movement. There was a contradiction in that I hadn't come to lesbianism as a political alternative. I feel my own history as somewhere between old and new dyke lifestyles. Old dykes were lesbian in isolation — they figured out that they loved women and that was that. New dykes came out on the upsurge of feminism. A third group to which I belong, connects to both parts: we were dykes before the lesbian movement, but were political as well.

My political confusions began to resolve themselves when I began to work in the gay caucus in the organising committee for the July 4th anti-bicentennial in 1975-6. I chose to work in the gay caucus as opposed to the women's caucus, a moderately scandalous choice. I was the only woman with eleven gay men, mostly political white gay men. My experience with them was good. It gave me a sense that there were men committed to struggles against sexism: men who were as moved by feminism in their own way as I had been. Not because they were guilty about being men, about being oppressors, but who were moved by the idea of a new way to be men. I hadn't met men like them before: I'd met gentle straight men but wasn't convinced. I hadn't met men before who passionately identified with parts of feminism as their own. I got a real sense of feminism reaching out beyond women, and touching and changing men and how they wanted to be, and impelling them to work against sexism. Feminism was bridging gaps between lesbians and gay men, and I began to spend more time in the Castro, and though the faggot lifestyle there was alien, it wasn't threatening.

Then the attacks started, and lesbians and gay men started to come together. First Richard Hillsboro was murdered and the Bryant thing started. There was a changing wind in the country. Harvey Milk was elected but he was virtually the only out gay official, proud to be a faggot and a progressive. As the repression increased there was an explosion of gay life that was more positive. People fled to San Francisco trying to figure out what being gay was all about, but with a consciousness that homosexuality was being threatened. The city wasn't mecca, and we had consciously to see that we were being attacked and that unless we fought back we weren't going to survive. Lesbians knew that before gay men, and Lesbian School Workers formed as an organisation knowing where the attacks would come. The lesbian community by now was the biggest in the US and it was a deeply politically conscious community.

And Bay Area Gay Liberation existed, which was a socialist, primarily faggot organisation that set the tone of struggle, maintaining links between the gay male community and the third-world communities. There was a model for coming together, and taking up sexism and racism. The Castro area exploded, and is now the gay capital of the US. It reflects a new way of being out, proud, defiant, very sexual and cruisy for gay men. For men it's very butch, and raises a finger at all the straight stereotypes. As the street evolved, lesbians were often unsure about how they fitted in, but at least we hassled: it was OK to be gay and hence OK to be dykes. It isn't enough but it's not tiny.

The change was the Briggs initiative. It was an explicitly political struggle. The gay left gave a lead, didn't trail behind. The liberal strategy was exposed for what it was — a cop-out. They argued that gay people should go back in the closet, and straight people should do the advertising and so on; that being gay wasn't really different, only a matter of sexual choice.

The whole strategy was overturned and issues of homophobia were debated. Before that every campaign that had been fought in the US had adopted that liberal strategy and we'd lost every time. . . in Eugene, in Dade County, in Minneapolis. Everyone knows that being gay is different. If we were afraid to confront our own fears we couldn't face others'. And we had no answer. If someone asked "Don't you want to recruit children?" we'd say "NO, we don't want anyone to be gay": but of course we did. We wanted other people to be gay because we were glad to be gay. We had to confront the repressive notion of recruitment, but we couldn't dodge the real issue. Bryant and Briggs said if we can take them on in California and win, we can win everywhere. We knew then that if we lost, we lost everywhere. It was frightening, a statewide confrontation. California is huge, a rural farm state. Farmers vote here, agribusiness controls things here. Doing publicity meant going to small farm towns, facing very conservative working people. We figured that even if we lost, if we told the truth we'd convince enough people that we could fight back some time and win.

In the face of the repression we became very gay to each other: we didn't know if we'd make it, and the only people you could trust were other gay people. It changed Castro: we were being filmed, photographed, interviewed, asked questions all the time, and we had to think, to come to see each other and the street, the community as survival. You couldn't trust straights, no movie stars flocked to our banner, no active liberal support would run the risk of being called dyke or faggot. All the other campaigns had lost because they'd relied on getting the liberal vote out and it hadn't come through: they hadn't gone into working-class communities and tried to change people's minds. We went to the farmers, to the union locals, to the schools, to the hospitals, the childcare units, all the places we hadn't been before and we came out and forced people to think.

Gay people who'd never been political before took amazing risks . . . everybody took three steps further out. If you weren't out you came out: if you were out to three people you came out to three more and so on. It changed our community because we began to respect each other: we were militant, fought and defended each other. The specific people who Briggs named, his accusations blew up in his face. For example, Larry Benner, a schoolteacher in Healsbury, a tiny town. Larry's fifty, a schoolteacher of thirty years' standing, a communist and also a well-known and respected member of the town. When Briggs attacked him, Larry was well grounded in the community, very out, was proud of being gay and got a lot of support and Briggs was discredited there. And it was the same everywhere. Gay people started taking care of their own people, their own community, saying, "We've had enough. We're gay, we have a right to be gay, and if you can't take it that's your problem."

And we won, won in every single area of the state where we went and did work. We won because we came out, and the community was politicised. A huge number of gay organisations sprang up, it was a real flowering of the movement. Lesbians and gay men worked together and created a renaissance of gay life in San Francisco. Two thousand people stood in line for a film benefit for the "No on 6" campaign. Everyone took literature and used it. If you used traditional political methods, you didn't understand the significance of what was happening. People went out where they had to confront homophobia in their own lives — not going to meetings. Telling your mother, talking to the busdriver on the way to work . . . No one knows how many people did things and told no one, took no credit, just acted in their own lives. We won and we created a self-conscious community in San Francisco, lesbians and gay men with a different level of respect for each other.

Then Harvey was killed.

He was important, a faggot, proud and a socialist. For Harvey to be killed by a man who was the epitome of a homophobe — white working-class ex-cop, family man and a Christian, was too much. In San Francisco, where it was wonderful to be gay, where you came because you couldn't be gay anywhere else, what did they do — they murdered one of us. We were none of us safe. The murder forced people to confront the ugliness of homophobia. Under our noses Harvey was killed by someone who felt he was safe to do that in San Francisco. And ultimately he was proven correct — he got six and a half years.

That action, on top of the sense of community that we'd built during Briggs, galvanised the community. It was dramatic, if unstated. If they could get Harvey, then we were next. Forty thousand people marched on the night of his murder, two hours after his death, they marched to City Hall to mourn him. Everyone knew it could be them. When Dan White was found guilty with such a light sentence, it was intolerable.

The day after the riot was amazing. If you catch a bus, normally you're nervous if you look gay, wondering who's going to jump you, who's going to sneer. The first thing next day I got on the bus, went to the back and there's these two black kids, sitting there. One said, "Are you a dyke?" I said, "Yeah, so what?" and this kid said, "Hey, you people are OK, you know how to kick ass. I didn't know dykes and faggots could do that." For a couple of weeks gay people knew each other and just grinned at each other. And other people responded.

Even people who felt unsure about the kind of violence, somewhere they thought we were right, were proud we hadn't taken it one more time. We had the right to be that angry, we felt we had the right, and feeling that makes being gay a whole different thing. We don't have to die to be gay, they don't have the right to kill us. The gay community too often doesn't resist, and doesn't respect the gay people who do. Sometimes we are our own worst censors. But not this time. Fifteen thousand rioting queers at City Hall: we didn't burn down our own ghetto, we went to where the power was and we burned it. Which was why they were terrified and why we weren't murdered. If we'd stayed in the Castro they'd have machine-gunned us. But they didn't want a massacre on their property, it's a different thing from killing people in their own ghetto separate where no one sees it, and it can be forgotten. Gay people moved from the Castro and said "You can't keep us home, just let us be gay there: we're coming here because you're here, straight San Francisco."

The violent reaction we had to that violence also changed the community. People said, "Fuck that! They can't do this. We're gay but we're not going back. We're going to be gayer than ever before, we're going to be queerer, more militant, we're going to take self-defence lessons. WE're gonna kick ass! You can't push us any more."

"We're going to be gay everywhere, we're not going back." It was the first riot by white folks. It was a revolutionary act by fifteen thousand gay people. It transformed the expectations externally about what the gay community is like, and it's transformed us: we have a different sense of how we're gay in this town. Not only gayer in the Castro, but gayer everywhere. And that's a nice place to start from.

Note: This article, based on an interview by Philip Derbyshire, was first published in *Gay Left* no. 9.

Notes on Contributors and Gay Left Collective

DENNIS ALTMAN was born in 1943 and graduated in 1963 from the University of Tasmania. A long-time gay activist and author of *Homosexual: Oppression and Liberation* (1971), he is also a frequent commentator on Australian politics and gay politics worldwide. He was until recently Senior Lecturer at the University of Sydney. His latest book, *Coming Out in the Seventies,* was published in 1979.

KEITH BIRCH has been involved in the gay movement in London since 1971, with GLF and the groups that followed in its wake, and he joined the *Gay Left* Collective in 1975 when the journal first started. He now works for the National Union of Public Employees as a researcher.

BOB CANT has been active as a socialist since the mid-1960s and as a member of the gay movement since 1971. He has written for *Gay Left, Outcome, Socialist Worker, College Rank and File, Socialist Review, Gay Marxist* and *Anti-Apartheid News.* He works for London Gay Switchboard and is Action Officer of his NATFHE branch.

SUE CARTLEDGE first became involved in the women's movement ten years ago. She remembers Saturday mornings doing free pregnancy tests, and Saturday afternoons doing street theatre on abortion in that Catholic city. She has lived with a husband, a lover, in a mixed group and in two households of women and children. She is still working on the politics of personal relationships! Becoming a socialist, a lesbian and most of all a feminist changed her life.

DEREK COHEN, aged 31, is a member of the *Gay Left* collective and has been involved in numerous other gay publishing ventures. After university he worked and then qualified as a residential social worker, and subsequently for a radical publications distribution service. He is now a co-ordinator with a left-wing printer.

EMMANUEL COOPER is a founding member of the *Gay Left* collective. He is a socialist who works within the autonomous gay movement and he contributes regular articles to *The Morning Star* and *Gay News,* as well as other journals. He is currently planning a book on the concept of "gay art".

MARGARET COULSON has been involved in left-wing and socialist politics for a number of years. She is the author of various articles on the oppression of women under capitalism.

PHILIP DERBYSHIRE was born in Manchester, where he lived until he went to university to study philosophy. After graduating he lived in America for a time, but it was not until he moved to London in 1976 that he came out and formed a commitment to socialist politics. He was a member of the IMG for eighteen months but left over questions of organisation. His present political involvements, apart from *Gay Left* which he joined in 1978, are focused on the need to develop a more flexible understanding of political organisation and the relation between the various levels and types of struggle and the present forms of the bourgeois state, and hence to move beyond the arid debates around the leninist canons.

RICHARD DYER studied French and worked in the theatre before doing research in cultural studies at Birmingham University. He has been involved in the gay movement since the early seventies, and helped organise the gay film season at the National Film Theatre in London. He teaches at Warwick University and lives in Birmingham with three other gay men.

STEPHEN GEE has been involved in the gay movement for a number of years, and was involved in the setting up of the Gay Activists' Alliance. He has also worked with the Brixton Faeries' gay theatre group in London.

SUSAN HEMMINGS is a feminist lesbian and a lesbian mother. She is a member of the *Spare Rib* collective which produces the monthly women's liberation magazine in London.

ALISON HENNEGAN read English at Girton College, Cambridge, and in 1970 embarked on a Ph.D. thesis entitled *Literature and the Homosexual Cult, 1890-1920*. She attempted to disguise her initial terror of the emerging gay movement by adopting a stance of lofty contempt towards it. Nevertheless her increasing involvement in gay politics led her to abandon her research in 1974 to devote herself to full-time but unpaid work in the movement. From 1976-7 she was the Vice-Chairwoman of the Campaign for Homosexual Equality, and from 1975-7 she was the National Organiser of FRIEND, the gay counselling and befriending network. Utterly exhausted and very broke by the summer of 1977, she joined the editorial staff of *Gay News*, whose Literary Editor she has been for the last three years.

MARGARET JACKSON is a lecturer in the Sociology of Education at Goldsmith's College, London, and has been teaching since 1962 in secondary schools and colleges of education. Her two marriages have enabled her to understand some of the ways in which men exercise control over women in the private sphere. She is now a lesbian and active in the women's liberation movement as a revolutionary feminist. She is a member of the Patriarchy Study Group and is currently researching into male sexuality.

PAT MAHONY is a lecturer in Education at Goldsmith's College, London, and has had a varied teaching career in both primary schools and universities in England and Australia. She became a lesbian after nine years of marriage, and she now lives with her two children and two other women. She is actively involved in the women's liberation movement, is a member of the Patriarchy Study Group and is currently researching into male sexuality.

JOHN MARSHALL studed sociology at the University of East Anglia and is now a graduate student at Essex University. His main research interest is the social control of male homosexuality during the post-war world. He is active in CHE, Gaysoc and the local telephone help-line.

FRANK MORT is a research student at the Centre for Cultural Studies, Birmingham, where he is engaged in examining the regulation of sexuality in the nineteenth century, and in the post-war world. He has published a number of papers and articles in this area.

JOHN SHIERS has been involved in the gay movement since joining GLF at Lancaster University in 1972, when he was nineteen. Since then he has lived mostly in Manchester, with a brief period in London, and is currently a community worker. Politically he identifies with the open, non-authoritarian socialist tradition to which he sees the women's and gay movements belonging and developing. He has recently become a reluctant member of the Labour Party.

SIMON WATNEY was born in Surrey in 1949 and studied Art History at the University of Sussex in the late 1960s. He was politicised as a teenager in the context of the Campaign for Nuclear Disarmament, and first became involved with GLF in the winter of 1970, helping to establish Sussex GLF in Brighton the following year. He moved to London in 1975 and joined the *Gay Left* collective two years later. He has been a teacher since 1972 and is currently a lecturer in Aesthetics and Communications at the Polytechnic of Central London. His history of *English Post-Impressionism* was published in 1980.

JEFFREY WEEKS has been involved in the gay movement since he joined the GLF in 1970, and was a founder member of *Gay Left*. He is the author of various articles on history and sexuality, and has written *Socialism and the New Life* (with Sheila Rowbotham), *Coming Out: Homosexual Politics from the Nineteenth Century to the Present* and *Sex, Politics and Society: the Regulation of Sexuality 1780-1980* (to be published in 1981).

TOM WOODHOUSE was born in Belfast in 1955 and has lived in London since 1977. He was a founder of the Anarchist journal *Zero* and is now a member of the *Gay Left* collective. He writes occasionally for Irish and English radical magazines, is a vegetarian and likes bicycles. He works as a cook.

NIGEL YOUNG is a gay activist socialist who works to unite socialist and sexual politics. He is a founder member of *Gay Left* and works in the National Council for Civil Liberties. He is also an infants' teacher and has been in the National Union of Teachers for ten years. He is his school's union representative and the present membership secretary of the Hackney Teachers' Association.

INDEX OF NAMES AND TITLES